Writing and Editing News

Studies in Journalism

The Studies in Journalism series will comprise monographs, edited volumes and textbooks on various aspects of the academic discipline of journalism and mass communication. The volumes in this series have been envisaged as interactive guides on reporting, coverage and opinion pieces. Ranging from the theoretically-bent to the empirically-argued, the books will draw cases from across the spectrum of practices, trends and visions within the journalistic profession in this part of the world. This series is aimed at students and teachers of journalism, journalists, freelance writers and media professionals.

Series Editor
Nalini Rajan, *Professor, Asian College of Journalism, Chennai.*

Writing and Editing News

K. V. Krishnaswamy

Orient BlackSwan

WRITING AND EDITING NEWS

ORIENT BLACKSWAN PRIVATE LIMITED

Registered Office
3-6-752 Himayatnagar, Hyderabad 500 029 (Telangana), INDIA
e-mail: centraloffice@orientblackswan.com

Other Offices
Bengaluru, Bhopal, Chennai, Guwahati,
Hyderabad, Jaipur, Kolkata, Lucknow, Mumbai,
New Delhi, Noida, Patna, Vijayawada

First published by Orient Blackswan Pvt. Ltd. 2015
This paperback edition published by Orient Blackswan Pvt. Ltd. 2016
Reprinted 2018

ISBN 978-81-250-6418-3

027491

Typeset in Goudy Old Style 11/13
by Jojy Philip, New Delhi 110 015

Printed in India at
Rakmo Press Pvt. Ltd.
Greater Noida

Published by
Orient Blackswan Private Limited
1/24 Asaf Ali Road,
New Delhi 110 002
e-mail: delhi@orientblackswan.com

Contents

Figures

Preface

A Journeyman's Tale

As a mini war broke out early in 2013 after Press Council of India chairman and former Supreme Court judge Markandey Katju called for minimum educational qualifications for journalists and entrants to journalism, there were counter-arguments which said that in this profession you learn on the job and that formal education, which helps in no way, is not an essential requirement. This was eminently true, for very practical reasons—those were early days after Independence when the media was starting to grow, when newspapers were themselves the school, when no one gave a thought to opening media training institutions or felt the need for one; a time when conditions in the industry were quite primitive.

Again—as veteran journalist V. Gangadhar wrote[1] soon after the controversy broke out—we learnt the ropes while at work, when trial and error was the only option. In some of the more conservative newspapers, error was punishable, but in some of the others it was all part of the game, and we regretted and moved on. The media scene today—more than 50 years later—is more complex and complicated, and much more competitive. Media houses can no longer afford to err if they care for their credibility. They need entrants who are aware of the professional tools, have learnt the basics of their use and developed a degree of skill. It was to meet this demand that several universities and degree colleges started undergraduate and postgraduate media courses, and some media schools also opened. These have over the years become an essential part of the academic scene. But the growth has been uneven and apparently unregulated, and—I would say, stuck as they are in the pre-digital era—mostly unrelated to the demands of the media industry. As Gangadhar had said in his article, many of these mushrooming media schools have neither the required course of study nor competent faculty. In fact, there are even fewer guidebooks to give the students a glimpse of the media world and the exhausting demands it makes on its practitioners. This is the felt need I seek to meet in a small way.

Today, technology drives the media like never before. This is both a blessing and a bane. By taking the drudgery out of the profession, technology has made the journalist's job more pleasant and enjoyable and less tedious. Whether you work in the field collecting information or on the desk putting it all together, technology has become a major tool at your service. It is no wonder then that as handheld devices emerge as the major delivery point for the reader-in-a-hurry, news online takes a hold on us. This, in turn, requires the journalist to continuously update the news. Even veterans are being asked to reorient themselves, learn and unlearn, adapt or perish. Journalism schools are being advised to include coding, where you learn HTML, etc., as part of the curriculum. On the negative side, I feel, technology has tended to take away some of the romance from the profession, the rough and tumble of news collection, the struggle with the mechanical typewriter—where the letter 'x' was the most used—and the even tougher world of making pages in the hot metal process in the furnace of the linotype department.

If loss of romance of the profession is to be put down on the debit side, where will this new development in 2015 go: Ten leading media organisations in the US, it is reported, are to test drones for news gathering. The plan is to deploy drones or unmanned aircraft systems to trouble spots where it might be too dangerous to send journalists to report. The tests could lead to 'a safe, efficient, timely and affordable way to gather and disseminate information and keep journalists out of harm's way,' said Virginia Tech University, which is a collaborating partner.[2] These are eye witness accounts of a new sort.

In the coming pages, chapters have been devoted specifically to the areas of reporting and editing and more. And in quite a few pages I have included anecdotes from my own years in the profession and the years I taught journalism. If the book helps new entrants in their journey into the exotic world of journalism even in a minor way, I would be happy that I have returned at least some of what I owe to the profession. I offer no apology for the fact that I mostly provide the perspective of the print journalist since this was what I was, though I have lessons for the other three streams as well. Media is certainly at a crossroads, but I am not ready to join the rising chorus of journalists and others lamenting the impending demise of print. Even at the risk of sounding like an ultra-orthodox practitioner of the profession, I say to prospective new entrants: Equip yourselves for multimedia, but train yourselves in print. For it is here that you will learn the basics of good journalism. Best of luck!

As a final thought, I quote David Carr. An article by him in the *New York Times* in October 2010, as the crisis in the newspaper industry was peaking, came as balm to old print hands like me who, mule fashion, refuse to acknowledge that our favourite medium has to share the stage with others like online and television: 'You can make news working in your pajamas and running stuff past your cat and no one else. But even in 2010, when a print product is viewed as a quaint artifact of a bygone age, there is something about that process, about all those many hands, about the permanence of print, that makes a story resonate in a way that can't be measured in digital metrics. I love a hot newsbreak on the Web as much as the next guy, but on some days, for some stories, there is still no school like the old school.'[3]

An explanation may also be in order. Many of the examples given in the following chapters are taken from the English dailies in Chennai. They could as well have been from any of the dailies in the other parts of the country and abroad. The only reason for this Chennai focus is that I have spent most of my professional life in the southern metropolis and so am familiar with the dailies available there. Reading them had become a habit.

In conclusion, a few acknowledgements: I owe a huge debt of gratitude to my first news editor late C. P. Seshadri, known to us as Master, of *Indian Express*, Madras, and my senior P. J. Mathew, who was a thoroughbred professional and full of promise, but gave us only a glimpse of it. I gratefully acknowledge the whole-hearted support of the *Hindu* and its editor, Malini Parthasarathy, and the Asian College of Journalism (ACJ), Chennai, whose chairman,

Sashi Kumar, first gave me the platform to teach and offered me all help in the preparation of key chapters in the book. My sincere thanks are also due to V. K. Raghunathan and Mohan Ramamurthi, former print media colleagues in the ACJ. Their contribution in the preparation of the lessons and related exercises and examples on reporting and editing for teaching at the college benefited me while I was part of the faculty, and has been useful in giving substance to the two chapters in the book. For trusting me to write the book, my thanks are due to Orient BlackSwan's Mimi Choudhury, Vice President (Publishing–Social Sciences), and for making it happen, many thanks to Antony Arul Valan Gnanapragasam, Assistant Editor (Social Sciences), whose role as editor made me realise that even veteran journalists needed to be disciplined by an editor. Lastly, I acknowledge the support and encouragement I have received from my constant companion Padma, daughter-in-law Monami Bhattacharya, and son Aravind, who has been my inspiration.

K. V. Krishnaswamy
February 2015, Bengaluru

NOTES

1. V. Gangadhar, 'Indian Journalism at Ground Zero', *Hindu*, Op-ed, 20 March 2013.
2. AFP, 'Ten news organizations to join drone-test programme', *MailOnline*, 15 January 2015, available at http://www.dailymail.co.uk/wires/afp/article-2912420/Ten-news-organizations-join-drone-test-program.html (accessed March 2015).
3. David Carr, 'A Vanishing Journalistic Divide', *New York Times*, 10 October 2010.

Publisher's Acknowledgements

For permission to reproduce copyrighted material in this volume, the publishers wish to make the following acknowledgements.

Sashi Kumar, Asian College of Journalism (ACJ), Chennai, for the following five permission clearances:

For extensively quoting and discussing his lecture on TV journalism in Chapter Four, 'Broadcast Journalism: In the age of 24×7 TV and FM radio', of this volume.

For permission to reproduce two photographs—'PTC during a programme' and 'PCR with control panels, monitors; Studio in the background'—appearing as Figures 4.1 and 4.2 in Chapter Four of this volume. © ACJ

For permission to reproduce the first page of *The Word: Lab Journal of the Asian College of Journalism* 10 (2), 31 October 2009, appearing as Figure I.1, 'Front Page of a Newspaper Illustrating the Various Parts', in the introduction to this volume. © ACJ

For permission to reproduce the news feature 'Rooting for the non-playing CSK', published in *The Word: Lab Journal of the Asian College of Journalism* 12 (2).

For permission to use exercises compiled during the author's term as member of the faculty at ACJ, appearing as examples in the main text and exercises in Appendices of this volume. © ACJ

The *Hindu*, for the following three permissions:

Image of the first page of the daily's 1 October 1934 edition, appearing as Figure 1.1, 'Front Page of a Newspaper of the 1930s', in Chapter One of this volume. © *Hindu*

Two reports, 'Thousands throng Birla Planetarium', 23 July 2009; and, 'Warangal software engineer shot dead in South Africa', 8 July 2009, appearing in Appendices and Chapter Five of this volume, respectively. © *Hindu*

For an extract from a report on the 25th year celebrations on 22 September 1903, appearing in Chapter Two of this volume. © *Hindu*

Deccan Herald, for permission to carry a report, 'A pipeline commissioned on Friday at the Indian Oil Corporation', 3 July 2010, appearing in Appendices of this volume. © *Deccan Herald*

Sitalakshmi Krishnamoorthy, Associate Editor, *DNA*, and Sonali Karsale, Assistant Manager, Research, Archives & Syndication-*DNA*, for permission to carry a report, 'Train to Kashmir becomes reality', 27 June 2013, appearing in Chapter Four of this volume. © *DNA*

V. Sudarshan, Resident Editor, *New Indian Express*, for permission to carry a report, 'Two Youth Choke to Death', 27 May 2009, appearing in Chapter Three of this volume. © *New Indian Express*

Isha Sharma, for permission to carry the rough and fair drafts of 'Surfing in Kovalam Waters', assignments written as a student at ACJ, appearing in Chapter Five of this volume. © Isha Sharma

Vinaya Patil, for permission to carry the news feature 'Rooting for the non-playing CSK', assignment written as a student at ACJ, appearing in Chapter Two of this volume. © Vinaya Patil

Introduction

The media scene today is completely and comprehensively different from what it was when I entered it. Especially in the past decade and a half, the industry in India has witnessed a silent revolution, spurred in the main by the rampaging advances in technology and also by the fact that it has entered a phase of welcome consolidation. The latter is provoking alarm among some sections of journalists, since it is naturally causing dislocations. But the industry has enough resilience and growth potential to withstand pressures from changes wrought by moves at consolidation and the frenetic march of technology. Every day there are reminders about the bumpy road ahead. No one apparently wants to mention the other c-word in public, but convergence is round the corner. The days when each media stream lived in its own splendid isolation are long gone; the print newsroom and TV newsroom are beginning to work together, sharing their resources and stories. Not that convergence is here and now. My strong belief is that print will keep centre-stage for some more years, in view of the lack of connectivity and large-scale illiteracy in the country. But it may come sooner than some of us wish to acknowledge. There is no escaping some form of convergence, where technological advances and corporate strategies meet, as in the US in the main. This may be difficult to envision for those of the earlier generations, who are not used to sharing content.

Every day one article or the other writes the obituary of the newspaper. In the West, online journalism or new media is posing an existential threat to the printed newspaper or print media, even as TV finds competition from the cloud difficult to counter. With newsprint, printing and distribution, apart from production, proving ever more expensive, even the mainstream newspapers in the US and the UK have turned to online editions to cut costs. Studies by professional bodies suggest that there may be a turnaround for the newspaper industry—the 2013 annual report on American journalism by the respected think tank Pew Research Centre's Project for Excellence in Journalism[1] says that 'for the first time since the deep recession that began in 2007, newspaper organisations have grounds for a modicum of optimism'. There may yet be little scope for optimism.

In fact, a situation may soon emerge where regional news will be purveyed by printed local newspapers, with readers going online for national and international news. It may be time for the four streams of the media to find their niche and survive, and maybe even flourish, in a collaborative, cooperative effort.

Converged newsrooms—that sanctum sanctorum of us print veterans—are not too far away. Already, most national newspapers in English, Hindi, and a few other languages have the online versions, which share content with the printed editions. Unlike five years ago, however, the online versions do not stop with converting what the print has published. Many of them keep updating the news and continuously publish breaking news stories as well. One step forward leads to another: newspapers which send photographers to cover important news developments have learnt to put many of their photographs online, while carrying one or two in the print edition which has space constraints; where they had two or three editorial staff lent from the main desk to take care of these online portals, today many have full-fledged staff especially trained for online work, which requires both editing acumen and technical know-how.

Four decades ago, Walter Lippmann (1889–1974), the legendary Washington-based political columnist and intellectual, had described journalism as an underdeveloped profession in one of his syndicated articles. In some ways it still continues to be so. Lippmann was writing of the 1950s and 1960s, when there were hardly any journalism schools to train aspirants in the demanding skills of the profession, no universally accepted set standards or textbooks. If you loved the profession for whatever reason—your father often talked of newspaper articles, your maternal uncle was a journalist, your mom wanted to write a novel—you joined one of the newspapers as an apprentice, which would invariably extend to two years. You learnt your skills on the job. It was a long, arduous process, with not many avenues for climbing up. The profession was also underdeveloped in terms of the working environment and the compensation one got. There were no fixed hours of work nor a well-structured pay scale. You went to work, of course as now, when the world around went to sleep; when everyone had a holiday, you had double duty to get material for everyone's entertainment. At work, the conditions were appallingly primitive. It was a luxury if your office had a 24-hour canteen to serve you tea, coffee and snacks. In one of the offices I worked in, we had a private-run canteen inside the compound where the owner doubled as cook and bearer, and cockroaches and stray dogs were permanent company.

Of the tools of the trade, the less said the better. Most reporting sections would have typewriters in working condition and in the years before cassette tape recorders came into use, they would do with shorthand notebooks and pencils. Portable typewriters were not yet in vogue, though an occasional roving correspondent would delight us with one. In the newsroom, all this was a luxury. Most reports, coming from part-timers at mofussil centres, would be handwritten or sent by telegraph. This meant that most of these reports needed to be deciphered, corrected, edited and typed. But managers would rarely agree that newsrooms needed typewriters. Some of us were ready to deal with a rattler of a typewriter and many preferred to edit in the copy, running the risk of misspellings and mistakes in typesetting from illegible handwriting. All the while, technology was keeping up the race with the printing industry, albeit at a slower pace. The tango began with the invention of the letterpress printing machine and the telegram. Technology has since marched hand in hand with journalism, giving the latter a leg-up at every step. Until the arrival of the computer and the World Wide Web at the turn of the century when technology took a giant leap. Journalism is still catching up.

Let me also touch on one new, worrisome development for the media. We are seeing that what technology has given with one hand it has counter-balanced with the other. For the Internet, which has been spearheading the media transformation, has also thrown up unprecedented challenges for the professional. One such development relates to the media coverage of terrorism in a milieu where perpetrators have had equally easy access to technology and its tools. The 16-hour hostage situation in a Sydney cafe on 15–16 December 2014, and the terror strikes in Paris, France, in January 2015 have put the media to a dramatically new test. Against its duty to accurately report the fast-moving news development, the media had to balance its responsibility to ensure that it did not aid the perpetrators, even unwittingly. The Australian media, for example, knew the demands of the lone hostage taker but refrained from broadcasting them and denied him the propaganda advantage he sought to gain. It is a totally new situation demanding the evolving of new norms for media coverage.

One consequence in the past decade has been that there has been a dramatic change in the presentation of news and news developments, with professional practitioners coming under unprecedented pressure to deliver; and deliver fast and accurately. The demands on those who are part of the media have multiplied manifold. There is a need for journalists to reorient themselves, for journalism schools to rejig their courses, without the journalists of course giving up the core practices which have stood the test of time, and which too have come under tremendous pressure for purely non-journalistic reasons.

The scene for the news reporter has also altered considerably. Technology has no doubt presented the reporter with a number of smart tools that greatly facilitate the job. On-the-spot reporting is literally done on the spot, without the reporter having to go to office, if there is one in town. The downside in a way is that it has become literally a 24-hour job; it used to be so figuratively in early times. The reporter no longer has the luxury of a systematic, even leisurely pursuit of news leads. Speed is of the essence in this electronic age and the age-old journalistic norm of checking and cross-checking facts and the higher value of truth telling are upheld more in the breach as deadline and circulation pressures become intolerable. Instant news and instant delivery are the new norm.

The result is that distortions are setting in and long-cherished professional practices are treated with scant respect. If you are the cautious type who wants to get your facts fully right before filing your copy, you are dubbed ponderous and slow. The new philosophy is, 'If there are slip-ups, say sorry and move on'. If there had been some distortion in the reporting, it is all part of the game. We have come a long way, from the days when a reporter came to office to type the report and file it with the desk where it was edited and sent to the composing section for metal typesetting and then on to page-making and printing. Today, from the field the report goes to the desk and on to the assigned pages and then for final printing, all in the click of a button. No journalist can ask for more in terms of working environment. The transformation is total.

Whatever the experience of the rest of the world, the present is a golden period for media in this country as it expands and prospers. I have only one advice for students of journalism: To be truthful to oneself and to the profession. Beyond this, I list other tenets in this book, all of which have been ingrained in me and my generation by seniors in the field at a time when there were as few distractions as attractions. In the following pages, I have tried to explain what is news, how it is gathered and a report written based on the information, how news travels from the field where it often happens to the pages of a newspaper or the screen, be it the TV or the monitor of a computer, on the ipad, a slate or a smartphone. I have also discussed some of the distortions that have crept in, such as 'paid news'.

The value of a textbook of this nature was underlined by an uncommon bloomer in the printed editions of the *New York Times*, dated 29 May 2014. In the main headline for its lead story on the front page was a typo which had apparently gone unnoticed. My attention was drawn to it by a tweet which reported the *NYT* acknowledging that the typo had remained uncorrected in all its editions. Trained precisely to spot such typos, I could not spot it from the accompanying screenshot with the headline. Not until I got an email via Twitter with the typo circled in red. It was then that I knew I could not be wrong in underlining the importance of some of these old-time practices of checking and cross-checking in journalism.

Before we move further, let us take a look at some of the terminology used in this book.

Important Terminology

angle: the point of focus or main point in a story

artwork: all illustrations, maps, charts and cartoons come under this head

banner: headline on the front page top stretching across all columns

body matter: the text of the copy that substantiates the lead

body type: the type of shape and style in which the body matter is printed

boil down: cut and shorten

break: a new story breaking out or emerging

broadsheet/tabloid: broadsheets are large size (55 cm/30 cm) newspapers such as the *Hindu*, *Times of India* and *Hindustan Times*. The trend worldwide today is for more and more broadsheets to go tabloid, which is roughly half the size. All pop or popular papers in England and even some sections in the heavies have converted to the tabloid format; the *Times* and *Independent* also have their tabloid version and call themselves compacts. In Europe and the US, most serious newspapers have gone tabloid.

copy: reports that come into the newsroom, viz., raw copy, agency copy, staffer copy, etc.

copy tasting: the process in the newsroom where reports are selected for possible use and others rejected (spiked or weeded in the pre-computer age)

drop: the first letter of an article printed in large size

dummy: trial run of the newspaper

exclusive: this means that the story has not been covered by any other newspaper or other media

fillers: short reports or video clippings to fill in when the main story runs short

font: typeface of letters (in printing and writing)

indent: the blank space at the beginning of the para or in the margins of the columns

intro: the first para or lede of a story

puff: story giving much unjustified publicity, more often to politicians, police and corporate houses

round-up: gathering together various strands of a story when the overall picture of an event is required. For example, during the monsoon season, floods in some regions happen even as in others drought conditions prevail and in a few rains begin; or, during a national strike action when a round-up is needed for the front page, while regional reports are published in the regional pages of the same newspaper

soft news vs *hard news*: soft news often relates to happy-ending human interest stories of endurance, trials and triumphs. These are published on the front pages of newspapers for their news value in terms of reader interest or sometimes because they are very well written. On the other hand, hard news relates to happenings and developments of immediate consequence. For example, the June 2013 landslide in Uttarakhand that devastated Haridwar during the pilgrim season was a hard story. It had all the elements that characterise a major news development. Four months later, there was a report that one woman whom her family thought had been washed away in the floods in Uttarakhand was spotted in a remote village begging for food. With help from the police and the villagers, the woman's husband took her home in faraway Haryana. The story hardly had any news value except that it appealed to the reader's emotions: it represented the triumph of human will and endurance and the strength of love that kept the family still searching for her. This is a classic soft story

spin doctors: people who attempt to influence news or political agenda (publicists and press officers). They are an accepted part of the scene in the UK; such paid professionals are emerging in India too.

stet: restore a deleted portion of a report or ignore the deletion. (Latin for 'Let it stand')

subbing: another name for editing

tabloidisation: the view that media in general are following the values of tabloids, prioritising entertainment, sensationalism and scandal over 'hard news'

whistleblowers: persons revealing newsworthy and previously secret information to the media; also called Deep Throat after the Watergate scandal. (Woodward and Bernstein of *Washington Post* exposed the scandal that ultimately led to the resignation of American President Richard Nixon.) The latest to join the ranks are former American sleuth Edward Snowden and Wikileaks founder Julian Assange. India has a whistleblower protection legislation on the anvil. Its importance to journalists can never be exaggerated

Parts of a Newspaper

Box: A story,mostly of six to eight paragraphs,used with a tint or, as in earlier times, framed with rules on all sides, the text in bold and the column ragged right. A side story to a main story or a human interest story, the box draws the reader's attention to it as it is highlighted with the tint or the rules.

By-line: The name of the reporter is often included at the beginning of the story, rather than at the end, or not at all. Or it could be tagged on to the end of the story in some cases or be part of the stand-first, a paragraph that summarises the story and is embedded under the headline.

Columns: The text in the entire page is divided into columns. Columns must be constructed carefully. If text columns are too narrow or too wide, they are difficult to read. For a broadsheet (the morning newspaper as we know it), the six columns per page format is gaining currency since it has some major advantages for the reader. The Indian advertising industry is yet to accept it since it involves major changes in size and tariffs.

Crosshead (subheads): This is a subheading that appears in the body of the text and its function is to flag an important point in the text. It is also used to break the monotony if it is a large body of text.

Feature: A multi-pronged story that is presented in detail and covering all aspects. It could be a package with a main story, side stories, photos and infographics. It could go into the human-interest angle and talk of the implications of a news story.

Gutter: The margin between columns and pages facing each other.

Headline: This is the main statement, usually in a large and bold font, describing the top story. A banner headline spans the full width of the page and is in the largest font.

Figure I.1 Front Page of a Newspaper Illustrating the Various Parts

Courtesy: Asian College of Journalism, Chennai

Kicker: A kicker is a smaller-sized headline, often underlined, just above the main headline. Kickers are often a one or two-word identifier used to help readers. Examples: Mumbai blasts or

Sensex crash inset into reports on the Mumbai explosions or Sensex crashing.

Lead story: The main story on the front page. It is also called a splash.

Lead or lede: The first paragraph of a news story, includes the 5Ws + 1H (what, who, when, where, why and how).

Masthead: The title block or logo identifying the newspaper at the top of the front page. Sometimes an emblem or a motto is also placed within the masthead.

Menu: Usually boxed, a prominently placed list of contents in the inside pages. Other names popular now: What's Inside or Must Read or In Other Pages.

Obit (Obituary): A report about the death of a member of society.

Promos: A panel on the front page with pictures and text directing the reader to look in the inner pages at a particular story or feature. It could run parallel to the masthead or vertically on the first or last column.

Ears (pugs or panels): These are at the top left and right hand corners of the front page of the paper. The price of the paper, the logo, a promotion and/or an advertisement are positioned here.

Second lead: The second main story on the front page. This could also be a picture and headline, which gives a sneak preview of a story that you might find in the inside pages.

Sidebar: A box or tinted panel that goes alongside a main report.

Spot news: This is the news directly witnessed by the reporter, such as reporting a riot.

Stand-first: This is an introductory paragraph before the start of a big feature report. Sometimes it may be in bold type.

Strapline: A headline above or below the main headline that gives more details of the news story that follows. It is much smaller in size than the main headline, and often different in typeface.

NOTES

1. Pew Research Centre, 'The State of the News Media 2013: An Annual Report of Americal Journalism', Washington DC: Centre for Excellence in Journalism, Pew Research Centre, 2014.

1

What is News?

Changing Definition in the Digital Age

News as we understand it today has evolved as a concept over the last six decades and more, the evolution acquiring lightning speed in recent years and perhaps rendering any attempt at defining it quite tricky. In this era of instant communication and 'citizen journalism', especially during a year which marked the demise of the newspaper industry's most indispensable companion of the last half-century, the telegram, it may be futile to define news. The sacredness and sanctity of news gets distorted in particular during an election year in India when the media gets as much infected by the poll fever as the political community and the voter. However, there is one constant amid the rapidly changing values in the media: the enduring value of information. This is solely because unalloyed, unadulterated information, from which news flows, continues to be a precious commodity in the age of the rampaging social media. In a direct sense, this reinforces the validity of the old dictum: News is Sacred, Comment Free. The purveying of news has admittedly seen a sea change, but news if anything has only acquired an edge in this era.

The old definition of news thus remains immutable. The traditionally accepted definition is that news is current information of interest to readers, viewers or listeners. This is the simplest way to define news, apart from the time-honoured description that the letters stand for the four main directions of north, east, west and south. Each of the three words is a vital part of the definition, with perhaps 'current', in the sense of the latest, trumping the other two.

'Information' is what the media is all about and 'of interest' sets the context in which news is reported, recorded and put out.

Information is news when it is topical and new or unrevealed. The *Oxford English Dictionary* defines news as 'new information, new occurrences as a subject of report or talk'. *Webster's Third New International Dictionary of the English Language* describes it as 'fresh tidings ... gaining the interest of newspaper readers' and *Chambers's Twentieth Century Dictionary of the English Language* calls it 'report of a recent event; something one had not heard before'. That news is 'new' goes without saying. If it is old news, it will interest no one and will cease to be 'news' which the media reports on. This is one reason why journalists vie with one another to get to the news first and report it or in the now familiar cliché, 'break' the news first. Even in the pre-electronic age, the newspaper which broke the news first always scored over its rivals symbolically.

The concept of news has been in continuous evolution. Till the 1950s, leading English newspapers in the country—including the *Times*, of London, the then global standard—carried only advertisements on their front pages, relegating news to the fourth or fifth page on the inside (Figure 1.1). In fact, when a leading daily moved news to the front page, an article in the satirical *Shankar's Weekly* magazine commented that it must have come as a surprise to the readers to be told that the best can be bettered. But the conservative approach to news continued, with newspapers continuing to devote much space for government news such as ministers' speeches and administrative orders. In the absence of other sources of communication, the newspapers were the main conveyor of information and for them government activities were the main focus of news.

The practice of publishing verbatim and in full speeches delivered, especially in the legislatures, was given up only by the late 1950s or early 1960s. By then 'bad news is good news for the press' had come to be accepted as a given. Bolder headlines and sharper writing of reports also appeared, injecting an element of professionalism into journalism. The style of reporting as well as the content changed and newspapers began to look for sources outside of the government. But the path ahead was not smooth. In the decade following the death of Jawaharlal Nehru, there was a churning of the political cauldron which resulted in the newspapers coming under subtle and not-so-subtle

Figure 1.1 Front Page of a Newspaper of the 1930s

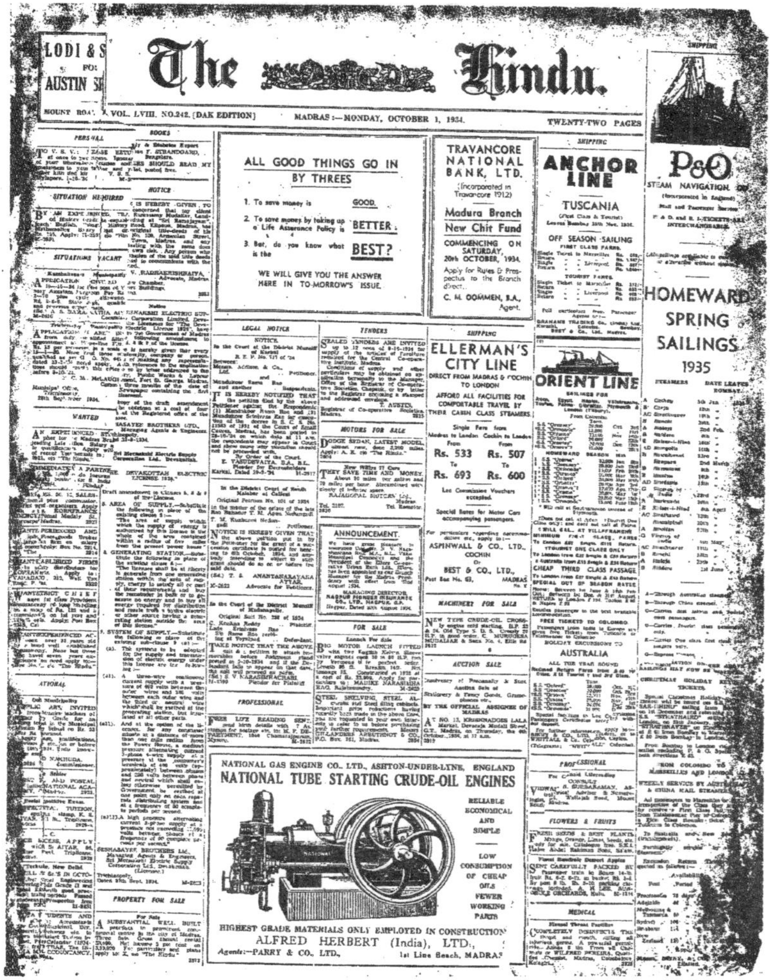

The Hindu.

VOL. LVIII. NO.242. [DAK EDITION] MADRAS:—MONDAY, OCTOBER 1, 1934. TWENTY-TWO PAGES

ALL GOOD THINGS GO IN BY THREES

1. To save money is GOOD.

2. To save money by taking up a Life Assurance Policy is BETTER.

3. But, do you know what is the BEST?

WE WILL GIVE YOU THE ANSWER HERE IN TO-MORROW'S ISSUE.

TRAVANCORE NATIONAL BANK, LTD.

(Incorporated in Travancore 1912)

Madura Branch

New Chit Fund

COMMENCING ON SATURDAY, 20th OCTOBER, 1934.

Apply for Rules & Prospectus to the Branch direct.

C. M. OOMMEN, B.A., Agent.

ANCHOR LINE

TUSCANIA

P&O

STEAM NAVIGATION CO.

HOMEWARD SPRING SAILINGS 1935

ELLERMAN'S CITY LINE

DIRECT FROM MADRAS & COCHIN TO LONDON

AFFORD ALL FACILITIES FOR COMFORTABLE TRAVEL BY THEIR CABIN CLASS STEAMERS.

Rs. 533 Rs. 507

Rs. 693 Rs. 600

ASPINWALL & CO., LTD., COCHIN

BEST & CO., LTD., MADRAS

ORIENT LINE

AUSTRALIA

ANNOUNCEMENT

NATIONAL GAS ENGINE CO., LTD., ASHTON-UNDER-LYNE, ENGLAND

NATIONAL TUBE STARTING CRUDE-OIL ENGINES

RELIABLE ECONOMICAL AND SIMPLE

LOW CONSUMPTION OF CHEAP OILS

FEWER WORKING PARTS

HIGHEST GRADE MATERIALS ONLY EMPLOYED IN CONSTRUCTION

ALFRED HERBERT (India), LTD.,

Agents:—PARRY & CO., LTD., 1st Line Beach, MADRAS

Courtesy: Hindu

pressure. Objective news reporting tended to see distortions but by and large the newspapers remained unaffected.

In the early 1970s, there was another trial. On the urging of Prime Minister Indira Gandhi, some of the leading newspapers resorted to featuring 'development news' on the front pages. Gandhi, who had by then established her supremacy in government and the Congress party and was demonstrating a streak of authoritarianism, felt that the press tended to highlight only negative news like violence and destruction and needed to project the programmes of her government or what her supporters called 'positive news'. In an apparent attempt to gain greater control over the flow of news, Gandhi floated the government's news agency Samachar by merging the two private ones active at that time, the Press Trust of India and United News of India. Simultaneously, government emissaries canvassed for featuring 'development news'. The dark period of Emergency rule (June 1975–December 1976) facilitated this attempt at muzzling the press.

Hard News and Soft News

Newspapers in those days, as now, concentrated on telling the reader what happened in the past 24 hours—for instance, about accidents, murders, political speeches and civic issues. This was considered 'hard news', as against 'soft news' which in general referred to stories of human interest and cultural news. In the 1960s, as governments began to project themselves, they persuaded newspapers to print reports on their programmes and popular schemes. These apparently had little 'news' value in terms of any fresh development, and began to be included under 'soft news' in a not very complimentary way. Under these circumstances, hard news took the back seat as newspapers featured official programmes. That this ploy of the government helped bury reports on the gross abuse of authority during the Emergency, which were revealed later, is a different matter. This mercifully lasted only a short while. Newspapers realised soon that 'development news' did not always make for interesting reading. News on murder and mayhem was not rejected anymore because they were 'negative'. Reader interest was far greater in these than in a report on, say, the progress of a road project in a rural area. News refused to be redefined. By then, the media had diversified and began to assert its independence. All the while, with new investments coming in, newspapers were benefiting by the intervention of technology for modernising printing and distribution. Simultaneously, with giant leaps in printing, newspaper organisations also speeded delivery by adopting modes of transport other than what they were using at that time, by train (the 'dak' edition) and vans (by road). Airlifting was one option, but not attractive because of its prohibitive cost. As technology provided more facilities, newspapers also tried out 'late news' fudges on the front pages that included the latest or breaking news. These were a small section of type matter in a box in the newspaper allowing late news developments to be included without the whole page having to be remade. The fudges, of length 15 to 20 cm in single column size, were inserted in a blank space provided at the bottom during page-making. Before the newspaper was put to sleep (i.e., finally closed at deadline time and sent for printing), brief reports of any breaking news, or 'flash' as they were called then, would be composed and fitted into the fudge and inserted on the front page. The fudge though had more style than substance.

The introduction of facsimile transmission with the advent of satellite communication was another turning point in the delivery of newspapers. Instead of establishing a newspaper office, complete with the editorial and reporting teams at different centres, newspapers took to facsimile transmission which ensured speed and could do with skeleton staff at the receiving end. It was a double blessing, in terms of economy of time and investment. It also enabled centralised control of news dissemination.

Then came TV in the form of Doordarshan (DD) which, like All India Radio, was never to pose a challenge of any sort to newspapers, in terms of news presentation or revenue. As a mouthpiece of the ruling parties at the state and central levels, DD lacked credibility like its older broadcasting twin. (DD is said to be gaining popularity these days). News for DD was never 'information of interest' but what was approved by the information and broadcasting ministry, vetted and sanitised. Even at a time when it was possible for Indian viewers with the necessary antenna to view satellite channels like the BBC and CNN, the government-run broadcaster refused to change. It could afford to at that time since it held monopoly over news broadcast. The absurdity was completely exposed on the day (31 October 1984) Indira Gandhi was assassinated. In the absence of private channels in the country, DD was the only source–and it waited an interminably long time before announcing an event that the entire world was aware of soon after it had happened.

The prime minister was assassinated by her bodyguards around 9:20 AM on the lawns of her official residence in New Delhi. When DD finally secured permission to telecast the information, nearly 10 hours had elapsed. All the while, BBC and CNN were reporting on the killing and its aftermath. DD waited for clearance which came only after the ruling Congress party had picked a successor—the chosen leader, Rajiv Gandhi, was away in Calcutta and had to be located and asked to fly back to Delhi. Only after he reached Delhi did DD announce the assassination of his mother. In an article in the *Telegraph*, V. Kumara Swamy narrated the way DD handled the news:

> On Doordarshan, it (Wednesday October 31, 1984) was a normal day—at least from the outside. "We were being informed about the developments at AIIMS (All India Institute of Medical Sciences, New Delhi, where Indira Gandhi was rushed) and were asked to be ready for the news bulletin. But when I read out the bulletin at 8 pm, which was the first bulletin of the day, I did not announce that she was dead in as many words," newsreader Salma Sultan recollects. "I said that there had been an assassination attempt on her and she was undergoing treatment. But all of us knew that she was no more. It was difficult for me to hide the shock and grief."[1]

Such attitude has prevented DD from reaching its potential as an instrument of public education with a nationwide network. The turning point came hardly a decade later with the commercialisation of programming when private television channels arrived on the scene in the mid-1990s, riding on the liberalisation era. The advances in communication technology resulted in an invasion from the skies and the coming of transnational television. The media scene saw a metamorphosis—and deeply impacted news presentation. Satellites brought the very latest news in video format into the drawing rooms. After reading news in the cold format of print for decades, this was a revolutionary change. This was news in celluloid flesh and blood.

The pioneering weekly news package on Friday nights under Prannoy Roy became a hit by the late 1990s, giving a new meaning to video news coverage to an audience resigned to the predictable DD News. But even this had only a marginal impact on the print media which continued with its presentations unchanged. There was not yet a compulsion to update the news presentation so that it did not read like a repetition of what prime time television news had presented the night before. This happened with the arrival of 24×7 news on TV in 2003. The media scene began to get crowded over the next few years. Round-the-clock news was a natural progression as was online news and continuous streaming. After 2003, news and news presentation were no more to remain the same. The scene today is somewhat bewildering. The advent of the social media has changed the definition of news, or at least given it new meanings that would have been unthinkable a decade ago. The discovery of the 'cloud' as a storage has opened up new avenues. The sky apparently is not the limit any more.

Impact of News on Target Audience

Apart from 'current information of interest', the definition of news has an additional dimension that includes the impact such information can have on the reader. In some instances, a breaking news may have little interest for the reader but the report will have value for him/her for the impact it can have on him/her. For a majority of readers of regular newspapers, the financial pages will carry little interest save on days when markets go erratic or the budget is presented. Even if the news is not interesting, it is newsworthy because of the personal impact it has, or will have. There are other criteria that the media employs to judge the value of news. For example, what is news of value for a newspaper catering for the general public may not be of same value to a business daily whose readers look for exclusively business- and finance-related news. We will deal with these criteria in later chapters. But I cannot resist the temptation to cite one criterion, the unusual, and mention the clichéd but apt example: 'Man bites dog' is news because it is unusual.

There are also times when news acquires importance even if it is not 'current' in the strict sense in which we have defined it. In this category fall news that breaks 24 or 48 hours after the event has occurred. Natural calamities are a classic example; when they happen there is little realisation of the magnitude of their impact. The ramifications of the massive floods and landslips that ravaged the Himalayan pilgrim centres in the summer of 2013 and the Fukushima nuclear reactor accident following a tsunami in Japan became known many hours after the disasters had struck. They did not cease to be topical or lacking in interest merely because the news was not 'current' in a limited sense.

Here are two other examples. A few decades ago, an earthquake of severe magnitude struck Iran's ancient city of Qom in the central region, but early reports gave no indication of the scale of tragedy. When communications were restored in two days and rescue teams reached the villages razed by the quake, the world came to know that more than 30,000 had died, not 60 or 70 as first reported. All media attention refocused on the story, late in fact by days. Not 'current' but of enormous reader/viewer interest and hence news of value.

The other example dates back a hundred years. When Archduke Franz Ferdinand, heir to the Austro-Hungarian throne, was assassinated in Sarajevo, thus ultimately triggering World War I, the news took days to travel to Bombay (now Mumbai) by (snail) mail. But for the Indian reader it was still news and the *Times of India* published a report on the front page three days later. The headline, in a relatively small type and in single column, was a true reflection of the fledgling media at the start of the last century. The headline in three decks read as follows:

AUSTRIAN TRAGEDY

FULL STORY BY THE MAIL

AN EYE-WITNESS ACCOUNT

With no other mode of communication save snail mail, a 48-hour-old development still gripped reader attention and interest.

Both the type of display that the news report received—as a single column, i.e., enclosed in one newspaper column against a headline for the report which can spread across one, two, three or more columns—and the headline (in small type) that adorned it must be revealing of the state of the media in those early days. In the slow, leisurely pace of life during the early decades of the past century 'news' which had but a small following had a different connotation and different impact. Today, if there is a delay of even 48 minutes, newswires lose out in the rat race that news reporting is. In effect, it is 'breaking news' at break neck speed. That this has landed some news services in deep embarrassment and trouble is another matter. If journalists had 24-hour news cycles till a decade ago, today they have a deadline every passing minute.

Also today, design and display of news play an important part in both audiovisual and print media, with the online models devoting as much attention to the visual aspect as to the content, both for easy accessibility and ease of reading. Single column headlines have vanished except on the inside pages of newspapers for local and other news reports. Packaging news has perhaps acquired disproportionate importance, but this appears unavoidable when you have to sell news in a buyer's market where the reader/viewer is the master. The media needs to dress up news to be able to sell and survive.

Yesterday's 24 Hours and Today's Second

In the internet age, thus, the latest is what happened just a second ago. Beyond that moment, it ceases to be 'current' and will no longer be considered worthy of being given the prime slot. This has implications for both the broadcast and print media. With their round-the-clock news feeds, TV and online portals have to keep a 24-hour watch to ensure that they do not lag while newspapers need hawk-eyed desk editors to ensure that what they print is not outdated by the time the edition reaches the reader. 'News of interest' had also by then begun to acquire its own connotations in terms of changing audiences and their changing tastes and special needs.

In a situation where the reader/viewer is spoiled for choice, the media has increasingly laid stress on the presentation of news. In the pre-computer era, newspapers had to contend only with a few aspects of this presentation. They had to ensure that they used the fonts that are easy on the eye when printed on relatively coarse newsprint paper, ensure that there is the right balance in use of the headlines in terms of size and typeface, and the right flow of printing ink. Today the situation is quite complex, complicated perhaps by the fact that newspapers without exception have their own online editions. Primarily this means that newspapers too have to deliver news on a minute-by-minute basis to feed the web portal. The arrival of television brought in some challenges, mainly related to writing and presentation. These challenges are child's play compared to the demands that are made now on the media to deliver news for the laptop, the handheld phone, the tablet and the mini tablet for the reader-in-a-hurry. The screen sizes have kept shrinking, challenging the media to find the right fonts that are both easy on the eye and equally clear to comprehend, with a generally accepted 20–25 word limit for a sentence. (I wonder how William Faulkner would fare as a journalist today.) The most brutal challenge is posed by the social media which have opened the floodgates when everyone with an internet connection can report, comment and analyse, and provide minute-by-minute news feed. The demands on the language of presentation, content, font size and screen background, have combined to make this the most challenging scenario ever faced by the media. One round-the-clock TV news provider of international repute claimed that it took two years of research to finally choose the font and size for use in its online version.

The electronic revolution in the field of communication is also making newer and newer demands on practitioners. The journalist today is called upon to play many parts. On the production side, s/he has learnt some of the software skills to edit reports, give headlines, handle photographs, make pages and transmit them. Journalists on online portals build websites, clear content through editing and writing and make pages with graphics and reports, after mastering design.

No wonder the advice to journalism schools is to include lessons on coding for all students, not just for those in the online or new media stream. The day is not far off when a reporter is asked to code his story so that it can be uploaded immediately. Especially for 24-hour news portals this may be coming earlier than for others. In the field, the journalist is being called upon to do a veritable act of jugglery.

Andy Schotz, a veteran American reporter, had spoken more than five years ago of the changing scene for the reporter. In an article, he wrote of how he simultaneously took pictures with one hand and shot video with the other. He adds: 'These days I'm several ounces heavier as I travel to my reporting assignments. That's because of the Flip video camera in my breast pocket. It's a little bigger than a credit card. Its stature in my newsroom, though, is large.'[2] He warned against overburdening the reporter, the quality of whose work may ultimately suffer.

The telecom revolution has not spared journalistic writing either. Of course, writing for newspapers and online portals is different from writing for the broadcast media. Because of their short durations, news capsules on both TV and radio broadcasts do not enjoy the luxury of time and space. If in the newspapers the reporter gives a word picture of the news development, in TV this is precisely what he or she needs to avoid for the simple reason that visuals on the screen give the viewer quite a broad picture of what has happened and all that the TV anchor or reporter needs to do is to explain the context and perhaps give a general background that helps the viewer understand what is on the screen.

One easy example is the reporting of a cricket One Day International (ODI) match which has live coverage on TV. In the pre-TV era, cricket correspondents could indulge in some descriptive reporting of key phases of the game, some paragraphs on a batsman's star turn, on a bowler's guile in getting a rival out or a fielder's agility and sharpness in close-in catching. Since in live coverage on TV every player and every key event can be seen over and over again, this type of cricket reporting has become redundant. Today, correspondents are called upon to go behind the day's play, to interpret and analyse, and forecast. A few of them resort to blatant gimmickry, in an attempt to look different, often with disastrous results.

INSIDE A NEWSPAPER OFFICE

Before we move on to the next chapter and to two of the main aspects of journalism–writing and reporting–let us see how all that happened in the last 24 hours is brought out in the form of a newspaper, every day without a break; how what a VIP declared only hours ago is reported in such detail the next day along with photographs, how a murder in the neighbourhood 12 hours ago is chronicled in such minute detail and from various angles. The advent of TV has demystified all this to a large extent with its own reporting of these events. However, the charm is in the detail and the TV lacks in it.

For an outsider the mystery and awe will remain till one enters the newspaper office or TV centre and experiences the frenetic activity around. Most of the tasks described below, from preparing news lists to tasting copy to editing reports, are common for all four streams of the media. The only difference is in the output; print will produce a news report on the computer, online will supplement the report with graphics and background and design the web page, radio will struggle to trim the story into the few minutes available for the entire story and TV will look for background footage and expert commentary. However, let us understand the various tasks in a newsroom by asking a very simple question: When does a day start in a morning daily?

A Typical Day

To answer that question, we must know when the previous day ends. Truth be told, the day never ends in a newspaper. It is a 24-hour non-stop run. For the two key players in the news section, the one in charge of overall news and the other concerned with regional/local news, the day starts when the day breaks. For the others 10:00 AM is the latest, unless you are a reporter who has been given an early morning assignment to cover. By 10:00 AM, all departments are on active mode. The first to face a deadline for the next day is the advertisement department where staff quickly review the ad flow and the overall position at the time the deadline is reached for accepting ads. By noon most newspapers have the 'dummy' ready, with advertisements allocated to different pages and the total number of pages fixed, primarily on the basis of the ad strength. It is now over to the news sections—the editorial and reporting departments. By now staff in the editorial, reporting, and design and page layout sections working on the weekend and Sunday and other supplements are already on their jobs. They have different deadlines, depending on the date of issue of their supplements. For example, the Sunday magazine section of most newspapers is readied by mid-week, mostly Wednesday, and printed the next day so that these do not clash with the printing schedule of the news sections and the special weekend sections of Friday and Saturday. Senior editorial writers have their discussions and choose the contents of the editorial and op-ed (short for 'opposite editorial') pages. Those writing the day's editorials begin working on their topics.

Around noon, the newsroom is just beginning to stir. Reporting staff, who have received their day's assignments the previous day, are out on the field or waiting for briefing by the chief reporter or chief of bureau on the possible highlights of the day. The chief has done a review of the previous day's performance, marking the hits and misses compared to the rival newspapers and is sending out reminders/memos. The chief reporter also has the day's news list ready, listing the main stories expected in the city/town and the reporters working on these assignments. Similar exercises are on simultaneously in the photography department, with the chief photographer preparing a list of possible news photographs that will be available for use during the day. The news editor–who was perhaps woken up at daybreak by the editor seeking clarifications, or some staffer seeking instructions or informing the chief of a sudden development in his/her area–checks in at noon. The news editor, the fulcrum around whom the entire news department rotates, will call the first of several meetings in the newsroom. The first one is attended by the advertisement department head (ad head) and the chiefs of all departments connected with news–the regional/city editor, national editor, business editor, sports editor and photo editor. The ad head briefs the news editor on the dummy, with the columns on different pages that have advertisements and the space available for news. This is the only news meeting the ad head attends. The first news meeting sees a review of the day's newspaper and the pluses and minuses compared to rivals. The different chiefs give explanations to the issues raised and the meeting then progresses to take a look at the news lists brought in by each. A rough picture of the next day's stories emerges from a general discussion on the prospects on the news front, with the news editor giving them instructions on what to pursue and what not. The meeting ends with an outline of the news budget, showing the likely allocation of space for each section–regional, business, international, national and sports. This allocation varies across months, and at times even across days. For example, when the annual budget is presented most space will be taken up by stories on topics that on any other day will be banished to the business pages.

It is early afternoon, and the editorial department is immersed in work—'tasting' copy. 'Copy' (the word has no plural form and has perhaps lost its moorings in these days of paperless offices) stands for all the reports pouring into the computers at the 'desk' or the newsroom. The mounds of copy, accumulated overnight, are sorted; those which have no chance of being used are 'spiked' or 'weeded' and the rest distributed to the different sections. This weeding out and sorting—called copy tasting—is done by a senior; a trained hand that does it swiftly, correctly and reliably, ensuring that no news leads are lost. Copy tasters also draw the attention of the chiefs of the different sections to 'breaking news' or emerging stories which may need to be followed up immediately. In some newspapers, copy tasters bring these to the notice of the news editor who will initiate the follow-up action. Once the day's production starts—that is, when the desk begins to feed reports into the computer for next day's newspaper—the chief subeditors take charge of all work, i.e., further copy tasting and revising edited copy. They report to assistant editors who in turn work under the direct supervision of the news editor.

By late afternoon, chief sub-editors and sub-editors who actually produce the first edition (deadline 10:00 PM) are streaming in. After briefing by the section chiefs—an assistant editor or higher in the hierarchy—the sub-editor begins to assess the copy in the desk or the computer for the right perspectives and implications and, in consultation with the chief sub-editor, begins the editing task. As we will see later, editing is one of the most vital aspects of media production, applicable to the four streams of print, online, radio and TV. This involves making the report read correct and cogent and sequential. At a later stage, it also means assigning it to the right column and page and giving the right heading and fitting it to suit the word length. The afternoon news meeting, held around 4:00 PM, does what is called 'budgeting' which, as the word suggests, primarily fixes the space allotted for each news section. The meeting sees the day's newspaper take some definitive shape. All chiefs who attended the 10:00 AM meeting (except the ad head) and the chief sub-editors who handle news stories and page-making participate. The result: news stories and photographs that go alongside the stories or standalones that are topical and illustrations, if any, are assigned to pages. The possible stories are sighted for the front and turn pages (where front page stories are continued) along with photographs, those that have already arrived or are expected later in the day. Follow-up actions required to be done are decided at this meeting and the news editor lays out the instructions. The meeting disperses, all have their tasks cut out and the newsroom fever grips everyone. Equally feverish activity is on at the reporting room where the rush to finish copy and deliver has reporters scurrying around. For the regional news stories, the deadline is closer and there is no time to be lost before all facts are checked and rechecked with the sources. Reporters file copy to the chief reporter who approves them and passes them on to the city desk. The chief reporter sits in with the city desk when decisions on fixing stories on regional pages are taken.

From now on, the core editorial group consisting of the news editor and heads of the different departments begin their hourly review of the position of the newspaper. At around 8:00 PM, the group takes final decisions on the front page and the major inside pages. The manner in which the stories and photographs/graphics are placed is decided by the team in consultation with the design editor and layout artist. As the 10:00 PM deadline approaches, the pages are made and transmitted electronically to printing presses located far away from the urban centres. Back in the newsroom, it is a little past 10:00 PM. The chief sub-editor in charge of the night shift has taken charge and is reviewing the news to check which stories need to be updated, which stories need to be brought forward to the front page and which should be eliminated because they are outdated. The editorial staff call it a day when they put to sleep the final 'late city' edition which then goes for printing.

In modern presses, computer files are converted to etched aluminium plates which are placed on metal cylinders that roll and stamp ink on to the newsprint. For colour pages four plates of cyan (blue), yellow, magenta and black are combined to create any hue. The printed pages are cut and folded and bundled mechanically as per requirement. In a modern press, up to two lakh copies can be printed in an hour. Agents of hawkers take charge at this stage in the pre-dawn hours for despatch to different centres. When printing and packing are finished, distribution begins. At the end of this, as the last copy leaves the press, it is at last all quiet. Not long after, cleaners are at the newspaper office clearing the pile of papers that seem inevitable even in a paperless newspaper office. The newsroom is ready for the next day.

For me, the mesmerising aspect is the part played by the computer. Its beneficial intervention is evident at every stage of production. The reporter does not struggle with mechanical typewriters and plain sheets of paper any more. The sub-editor does not put pen to paper for all the editing that goes into the newspaper. In the pre-computer days, from the reporter's notebook to the printing press, a news report would have gone through several hands—the chief reporter, news bureau, section heads, sub-editors, composing room, proofreading section, page-making section, the mangler—and then to the rotary press for conversion to plates ready for print. In the electronic age, the report traverses just three steps from the reporter to the subeditor to printer instead of the earlier minimum of 8. In the press, the whole range of machinery which depended on hot molten lead metal for every process of composition—which turned the composing hall into a veritable cauldron—has disappeared as has the mangler which used to convert pages of metal slugs into flongs to be recast to fit the rollers in the presses. In fact, 'go through the mangle' has dropped from the book of English idioms.

Newsroom Hierarchy

Just as the editor is responsible for all that the newspaper publishes, the news editor shoulders the task of organising the entire news section. All editorial departments work under the news editor—the news gathering section which includes all senior special correspondents, the chiefs of bureau, chief reporters and reporters, the photography department led by the photo editor and the desk comprising assistant editors, chief sub-editors and subeditors. The heads of the other desks of the editorial—business, regional, sports, entertainment, national and international—also report to the news editor. Assistant editors heading each section coordinate and liaise with the news editor while also supervising the editing staff under them.

The news editor plays a pivotal role coordinating and directing the

Figure 1.2 Newsroom Hierarchy

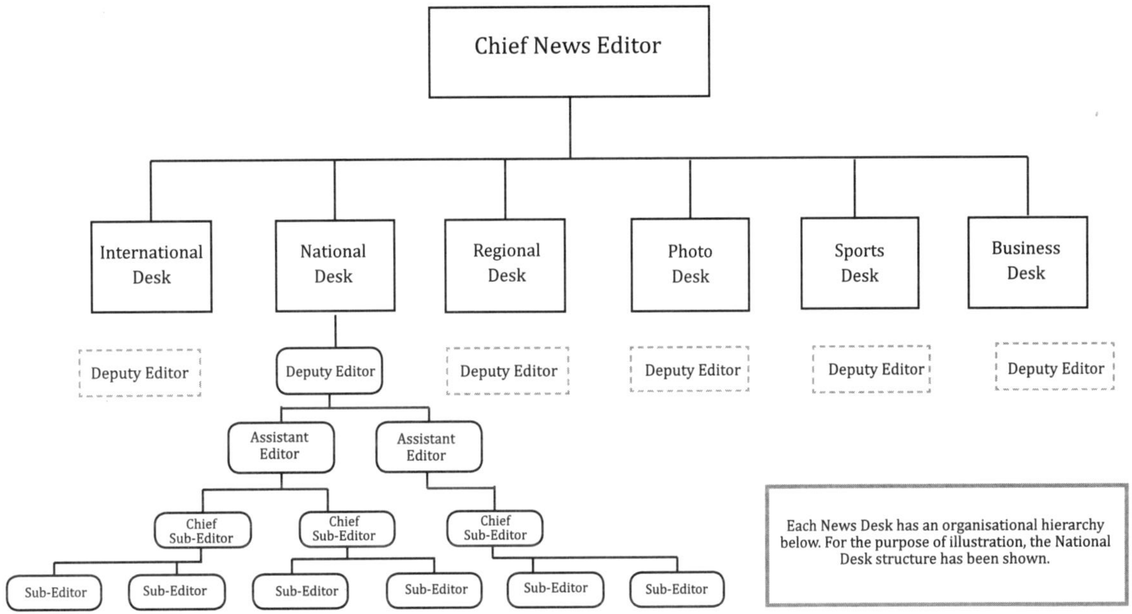

Source: Drawn by the author.

entire network with the help of a few assistant news editors. Thanks to the communication revolution, the news editor today controls all editions printed at different centres through the click of a button. From a laptop or PC, the news editor can monitor the entire activity from the headquarters in Delhi, Chennai or Chandigarh, every report being filed from Mangalore to Moscow to Washington, every page being made at the different centres, every copy being processed and every photograph coming into the system. The news editor's is a formidable task, especially if it is a multi-edition national newspaper. Such newspapers compete with other national rivals but have also to contend with the local interests and local newspapers, catering to local news in a way that does not distort the national perspective that the newspaper wants to project. Today a national newspaper's front page can look different at different centres such as state capitals as the editions would keep regional interest in mind while deciding on the stories. The Mumbai edition of *Times of India*, for example, may feature as the main front page story a new scheme the state government has launched while the Bengaluru edition may highlight the floods in a part of the state. A decade ago such flexibility would have been unthinkable since making major changes in the front page with the concurrence of the news editor was impossible. Here is one more instance where technology is driving the media. We will see more of this in the following chapters.

NOTES

1. V. Kumara Swamy, 'Where Were You When Indira Gandhi Was Killed?', *Telegraph*, 26 October 2014.
2. Andy Schotz, 'Fundamentals Should Still Apply, Even in Digital Age', *Quill*, 1 August 2008.

2

Writing the News

The No-frills Language

How does information, which is nothing more than a string of facts collected by a reporter, become a news report? The reporter who gathers the details puts them together in a standardised format. This then is edited—that is, the report is checked and prepared for broadcast or publication as news. To help them in this task, the reporter and the sub-editor have certain guidelines and criteria which they follow strictly. The reporter and the sub-editor play a complementary role in the preparation of news.

With the avalanche of information that is now inundating the knowledge world, we are in a situation of excess which places increasing demands on the journalist to perform and survive. Additionally, the journalist's unique position in the world of writing imposes greater responsibilities to adhere strictly to evolved standards. In one's professional duties and objectives the journalist is different from the blogger, writer of books, freelancer, advertising and public relations professional and others who also put out information for public consumption. The fundamental difference is that in the case of the journalist a very high degree of objectivity is demanded while for the rest there may be more freedom to write and comment. In this straight and narrow path, one trains to sift the truth from propaganda, and bias and comments from self-serving sources. It is a continuous, life-long effort.

Professional journalism has over the years evolved a set of rules and regulations, techniques and practices, ethics, values and principles. These help to ensure that the information gathered and put out is credible and in the interest of the reader. Before we go on to see what these standards and principles are, let us first see what news writing is, what its characteristics are and in what way it is different from other kinds of writing. Let us also learn about the 5Ws + 1H, the heartbeat of news writing.

The first lesson in news writing is that the journalist, whose objective is to convey some idea, some detail, some news, writes the way one speaks. Tell it the way you will tell your friend on the phone, is an advice that journalism schools give. The stylesheet of the *Economist* quotes William Hazlitt as saying, 'To write a genuine, familiar or truly English style is to write as anyone would speak in common conversation ... setting aside all pedantic and oratorical flourishes.'[1] The campaign for simple writing had been joined decades ago and it is a measure of the difficulty of imbibing it that you keep seeing much flawed writing in journalism. 'When a sentence is made stronger, it usually becomes shorter', wrote William Strunk Jr, an English professor, in a 43-page self-published manual called *The Elements of Style*.[2] He added, 'Vigorous writing is concise'[3]—a mantra that all journalists must be chanting in this electronic age when time and space have shrunk to the miserly hand-held mobile phone-cum-news provider.

Strunk wrote it at a time when both journalism and journalistic writing were still underdeveloped. His manuscript was republished decades later by E. B. White, future *New Yorker* writer, who added an essay of his own. The combined publication titled *The Elements of Style: With Revisions, An Introduction, And a New Chapter* (commonly known as 'Strunk & White'),[4] first out in 1959, is considered a manual on good writing. In his essay White wrote: 'Rich, ornate prose is hard to digest, generally unwholesome, and sometimes nauseating.'[5] If only today's journalists imbibe this advice. Strunk and White is a must-read for all journalists.

In simple but blunt language, the Strunk-White advice will read: Be clear and concise, or perish. With the social media adding to the news-views avalanche, no media outlet can survive if it does not adhere to this advice. What is clear is that like the media itself, newspaper language is being driven by technology.

As it has for long been. Till a half century ago when the teleprinter came into being, the language was governed in the main by the telegraph, which incidentally was given a final burial on 14 July 2013 after serving communication for more than 150 years. Decoding the telegram posed its own challenges. The script would quite often be garbled and messy, lines and words missing. In the telegraphic code, for example, the symbols for full stop (.) or paragraph marking ([) were avoided to prevent confusion in transmission. So when a sentence ended, they needed to write out STOP and when a fresh paragraph began, PARA. Quite often, the tricky word PARA has got into print as such. The teleprinter put a stop to the agony of deciphering the telegraphically transmitted text which most juniors would shy away from.

From the teleprinter to the present was a smooth transition. Today, the computer is driving the media and in this age of multimedia speed has become of the essence. To meet this demand the language that media uses has also evolved. Besides, readers/viewers have neither the time nor the inclination to read long winding reports like in the earlier eras. They want information on their doorstep, especially designed to ensure minimum effort on their part. They want information that is clear, precise and crisp. For this, successful news editors have key criteria. From these demands has evolved the language of news. It is somewhat similar to SMS language, though its role is weightier and much more serious. You have to learn and practise it. By no means can you gain proficiency through classroom lessons nor is there a quick fix. Learning it needs constant practice and a mindset that keeps reminding you of the ultimate goal: of attracting and retaining reader attention. If the writing is dull and unattractive or if it demands much attention and effort to understand, the reader will skip the report, leave the page and switch to other newspapers. The guidelines are the same in whatever language you are writing. This news language is for all languages.

It is not an easy language to learn and practise. Those of you fresh from college may find it easier to write a 2,000-word essay than a 300-word news report that is sharp, where every word counts. The essay is less demanding in terms of content and style of writing. In a news report, you are accountable for every word/phrase you use in the sense that it should be understood easily and should have a purpose in being included. You cannot dawdle and need to tell the story fast.

Every word you use should speed the delivery of information. This is best achieved through clarity which should begin with you, at home in more senses than one.

With clarity comes uncluttered writing, just as without it sentences are constructed badly and end up provoking anger and frustration. We will later see some examples of cluttered writing which results from a lack of clarity in thinking and/or insufficient information which is sought to be concealed.

The news motto is KISS and Tell: Keep It Simple and Straight and Tell. Simplicity in writing needs to be emphasised and imbibed by all journalists. With it comes precision and it enables you to strike a degree of rapport with the reader over a period of time. 'Read over your compositions [reports] and wherever you meet with a passage which you think is particularly fine, strike it out,'[6] advised Samuel Johnson. Your goal is to convey information, to communicate. The extent to which news language has evolved will be evident from the illustration that *The Newspapers Handbook* provides.[7] The *Handbook* provides the following as a report in the *Times*, London, in the year 1855:

> Three notable members of the Peace Society and of the Society of Friends spoke at a Christmas meeting of workmen in Gloucester, on Thursday night, on the subject of the (Crimea) war. Mr Joseph Sturge, member of a deputation to the Czar, Mr Bowly and Mr T M Sturge. Mr Joseph Sturge, after alluding to his mission to St Petersburg, with the view of bringing about a termination of hostilities, expressing his firm belief, notwithstanding all that had been said against the Emperor of Russia, or whatever might be the evils existing in the government, that there was no man in Europe who more earnestly desired a return to peace than that monarch, provided it could be done consistently with what he regarded as the honour of the country.[8]

The *Handbook* goes on to illustrate that if the news is reported today, it may read as:

> "The Russian emperor urgently desires peace in the Crimea," Joseph Sturge, who has returned from a meeting with the Czar, said on Thursday.

> "But any peace for the Czar must preserve the honour of Russia," he told a meeting of workers at Gloucester.
>
> Mr Sturge met the Czar in St Petersburg on a peace mission for the Society of Friends.[9]

Here is another example from a daily in Madras, dated 22 September 1903:

> As announced in our issue of Saturday last, the completion of the 25th year of *The Hindu* was celebrated yesterday (September 21, 1903). Public enthusiasm marked the event and the success far exceeded our best expectations.
>
> Mr G Subramania Iyer, one of the founders and former editor, said in his address "... as long as I was in charge I never underrated the responsibility of the Press in regard to our own social disabilities. I want to stress the responsibilities of the exponents of public opinion in the country to courageously and honestly press the importance of redressing our social wrongs as well as the errors of government."
>
> With "God Save the King" and the distribution of flowers and '*pan supari*', the party broke up.[10]

A full eleven decades later, how will this be reported? Here is an attempt:

> The *Hindu* today completed a quarter century, with a call from one of the founders and former editor G. Subramania Iyer to the leaders and the Press to rededicate themselves to redressing "social wrongs" as much as to exposing errors of government.
>
> "As long as I was in charge I never underrated the responsibility of the Press in regard to our own social disabilities," he said.
>
> Public enthusiasm marked the event.[11]

The Bare Bones Style

There are several criteria which govern the language of news. Here are some of them.

1. The most basic is: Be precise in the use of words. Using the correct word is more easily said than done. You need to sensitise your ear to the right word and the intended right meaning.

For example, not many will be aware that the words rob, steal, pilfer and swindle appearing quite similar and interchangeable, stand for different things. Theft and robbery are by definition different. Theft does not involve violence or the threat of use of violence. If that happens, it is robbery. If you are in doubt, look up the word in a dictionary or delete it.

2. Flowing from this almost as a corollary is the next one: be specific. This comes from knowing precisely what information/message you want to convey and knowing the correct word and usage to pick. Imprecise language betrays lack of confidence and abstract writing, characteristic of official communication, hinders the flow of reading and is unfit for newspapers. This disease of hiding in abstraction, which Fowler calls 'abstractitis'[12] does not affect journalists except in rare instances. The victims soon learn either that it is unsuitable for journalism or that they themselves are unsuited to the profession.
3. The third criterion is to be concise. Being concise has even more weight than the earlier ones. Either by force of habit or the demands of college education, we have developed a tendency to go into the essay mode and use long-winded sentences, well-worn clichés and obscure, long words. Such essay writing is never popular and should be anathema to a journalist whose job it is to convey news and information.

    Redundancies are another bane. Don't prefer five words when one will do as well. Some meaty samples of redundancy: future plan, over-exaggerate, general consensus, loud scream, new record, very first, past history, definite proof, 7:00 AM in the morning, concrete proposal. The last phrase once invited a comment from an editor: he asked what was 'concrete' about a proposal? Was it heavy like it was made of concrete? Delete such redundant words and phrases that add nothing of value to a report.

    Take this as an example:[13]

The City corporation has raised its objection to the planned construction of an eight-storey-high building to be used for offices, which would be located on the main thoroughfare in the heart of the metro. The civic body said its main objection was to the possibility that the structure and the advertisement hoardings it will carry may prove a distraction to drivers and result in traffic accidents on the main road.

There are so many redundancies in the paragraph that whatever information it seeks to convey can be done in half the number of words. Read this: 'The City corporation has objected to the construction of an eight-story office building on the main road (name it), saying it may prove a distraction to drivers and result in accidents.' Why 'eight-storey-high' where 'high' has no meaning here?

There is a long, long list of phrases and word strings which can safely be replaced with one word or two. Some examples are:

'to' is as good as 'in order to'
'at this point in time'/'at the present time' is 'now'
'take action' is 'act'
'with the exception of' is 'except'
'in the event' is 'if'
'along the lines of' is 'like'
'in the near future' is 'soon'
'for the purpose of'/'in an effort to' is 'to'
'personal feelings' is 'feelings'
'approximate estimate' is 'estimate'

4. Beware of errors over homophones—i.e., words pronounced the same way but differing in meaning or spelling or both. These are a bugbear for all journalists. Some homophones are bear/bare, defuse/diffuse, rights/rites, effect/affect, censor/sensor, break/brake.
5. Translate/interpret jargon sneaking into everyday use in the garb of specialised language. It is best not to use technical/scientific terms and puzzle the general reader. If they have to be used, sometimes to familiarise the reader with these terms, use them in their proper context and try and provide a clue to their meaning in consultation with experts. Taking care not to endanger accuracy, change long and complicated words to short and clear ones. For instance, if a scientist says that the atmospheric lifetime of greenhouse gases ranges from a few

years to a few thousand years, you can explain it to the reader that atmospheric lifetime can be taken as the average time taken by a human-caused emission of gas to return to natural levels of concentration and become less harmful. Also beware of clichés. Safe and sound, slow but sure, chop and change, followed in the footsteps, few and far between, heated exchange, uneasy truce, brutal murder and bottom line have over the years been overused to such an extent that they have lost their meaning or at least readers must have wearied of them. Don't use them unless they are relevant. Copy, especially in sports and entertainment, can also be prone to tired clichés. Replace them with straight talk. There are now dictionaries of clichés which can be a useful guide to avoid them.[14]

6. Don't clutter sentences with too much detail or too many clauses. Often reporters are so full of information about an event they have just covered that they feel unable to write a clear, straightforward account. In such a frame of mind, they tend to write tangled, cluttered sentences. The advice to them is to sit back, relax, refresh and then attempt to write the story. They should keep in mind the rule that a sentence should make no more than one or two points. Likewise, there should be one idea in one para.
7. Write in the active voice, i.e. subject-verb-object, to the extent possible. It is more direct and appealing. Instead of 'A meeting will be held by the dean at the ACJ to discuss the mess menu', say 'The dean will hold a meeting to discuss the mess menu.' Use of the active voice also helps to quicken the pace of reading.
8. Also use active verbs which power most strong sentences. For example, compare the two sentences 'The CEO left this morning by plane for Mumbai' and 'The CEO flew this morning to Mumbai.' The second sentence reads better and faster because it is powered by an active verb which combines the weak verb 'left' with the mode of departure 'plane' to make it 'flew'. 'Government staff ask for more pay, go on strike' versus 'Government staff strike for more pay'. 'Condemned man asks for clemency' versus 'Condemned man pleads for clemency'. Let verbs drive your sentences.

There are some special features characteristic of each of the media streams on news writing. News is the same for all the four streams and approach to news writing in terms of language—being straightforward and simple—is similar, but news writing in terms of content is not, nor is the news presentation. For print and online, news writing is more or less the same, differing in the way it is presented. Newspapers and magazines now have software that help the desk design pages. For web pages, there is an endless stream of software being developed on an everyday basis for designing and display of content.

For the two broadcast media streams—television and radio—news writing is more restrained and equally if not more challenging. Especially because in both an additional factor is that there is no way a viewer or listener can rewind and get a repeat if something is not clear. In the first, on television, the writing has to supplement the visual on the screen while in the second the writing has to be extremely simple and the pronunciation and diction of the news reader clear and uncluttered. Voice culture, in both, and appearance and mannerism of the anchor, in television, matter in a way they do not in the other two media. We will see more of these in the next chapter.

5Ws + 1H

As vital as the rules on news writing are the guiding principles that govern content. These are centred on the classic 5Ws + 1H of news that form the heartbeat of a news story. The five Ws are What, When, Where, Who and Why and the one H is How. The answers to these questions are an essential part of any news report and should come in the early paragraphs. Answers to the 5Ws + 1H in fact help frame the report, especially the lede, which conveys the essence of the story.

The five questions also provide a checklist of sorts for the reporter and the desk to ensure that the news report is complete and does not lack in detail. In most news developments, the answers to the first four Ws will be clear. It is only the fifth W—i.e., the Why—which has an alternative H or How. A news story has invariably answers to either why or how, not both. The Why will have an answer in a story that involves motivation. Why did the government announce a tax concession in the middle of the year? Because elections are due. If it is action, you will have the answer for the H. The teenager fell off a moving bus and fractured his leg. Ask the question How and you have the answer. There is normally no answer for the question Why.

The question What perhaps is the most important in a news story since what happened goes to the heart of the matter. In a house collapse during the monsoon in which two persons are killed, what happened has overriding importance. Answers to other questions are important but they will provide details. The core news is the answer to What. Two persons dead in a house collapse.

In the same report, Who is the question that crops up next. Who died? Two persons. If either of them is a child or a woman, the answer to Who needs to be in the lead para along with what happened. It will read: Two persons, including a child, were killed in a house collapse. When answering the question, often it might suffice to make a brief description of the Who. It would be absurd to give in the lead the names of the two if they are little known. The names will mean nothing to the general reader. These details can be given in the later paragraphs if need be, but not in the lead. If one of the dead is known in the neighbourhood, you give the name in the lead. In answering both When and Where, the reporter has to assess the manner in which the report has to go into the details. The time a train accident takes place may need to be spelled out since there could be dislocation in the services and there will be reader interest in that detail. But it may be meaningless to specify that a local car accident took place at 5:52 PM. A broad indication that it occurred early evening would suffice. The same logic applies to Where.

In terms of the value of a news report, perhaps the answer to the last question Why/How carries more weight than the others. The answer in fact completes the story, tying up loose ends and providing explanations for the reader to understand the story. Sometimes both questions will have answers in a story but only one of them will provide the decisive response. The answer to Why provides the motivation, as we have seen earlier, while How refers to the action. In a murder, for example, the answer to why it took place may provide key answers, though how it took place may also have an answer. For the print media, which will report on an event some hours after it has been covered on the air and the television channels, the Why and How often have greater significance.

Beginning with the Climax

Bruce Porter, formerly of the Columbia School of Journalism, who lectured at the Asian College of Journalism in Chennai for some years, has explained in a telling manner and with a classic example the crucial role of the classic 5 Ws + 1 H for writing breaking news leads. He takes the story 'The Pied Piper of Hamelin' which tells about a village in sixteenth-century Lower Saxony, Germany, being plagued by rats and its attempt to get rid of the menace.

The Brothers Grimm tell the fairy tale by starting at the very beginning: how there was once upon a time a sleepy village which found itself plagued by rats. The narrative moves on to the manner in which the village got the Pied Piper to help, promising to pay him for his labour, how he led the rats out of the village by playing tunes on his pipe and the way the villagers reneged on their promise to pay him. And then, the climax: The Piper in revenge lures the children of the village away into a hole in the mountain.

The most interesting point in the tale comes at the very end. Till one reaches the very last para one has no inkling of the most newsworthy element–the abduction and loss of the children. 'A newspaper reporter writing a breaking news lead to the Hamlin story would begin quite differently, revealing the news in the very first sentence,' says Porter in a book he co-authored with Timothy Ferris.[15] The reporter would begin with the children being abducted, and the Piper's revenge on being denied his due–the breaking news. His lead para gives the essence of the story. The climax is up front, unlike the fairy tale where it is told at the very end. This is the inverted pyramid in operation.

These are examples of the lead given in the book:[16]

> All the children of Hamlin were abducted today by an exterminator who was angered over the town's refusal to pay him for getting rid of its rats.
>
> An exterminator calling himself the 'Pied Piper' today abducted the

children of Hamlin after the mayor reneged on a promise to pay him for ridding the community of rats.

Angered by Hamlin's refusal to pay him for ridding it of rats, an exterminator called the 'Pied Piper' today led the town's children through a hole in a nearby mountain to an unknown destination.

The authors mention about how by asking each of the questions in the 5 Ws + 1 H the reporter can arrive at a slightly varying lead around the climactic point of the abduction of the children. Answers to the questions 'what' happened, 'when' and 'where' give the straight-forward answer, with answers to 'why' and 'how' lending more value by giving the reason for the abduction (why) and the manner of it (how). Describing the lead options listed above, they say: 'Each of these leads approaches the news from a slightly different angle. The first emphasises *what* happened, the second *who* did it, the third *why* he did it. But each delivers the essence of the story in a tightly wrapped package. That is the idea behind the breaking news lead. We may still have plenty of questions: Who is this Pied Piper? Why did the children go? Why didn't the police try to stop him? But the lead has conveyed the essence of the story.'[17]

The 5Ws + 1H principle plays a pivotal role in news reporting. For, fix the lead right and half the job is done; the rest of the story quickly falls into place. Most journalists follow the principle and yet on some days incomplete reports get into newspapers that beg many of the questions. Here is a sample of poor writing and poor editing. If only either the reporter who wrote it or the sub-editor who edited it had cared to ask the right questions, the report would not be lacking in vital details. The first example is a report of an accident involving a goods train and two buses. It was on the front page of a daily last summer.

4 Killed as Train Rams Vehicles Stuck on Track[18]

In a multiple collision, four persons—two drivers—were killed on the spot and seven others sustained serious injuries when a speeding goods train rammed a private van and a school van, which were on the track following a collision at the manned level crossing on Sunday.

The school van, fortunately without students, reportedly hit

> the private van, which was at that time waiting at the closed level crossing for the freight train to cross. The school van pushed the van from behind, which broke through the level crossing gate. Both the vehicles came to a halt on the track.
>
> Before the drivers could move the vehicles, the on-coming train hit their vehicles killing three persons. One of the train drivers lost two fingers in his right hand when a mangled sheet severed them off.
>
> Senior officials, including Collector Raman Singh, Superintendent of Police Mooshikavahanam and Railway Divisional Manager Rambo rushed to the spot and conducted an enquiry. Trains in the sector suffered no significant detention.
>
> Preliminary investigation pointed out that while the private van with a few passengers was proceeding to Vadapalani, the school van was reportedly driven by a learner who lost control of the vehicle.
>
> "Since the train was cruising at a moderate speed, others in the private van could jump out and escape. Otherwise, the toll would have been higher," said a senior Railway official.

There are too many unexplained details, apart from poor writing. Do you understand what had happened at the manned level crossing? Why were two drivers among those killed in the van? Was 'pushed' the right word to describe what the school van did to the other van from behind? Is 'to cross' the right usage for the freight train that would 'pass'?

It is from other newspapers that I learnt that the school van was being driven by a new recruit on training and that three trained drivers were sitting inside the van to help and supervise him. The driver apparently lost control and the school van rammed the other van from behind and propelled it across the level cross gate and on to the track where both got stuck and were unable to clear out before the train ran into them.

As the 5Ws + 1H guideline tells you, the question Who has been answered in the worst possible manner. Names of local officials may mean nothing to the general reader.

Writing Features and Analyses

The lean and mean writing style, of course, is not the only one used in newspapers. Only when it comes to news does the language in which it is presented is demanding because the ones for whom it is intended don't have too much time at their disposal. There are space constraints as well, and most importantly, there is the pressure of time. Since nearly all of it is spot news, there is little scope or need for descriptive writing.

'Soft' news writing such as for news features and human interest stories is, on the other hand, less demanding in some senses but can be more challenging. There is less rigidity in the style of writing here. These carry special, extra, often in-depth information which cannot be just browsed through and understood. Such writing includes news features, news analyses and magazine features. Each has its own parameters and life spans. Deadline pressures and barebones writing do not hamper these modes of writing where the descriptive style plays a prominent role. And, unlike a news report which is dead as a dodo in 24 hours or less, the features have a longer lifespan. For example, written a day or two after an event, to explain its significance, a news feature and a news analysis can stay alive for four to five days. A magazine feature has a longer life.

There are some broad guidelines that govern the writing for news reports, news features and news analyses and magazine features.

News Reports

1. News reports usually break news, describe what happened such as an accident, riot or murder. They are immediate and do not have a shelf life.
2. News writing is direct and without comment. The focus is always on the news.
3. News reports are normally not long, the length depending on the importance of the development.

News Features

1. News features are big-picture write-ups that place the news development in context, giving the perspective. They are detailed write-ups and can be about an individual or event, incident, accident, shoot-outs and celebrations and deaths. They can be about a series of events that may reflect a trend or a comparison of different incidents. They can also relate to the impact or consequence of an event or action.

2. The writing style is different from news reports. It is more descriptive, with the use of some colourful language and clever turns of phrases, without any of the restrictions that are listed in the language of news. Unlike a news report which goes to the heart of the matter straightaway, features don't follow the inverted pyramid style and can begin with anecdotes and question marks and exclamations, and are not bound to reveal their main point in the lead paras. In some human interest stories, the climax is at the end like in a novel. They provide background, history and sometimes even projections into the future. They can profile people and places.
3. Features can be long and extensive and take up an entire page or, sometimes, longer. To make it easy to read, different but related elements can be put together as a full blown feature. This means that when there is a major development which has several ramifications, say for example, the assassination of Indira Gandhi in 1984, there is need to report on all related topics—the killing, the political and law and order implications, succession struggles, regional rumblings, etc. If all of this is strung together in one news report, it will be too long and unwieldy and tend to drive the reader away. To make it easy for the reader to quickly grasp all the implications, the practice is to separate the different elements of the story with boxes and suitable graphics and display them in such a way that they form part of a whole in one part of the page or the full page, like a full-blown feature. To take the assassination example, there were different reports on the different angles or topics and all were grouped together. In fact, in this case, because of the magnitude of the event, the next day's newspapers—private television had not yet arrived—had placed all news reports unrelated to the assassination in a corner in an inside page.
4. Unlike a news story, deadlines don't threaten features. They can be run a few days after the main news development. Their life span is three or four days.
5. In the last few years, the best example of all three of these came in the *New York Times* on the day it reported a shooting incident in front of the Empire State building in New York (24 August 2012). Even from the headline and lead para that I have given

here, it was clear that the daily was taking an exhaustive look at all angles to the story, from the actual report (hard news, on the front page) to the history of shootings in the area, the internal office squabbling which might have led to the shootout and the consequences of police reaction, all news features, and finally to the gun used in the shootout and how it had featured in the gun control debate, an analysis. An excellent lesson for students of journalism on writing news features.

The following stories were carried in the feature:

1. The main report on the front page. 'Gunman dies after killing at Empire State building: A man fatally shot his coworker and then was shot and killed by police in gunfire that also injured several others outside the Empire State building, police said.'
2. Long before carnage, an office grudge festered. 'An animosity between the two men at the centre of a fatal shooting at the Empire State building evolved over years at the workplace.'
3. That yet again a landmark is the backdrop to violence. 'Since a 1977 shooting on the Empire State building's observation deck, the police department has increased security measures in and around the building.'
4. That the decision by two police officers to open fire in busy midtown leaves bystanders wounded. 'Investigators believe that at least seven of 16 bullets fired by two officers during the shooting struck the gunman but the rest may have injured bystanders.'
5. That the gun used by shooter is known for its deadly power. 'The pistol used in the shooting outside Empire State building is among the more lethal handguns in the American firearm market and had a key role in the gun control debate.'

One advice is to think of a feature story as a news story written like a piece of short fiction. You must, of course, combine the rigours of factual reporting with the creative freedom of short story telling.

Here are two versions of an event, a cricket match, that demonstrate the difference between a news report and a news feature. The first tells the news in a straight-forward manner. The second attempts to capture the festive atmosphere at the stadium during a match, where the result takes a back seat.

Mumbai Indians Win[19]

Chennai: Mumbai Indians defeated Royal Challengers Bangalore (RCB) by 36 runs in the final match of the Champions League T20 at the Chidambaram Stadium in Chennai on Sunday. MI's captain Harbhajan Singh was declared man of the match.

In a low-scoring match, MI was all out for 136 in the allotted 20 overs, losing their last wicket to the last ball. In the slow pitch, RCB could muster only 100 runs for the loss of eight wickets in the 20 overs.

There was a sizeable crowd at the stadium, though the local heroes Chennai Super Kings (CSK) were not featuring in the match and there was little interest in the game since CSK had already been knocked out of the championship.

Rooting for the Non-playing CSK[20]

VINAYA PATIL

"CSK ... CSK" the crowd was shouting at the Chepauk stadium on that humid, hot Sunday (Oct 9) evening. If you thought it meant Chennai Super Kings, you were right. If you also thought that the fans were cheering a match between CSK and some rival team on the ground, you were wrong.

The huge crowd, the shouts, screams, lights, waving of fans, and security checking–everything was normal, as it is for any cricket match these days. In a cricket crazy land, it was also not surprising to find people going wild over a match and shouting the name of their favourite team even before they entered the stadium. Once inside, there was absolutely no boundary to the excitement and curiosity on every spectator's face.

This was the perfect setting at the Chidambaram Stadium for the final match of the Champions League T20 between Mumbai Indians and Royal Challengers Bangalore (RCB). Yes, you read it correct. Chennai Super Kings was nowhere in the picture, but the venue being Chennai, the crowd couldn't stop cheering for their home team, despite its early exit from the championship.

Amid the cheers and boos, the match began at a quite slow pace. With a slow pitch, as indicated by experts, there wasn't much scope for high run scoring and the crowd shouting for every other boundary and a six hit. But, as the fall of wickets began for Mumbai Indians, the RCB supporters definitely had an opportunity to sing and dance. This was precisely where one got to see the drama and fun of watching a cricket match in the stadium.

Among a variety of fans, there was one who removed his t-shirt right in the stadium and began dancing on the chair. "That's (Saurav) Ganguly for you" someone commented, reminding everyone of the incident where the then captain of the Indian cricket team had removed his t-shirt and swirled it around in his hand to express his joy over an impossible victory in the Natwest Trophy way back in 2002.

As the first innings came to an end, Mumbai Indians had scored 136 runs, with their last wicket falling on the last ball of the allotted 20 overs. Now tension became palpable in the stadium as people began to predict the result. After a short break of 15 minutes, just before the match resumed, the Bollywood actress Priyanka Chopra was interviewed and the crowd was pleasantly surprised. Fans blew kisses and waved and expressed their love by shouting their hearts out in a bid to capture her attention.

The Royal Challengers Bangalore had begun batting now and they did start off with a bang. Their supporters happily cheered and the Mumbaikars booed, but all the cheering for the home teams went for a toss, when none other than the master blaster Sachin Tendulkar was shown on screen. The entire stadium shouted in unison as if paying a tribute to the legend. "He is our God, no one can ever equal him," said Mr Kumar Swamy, an RCB supporter.

The match had now begun to slow down, with the run rate falling and a few wickets already taken. But, the wicket that made the Mumbai girls both happy and sad was that of RCB's Virat Kohli. As the girls cheered for Mumbai, there were signs of sorrow at the fact that they wouldn't be able to see their heart throb playing. "He is freaking hot," exclaimed Shreya Sinha, a Mumbai Indians supporter and a Kohli fan at the same time.

The next big scream came when the *Badshah* of Bollywood, Shah Rukh Khan was on screen. Girls couldn't control their blushes. It was as if their eternal desire of seeing him had come true. Among all this drama, the RCB had managed to make 100 runs for the loss of eight wickets. The last few overs saw the remaining wickets being taken and Mumbai Indians emerging winners by 36 runs. The icing on the cake for Mumbai Indians was that their captain Harbhajan Singh was named Man of the Match.

"It was worth watching the match, in spite of not being a supporter of either contestants. I had come to watch a good game, and I did," said Shankhayan Ghosh as he trudged out of the stadium. For a country of cricket lovers, there was not just the match to enjoy on the ground but the parallel entertainment in the stands that the spectators provide.

News Analyses

1. A news analysis contains comments and views on the news event which is analysed for its implications. The analysis can be on an incident, major decisions, personal foibles, killings, coups and wars. Not all news stories have scope for analysing.
2. A news analysis is meant to educate the reader and explain in detail why an event or action has taken place. A journalist's experience and expertise come into play when presenting an analysis, which is an incisive commentary on a given event.
3. It can be an interpretation of the event sometimes to project a point of view.
4. The writing style is direct. The focus is more on the comments and analyses than on the details of the incident/action in question.

Writing for the magazine sections of newspapers has few constraints and fewer rules. On the other hand, articles on the editorial and op-ed pages are in a different genre altogether. The two pages that stand out in a newspaper because of their weighty content are its editorial page and, since the 1990s, the op-ed (Opposite Editorial) page. While every effort is taken to ensure that the opinions of the reporter and the desk do not intrude into the news pages—remember the injunction 'Do not editorialise'—the editorial and op-ed pages are devoted precisely to views, analyses, debates and discussions, to provoke thought and in effect to mould public opinion. Among the four streams of the media, only print has this privilege as there is no scope for editorial exposition in TV, radio or, to a large extent, online. TV channels have, in recent times, sought to claim the space through their web versions where they carry opinion pieces by contributors.

Editorials stand for a publication, be it a daily, weekly or monthly. They reflect the publication's views on a given subject, as enumerated by the powerful editorial board. An editorial, or 'edit' in short, takes a clear stand on a subject and gives the arguments for and against and states where it stands and why. Under normal circumstances, an edit has a word limit which is exceeded only if the gravity of the occasion demands. On rare occasions, such as the day the country attained Independence, the assassination of Mahatma Gandhi, the death of Nehru and the killings of his daughter Indira Gandhi and grandson Rajiv Gandhi, newspapers have published edits on the front page. A well-argued editorial has in the past swung public opinion during crucial debates. The op-ed page, which debuted during the media boom, publishes syndicated articles and those commissioned from regular contributors on topical subjects. These are subject to editorial vetting.

NOTES

1. William Hazlitt, '*On Familiar Style', quoted in Style Guide: The Bestselling Guide to English Language, London: Profile Books Ltd, 1.*
2. William Strunk Jr, *The Elements of Style*, Ithaca, New York: Private printing, 1918, quoted in Adam Haslett, 'The Art of Good Writing', *Financial Times*, 21 January 2011.
3. Ibid., quoted in Haslett, 'The Art of Good Writing'.
4. William Strunk Jr and E. B. White, *The Elements of Style*, New York: Macmillan, 1959.
5. Ibid., quoted in Haslett, 'The Art of Good Writing'.
6. James Boswell, *The Life of Samuel Johnson, LL.D.*, 1791.
7. Richard Keeble and Ian Reeves, *The Newspapers Handbook*, New York: Routledge, 1994, pp. 136–38.
8. Ibid.
9. Ibid.
10. Reproduced by permission of the *Hindu*.
11. Written by the author for this publication.
12. *Fowler's Modern Engish Usage*, second edition, revised by Sir Arnest Gowers, 1965, 5.
13. Written by the author for this publication.
14. For example, Christian Ammer, *Viva-Facts on File Dictionary of Writer's Library–Cliches: Meanings and Origins of More than 3500 Terms and Expressions*, Viva Books, 2005.
15. Bruce Porter and Timothy Ferris, *The Practice of Journalism: A Guide to Reporting and Writing the News*. Englewood Cliffs, NJ: Prentice Hall, 1988, p. 93.

16. Ibid.
17. Ibid.
18. R. Ilangovan, '4 Killed as Train Rams Vehicles Stuck on Track', *Hindu*, 1 July 2011, Salem edition. Reproduced by permission of the *Hindu*.
19. Unpublished news report written by the author for this publication.
20. News feature published in *The Word: Lab Journal of the Asian College of Journalism* 12 (2). Reproduced by permission of the author and ACJ.

3

Reporting the News

Multitasking, Changing Tools and Rising Demands

Reporters are the eyes and ears of a newspaper, they say. They are the ones who go out on the street, rain or shine, to gather information and they certainly are the ones who will never lose their job, computer-internet-social media-whatever else threatens. For, without the facts they bring from the field there is no reporting, no printed version of events, no broadcast or online version either. What does a reporter do each day? What is reporting? In what way is a reporter's task or goal different from the other wordsmiths like public relations personnel and bloggers who also mine information or use it? What are the instruments at the service of the reporter to sift the truth from propaganda and bias and comments from self-serving sources?

Over the past few decades, all these facets have seen major transformations and the profile of the reporter has seen a metamorphosis. Today, the task of the reporter is much more demanding. Often doubling as information gatherer and videographer, the reporter is called on to perform multiple tasks, each requiring different skills.

Basically, the reporter gathers information and fits it into a structured 'news' mould. The process of collecting such information is bound by certain well acknowledged professional rules—objectivity, fairness, independence, balance and accuracy. The reporter keeps foremost in mind the interest of the reader—and not that of the newsmaker. In contrast, others in information dissemination could have agendas, need not be and are mostly not objective and may be serving newsmakers and paymasters instead of the reader. Public relations professionals, speech writers and spin doctors put information to the service of those whom they serve and who pay them.

As for bloggers—many journalists have active blogs—they do not subscribe to the time-honoured dictum 'News is Sacred, Comment Free'. What they put out in their blogs is coloured by their subjective view. They make no effort to conceal this—which in some ways serves as a warning to the reader. When subjectivity intrudes, 'news' loses its sacredness, its sanctity. The presumed element of objectivity vanishes. However, most of these blog posts, cited by the newspapers where they contribute columns, do not masquerade as news posts. Readers know that they are reading someone's views, not pure unadulterated news. Clearly, the journalist belongs in a different field where truth telling should be the only goal.

Let's take an example from the day's newspaper and see how a journalist makes the information credible to the reader by the transparency of gathering and reliability of sources. There was a road accident resulting in the death of a motorcyclist who was knocked down by a public transport bus. The first thing a journalist needs to do is check the veracity of the information from contacts, hospitals and other local sources. The reporter checks with the local police station and other sources like friends and colleagues in the area where the accident took place; goes to the accident spot and then to the hospital and checks the records in the casualty section and the morgue; talks to the traffic police who have by then registered a case; talks to eyewitnesses to get as much information as possible in the time available.

Unlike others who may have come to know of the fatal accident through friends or relatives of the victims and would have received only one version of the occurrence and not any other—for example, the version of the bus crew and eyewitnesses—the reporter talks to and visits a variety of sources and gets a nearly complete picture of verifiable information. Unlike others, the reporter does not have a vested interest in projecting a particular viewpoint—supporting or damning one side or the other. After hearing all the sides, the reporter can present the picture as objectively as possible, without resorting to conjecture or hearsay and his facts verifiable by any independent observer.

Assessing Newsworthiness

Another aspect of news reporting is to assess the newsworthiness of an event. How is a reporter/newspaper to assess the 'newsworthiness' of an event or development?

Here are broad, basic criteria:

1. At the most basic level, the information should be useful. For example, interruptions in water or power supply, traffic diversions, disruptions to normal life because of a *bandh* (strike), demonstrations, weather forecast warnings of unprecedented rain or an approaching low pressure or cyclone.
2. The information should be relevant and meaningful. For example, the new Karnataka government is to present a fresh budget with additional tax proposals to finance the city's infrastructure which is grossly inadequate. This is very relevant to all Bangaloreans and meaningful in the context of their daily struggles with civic and other problems.
3. The information should increase awareness and understanding. For example, advice on healthcare during outbreaks of diseases or debates over global warming that serve to raise awareness of the dangers flowing from human profligacy with energy sources.
4. The information should help in forming opinion. For example, parliamentary debate on the food security legislation, giving the remarks of members belonging to all political parties. The different shades of opinion will help readers draw their own conclusions about the relevance of the legislation. The information should help decide support: A logical follow-up relates especially to decisions at the time of elections.
5. The information should be of educative value. For example, the reality that urban lifestyles are leading to increase in lifestyle diseases may provide some timely warning to readers about their food and other habits.

Not all news can be neatly categorised to fit into this framework. Reporters therefore seek newsworthy information. There is a veritable variety of sources from which they gain information of interest. Some are familiar—the routine beat that the juniors do every day to the offices of civic administrators, police (crime and traffic), hospitals and party offices, officials who hold briefing sessions, press conferences and seminars and more. Some news comes to them on the phone, through press releases and by email. Many newspaper offices have their sources book containing contact information of all relevant government institutions and experts in different fields who can be tapped in times of need. Reporters also cultivate their own sources over time—by keeping in regular touch with their sources. Other sources of information include:

- Spot reporting done where news occurs. Under this comes reportage of accidents, crimes, protests and demonstrations, police action and public gatherings.
- Political reporting of briefings by party spokespersons, supporters/opponents and interviews. Reporters also track political parties on a regular basis and get their views on important developments.
- Legal reporting is gaining importance and court proceedings are increasingly being covered by reporters.

Let us look at the stories in two newspapers on a randomly chosen day and explore how the stories must have been put together to see how news gathering has been done. Here are examples from the *Hindu* and the *Times of India* of the same day in mid-2012.

The main story in the *Hindu* is about an all-party meeting convened by the government the previous day to discuss the draft Lokpal bill. How has the information been gathered? There were different sources: the government through its spokesmen, the ministers directly, opposition leaders of various parties, civil society leaders. Perhaps this story was written by the chief of bureau with inputs from a number of reporters who would have got the views of participants and parties and activists, directly or over phone or email. Apart from briefings from parties, the report also quotes the main observations of the prime minister. When major developments such as this take place, there are many angles to the story that need to be reported on. A number of reporters are sent out to the different sources of information to gather news and views. Their reports are collated and put in context to get the national picture. In a larger office where a news bureau operates, the reporters file their reports and brief the bureau chief. The bureau chief files the main report covering all the developments of the day, giving the overall picture. This report is invariably the lead for the day. The practice holds good for all the four streams–print, online, radio and TV.

There is no spot reporting in this report in the sense that nothing has happened at any specific spot unlike in the following second story. The main story has been put together by tracking news developments and is primarily political reporting. There is also no side story on the page to go with the main story or first lead. Two reports in the inside pages plus photographs (page 14) go without a reference on the front page.

The second most important story relates to the death by shooting of a 13-year-old-boy inside the army residential complex in Chennai. This is spot reporting and involves several reporters. We have the police version, defence authorities' version, eyewitness accounts, reactions. And vitally, a human interest story of great interest where every detail has been included. The development, which may have wide repercussions, is the lead story in the *Times of India* while the *Hindu* takes it as the anchor (at the bottom of the front page that the paper normally allocates for regional news).

A second political report relates to the sacking of a minister for his alleged links with the opposition. The *Hindu* makes no mention of the allegation against him, without which the story is incomplete. The *Times of India* focuses on this point. Crime and killings are of perennial reader interest: the *Hindu* has a report on the arrest of an aide of Chhota Rajan in connection with the killing of journalist Jyotirmoy Dey in Mumbai.

The day after the Wimbledon final is the best occasion to bring sport to the front page: the *Hindu* has an excellent photograph of winner Djokovic getting a taste of the Wimbledon grass, with a nice caption too.

Interview and conferences/seminars need not always be hard news. But they provide background, provoke controversy. Interviews are a major source of information. There are none here.

Spot reporting: On an inside page in the *Hindu* is a report of a controversial action by city corporation officials–a classic case of

Figure 3.1 Reporting Setup

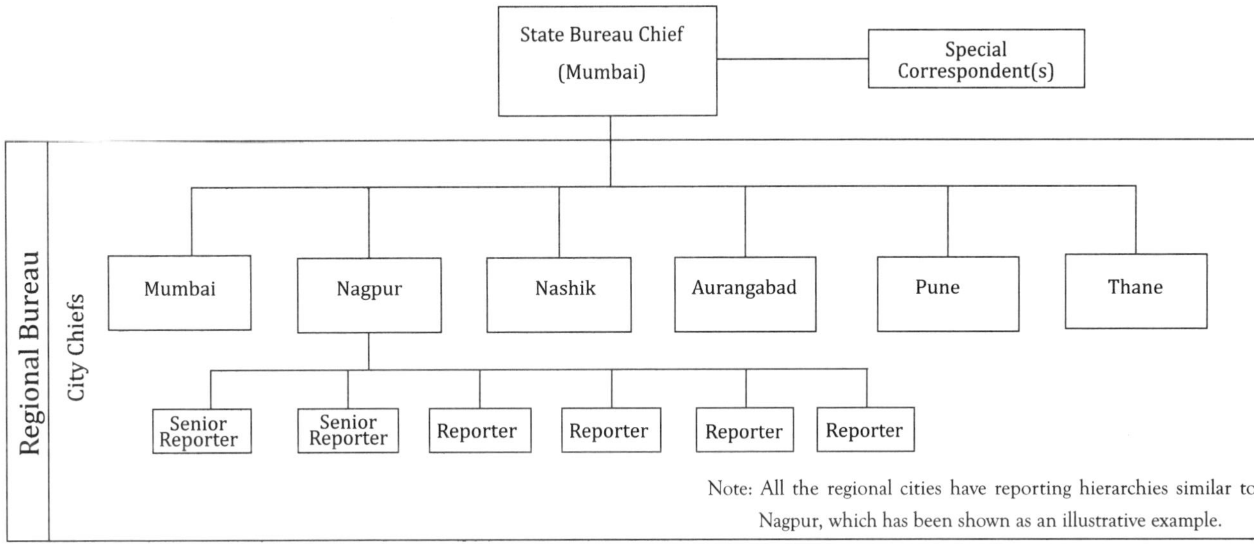

Note: All the regional cities have reporting hierarchies similar to Nagpur, which has been shown as an illustrative example.

Source: Drawn by the author.

spot reporting. The reporter was on the spot with a photographer to report on both sides of the controversy.

Courts: Courts are part of the regular beat of reporters. Not many of them need to hold a law degree but must be able to convey the implications of a judgement or the arguments in a clear, understandable manner.

Spot news of the best sort: On another inside page (in the *Times of India* partially on page one) is a report on an accident in a factory which led to the hospitalisation of several employees. The reporter visits the factory and the hospital, talks to police and the district administration, and the employees and employers. Does the report give fair coverage to both sides? This is an excellent example of spot reporting, the dream of every budding journalist.

Reporters, who cover ministries regularly, also file reports on new programmes and schemes that the different ministries plan to launch. On the last page in the *Hindu* two days ago, there was a report on the Centre finalising an urban health scheme. No specific sourcing is given for the report nor is one required. It is the result of informal official briefing, an accepted practice to disseminate official viewpoints and programmes. The reporter must only guard against PR attempts and must be able to separate information from propaganda. This comes without effort to a trained reporter. This type of reporting provides information of interest to readers.

Analysis/background: Another important report in the *Hindu* analysed the killing of several Right to Information Act (RTI) activists in the past seven months. It seeks to give some perspective and background to the murder of an activist in Gujarat, using it as a peg to analyse the national picture on a legislation that is under constant attack by officialdom and sections of the Executive and one that the media must cherish and guard as a vital tool of its trade. As yet, the Act is hardly used by newspapers, though magazines which have the time to await a response have used it to advantage.

Putting It Together

Reporting in essence boils down to writing about an event, finding out the consequences or implications of an event or a decision and seeking the views and reactions of experts on possible outcomes of events and developments. Under the rubric of 'events' come accidents, happenings, celebrations, political activity, riots, calamities, wars, terrorist attacks and sports. Talking to people connected with events such as politicians, bureaucrats, corporate leaders, and celebrities from the field of entertainment and sports yields newsworthy information.

The journalist ends up collecting a whole lot of information and all of that cannot be published. Even the information the journalist decides to convey has to be presented in a comprehensive, understandable manner. It is here that the news writing technique comes to the journalist's help—it teaches the journalist to present simple to complex details in an easily-digestible format.

How does the journalist go about the writing? What goes into a report? What has happened/What is happening? Where did it happen?[1]

As we have seen in Chapter Two—in the discussion on 5Ws + 1H—a storyteller begins at the very beginning and comes to the climax at the end while the journalist inverts the process and begins with the climax, the most newsworthy element. (Remember the Pied Piper analogy.)

The journalist has nothing to do with chronological narration. The technique used is called the Inverted Pyramid style. A terse lead, the most vital part of a news report, captures some of the answers flowing from the 5Ws + 1H. In this time-tested inverted pyramid style of reporting, the lead para is followed by the body of the report which elaborates on the lead points in descending order of importance. For example, in the report on the theft of *panchaloha* idols which we see later in this chapter, their recovery is the most important point though the official police briefing begins with the disappearance of the idols some time earlier. Once the main point of the story has been indicated, the report moves on to elaborate it. In the idols story, it provides answers to all those questions about how police recovered them, from where, were there any arrests, who were the arrested persons, was there an idol lifting gang behind. The news story then expands—who were the people behind the theft, to which temple did the idols belong, who helped sell them, etc. The reporter talks to temple authorities on the safety of idols, consults experts in the field and refers to earlier cases for a background.

You move from the lead para step by step, listing the points in the way the questions will arise in you about the story.

There are standard structures for presenting the different types of news stories. For example,

1. Cabinet or official meetings: final outcome/decisions taken, the conflicting positions and debates on it, the resolution of differences.
2. Speech: the most important point made by the speaker. Merely stating that so-and-so spoke at a meeting cannot be news.
3. Traffic accident: the number of casualties, including dead and injured, how it happened and status of the injured, the possible cause, etc.
4. Controversies: balanced presentation of opposing views in the lead para, followed by objective presentation of the conflicting views.
5. When covering court proceedings, there is a certain order in which the story is structured. You lead with the judgment if it has been delivered, followed by the issue contested and the arguments for and against.

The news structure in the inverted pyramid style approximates as follows:

Introduction/Lead Para:[2] The climax or the most newsworthy point
Para 2: The context which explains the action in the lead
Paras 3 and 4: The cause of the action described in the lead
Paras 5 and 6: The effect/consequence of that action

For stories witnessed by the reporter or for stories based on multiple accounts, attribution may not come in the first paragraph or may not even be needed. For example, 'Incessant rain throughout the day has led to waterlogging and disruption of normal life.' The fact or assertion that it rained needs no attribution. The statement, 'It was a sweltering hot day' needs no attribution; but if you report that the day temperature was 39 degrees, you need to attribute it to some authority or monitoring equipment.

Fact files to Reports

Let us see some examples of ways to write news reports based on given facts or from a file of facts. Most often, reports by police take the form of a fact file. Under normal circumstances, journalists read the fact file, note down the key points and prepare their report. As you will see later, occasionally, such police fact files in the form of a press note can be a veritable puzzle.

I

Fact File: Housewife Murder (Crime)[3]

A report is prepared based on the fact sheet for the newspaper dated 10 August. The dateline, that is the date and place, is Bengaluru, 9 August, when police claim to have solved the murder and released details.

1. Radha, a housewife, is found murdered in her apartment in JP Nagar on 6 August. She was 41 years old.
2. Gopal, her husband, works in an accounts company in Dubai and was on holiday. Sridhar is their nine-year-old son studying in Class IV in a school nearby. They have no drivers and other assistants. They employ a maid servant who has been with them for three years now.
3. Radha was found in a pool of blood in her drawing room by a friend and neighbour who usually visits her after the hustle and bustle of the morning hours are over. On 6 August, the friend found the main door ajar and opened it to see Radha in an unconscious state.
4. Gopal had gone to visit his relatives in Tumakuru (another town) and was due to return on the night of 6 August. He was informed on the phone immediately and was on his way back.
5. 7 August: Police question neighbours and, on his return, interrogate Gopal who informs them that some valuables, including jewels and silver and expensive watches were missing. The almirahs are intact.
6. 8 August: After extensive probing, police interrogate three persons who were seen in the apartment complex where the Gopals live on the morning of July 3. One of the three is the auto driver who takes Sridhar to school every day. He also happens to be the husband of the house maid. The other two were his friends.

7. 8 August: Following the interrogation of the auto driver, he is arrested and on the basis of information provided by him. Ramasami, a relative of Gopal, is also taken into custody for questioning.
8. 9 August: Police Commissioner Natrajan says they have cracked the murder with the arrest of the relative. He told newspersons, 'The relative has confessed that he arranged to get Radha murdered since she was not responding to his amorous advances. He knew that Gopal, who is a distant cousin through his father, had brought gifts for all and also jewellery from Dubai. He used to visit the Gopals regularly and began to get interested in Radha. She was unresponsive. Frustrated about this, he decided to kill her and use the opportunity to steal some of the valuables at home. He paid Rs 20,000 to the auto driver whom he knew to help him.'
9. 9 August: Police arrest auto driver's wife as an active accomplice in the crime. Police said it was she who kept the other two informed of Radha's movements.

Where is the most newsworthy information in the report? The murder which took place three days earlier would certainly have already been reported and so is no more the lead point. The arrest of a relative was the latest and has the focus of reader interest.

In murders, the first question that arises in a reader's mind relates to motive and this comes in the second para of my report which follows. Note that instead of saying that the murder took place on 6 August, I have said 'three days ago'. This is reader-friendly reporting: if you say 6 August, the reader would have to remember this report is dated 10 August and that police were reporting on 9 August.

Once you have the lead, seek the answers for the other questions in the 5Ws + 1H format. Tell it as you would tell a friend on the telephone.

Kin Arrested for JP Nagar Murder[4]

BENGALURU, 9 August: Police have arrested Ramasami and two others in connection with the murder of Radha, a housewife, at her JP Nagar residence three days ago.

Ramasami is a distant cousin of Radha's husband, police said. During interrogation, he told police that he was interested in Radha, 41, but that she never responded to his advances. "Frustrated about this, he decided to kill her and use the opportunity to steal some of the valuables at home," Police Commissioner Natrajan told newspersons following the arrest. Ramasami bribed an auto driver who took Radha's son to school to commit the crime. The driver's wife is the maid in the Radha household.

Gopal, husband of Radha, was on vacation from Dubai where he worked and was out of the city to meet relatives when the murder happened, police said. He reported that some valuables, including jewels, silver and expensive watches were missing. Being a frequent visitor to the Gopals, Ramasami had an eye on the gifts and the jewellery brought by Gopal from Dubai. Ramasami was taken into custody following the interrogation of the auto driver who confessed to the crime and told the police he received Rs. 20,000 from Ramasami for executing the plan.

On July 3, Radha was found unconscious in a pool of blood in her drawing room by her neighbour.

II

Fact File: Red Sanders Smuggling

1. Andhra Pradesh police arrest a Chinese national for alleged smuggling precious red sanders logs. Chittoor district police effect the arrest and present the Chinese national, identified as Yang Ping, before a district court.
2. Police action comes within 15 days of the arrest of an actor in a town in Kurnool, Andhra Pradesh. On her way to Bengaluru, she was on the run after being named as one of the accused in a red sanders smuggling case registered in Hyderabad.
3. A month earlier, more than 20 woodcutters from across the border in Tamil Nadu were shot dead by the newly-formed A.P. Red Sanders Anti-smuggling Task Force in the border district of Chittoor.
4. "One task force group moved towards Eethagunta and the other towards Cheekateegalakona. On finding over 100 woodcutters felling trees and carrying logs away, the officials asked them to surrender. However the woodcutters rained stones and hurled

sickles at the team, injuring some of them," said a police spokesperson in Chittoor. "We fired random shots in self-defence."

5. The woodcutters from Tamil Nadu allegedly hired by mafia gangs operating from that State. Most of these men living across the border, it is said, do not know that they are indulging in clandestine activity nor who pays them handsome money for their work.
6. "I congratulate my force whose men have toiled hard to put down red sanders smuggling. It is an onerous task as many gangs, national and international, are involved," claimed the State police chief.
7. `Arrest of Chinese national comes even as State police come under criticism for gunning down the woodcutters in Chittoor. It also brings to the fore the role played by Chinese mafia in the smuggling of this rare wood from Andhra Pradesh, the only state where it grows. As many as 55 Chinese nationals have been arrested for being in possession of red sanders in the past four years.
8. Also called red sandalwood, smuggling of red sanders increased after the trees were put on the endangered list in 2000 and the Centre banned its felling, movement, sale and exports.

This is how a report was published in a daily:

Chinese Held for Red Sanders Smuggling[5]

HYDERABAD: A month after the controversial gunning down in Chittoor of 20 woodcutters from Tamil Nadu and a fortnight after the arrest of a film actor, the newly-formed anti-smuggling task force today arrested a Chinese national for alleged smuggling of precious red sanders logs. Chittoor district police who made the arrest presented the Chinese national identified as Yang Ping before a district court.

"I congratulate my task force whose men have toiled hard to put down red sanders smuggling. It is an onerous task as many gangs, national and international, are involved," said the State police chief.

The police action comes within 15 days of the arrest of an actor in a town in Kurnool, Andhra Pradesh, while she was on her way to Bengaluru. She was on the run after being named as accused number 10 in a red sanders smuggling case registered in Hyderabad.

Hardly a month earlier, more than 20 woodcutters from across the border in Tamil Nadu were shot dead by task force personnel in the border district of Chittoor. Questioned about the encounter, police said the dead men were part of a big gang of over a hundred people found felling red sanders trees and defended their action by saying the men refused to surrender when challenged

"One task force group moved towards Eethagunta and the other towards Cheekateegalakona. On finding over 100 woodcutters felling trees and carrying logs, the officials asked them to surrender. However the woodcutters rained stones and hurled sickles at the team, injuring some of them," said a police spokesperson in Chittoor. "We fired random shots in self-defence."

The arrest of the Chinese national has come as a needed boost for the State police. The force had come under strong pressure to defend its action in the Chittoor firing on woodcutters, forcing the State Chief Minister to call the Union Home Minister and brief him on the action as the killings had provoked anger and unrest in Tamil Nadu from where the labourers hailed.

The arrest of the Chinese national also brings to the fore the role played by Chinese mafia in the smuggling of this rare wood from Andhra Pradesh, the only state where it grows. As many as 55 Chinese nationals have been arrested in the country for being in possession of red sanders in the past four years.

Also called red sandalwood, smuggling of red sanders increased after the trees were put on the endangered list in 2000 and the Centre banned its felling, movement, sale and exports. The current crackdown and the resultant shortage in the market may push the prices of legally sold red sanders to Rs 9 lakh a tonne, say sources. At present, sale of old stock is permitted and the price is said to be Rs 3-5 lakhs a tonne. The asking price in China, say sources, is around Rs 20 lakhs.

Let us take a close look at the news report. The inverted pyramid style of news writing tells us that the lead should start with the most newsworthy element in the file, here the arrest of the Chinese national. The report here starts with the gunning down of woodcutters a month ago and the arrest of the actor and then comes to the vital element. The reader does not care for the name of the Chinese national, or who arrested him or where he was produced after arrest. Go straight to the point and go on to place it in context by saying that this was part of a crackdown on red sanders smuggling. This would lead the reader to wonder whether there was an international gang behind the activity. Also, the qualifier 'precious' here is redundant. As seen in Chapter 2, the lead para suffers from too many details. The 'encounter' with the woodcutters and the arrest of the actor are important, no doubt, when presenting the big picture and giving the context but certainly not necessary in the lead para and can form part of subsequent details. I would also push the second para down, if not out. The police chief praising his men is no news and it is undeservingly placed so early in the story. (See elsewhere for comments on how a journalist should avoid giving such 'puffs' or unmerited praise to those in positions of power). The fifth para, quoting a police spokesperson in Chittoor, also falls under this: first, the village names will mean nothing to the readers, except the locals, and second, caution should have been exercised in giving the quote about the police being rained with stones, etc., since this was a controversial point which was disputed by human rights groups later. More caution should also have been exercised while reporting on the misdemeanours of people, with proper attribution, which is essential but missing in the third para.

I have mentioned about the encounter and the actor's arrest providing the context for the arrest of the Chinese national. The last two paras in the report serve a different but equally important purpose. They provide the background to the story. The difference between context and background is fundamental and should be kept in mind when details are included in a report. Without the context a news story can be incomplete and may prove incomprehensible for first-time readers. Background, on the other hand, is not essential to the story, which is complete even without it. Background helps to tell more about what is happening in the region and enhances the value of the story. Context places the information in perspective and is given as close to the lead paragraphs as possible, especially if the story is linked to the past and will have implications for the future. Context, therefore, gives needed meaning to news development. For example, when the judgment against the Pakistani terrorist Ajmal Kasab was delivered, almost every newspaper and television channel referred to the '26/11' attack case. Not one explained what 26/11 was. It was the media's collective failure: the first lesson journalists learn is to tell a story in full detail so that a person who reads about the subject for the first time can understand it. The reference to 26/11 provided the very essential context to the judgement and case, and the media should have recalled that in a terror attack on Mumbai on 26 November 2008 more than 160 people were killed.

Here is a reworked version of the report:

Chinese Held for Red Sander Smuggling

HYDERABAD: A Chinese national was arrested in Chittoor district of Andhra Pradesh today in the continuing crackdown on red sanders smuggling.

The arrest of Yang Ping in the A.P.-T.N. border, which has seen much police action, hinted at the possibility of an international network behind the clandestine activity, and climaxed a month and more of vigorous effort to curb red sanders smuggling. A fortnight ago, an actor was arrested for alleged links with red sanders smugglers in the State. More than a month ago, the anti-smuggling task force had gunned down 20 woodcutters in the same district. They were alleged to be part of a 100 member gang that was collecting red sanders logs to be shifted to Tamil Nadu from where they hailed.

The Chittoor "encounter" has provoked a controversy, with allegations by humans rights groups and political parties in Tamil Nadu of deliberate killing of unarmed civilians. The arrest of the Chinese national in the same district has come as a morale booster for the task force, which has come under pressure to defend its actions against the woodcutters.

The arrest also reinforces reports that a mafia based in China may be driving the smugglers of this rare wood from Andhra Pradesh, the only state where it grows. As many as 55 Chinese nationals have been arrested in the country for being in possession of red sanders in the past four years.

Also called red sandalwood, smuggling of red sanders increased after the trees were put on the endangered list in 2000 and the Centre banned its felling, movement, sale and exports. The current crackdown and the resultant shortage in the market may push the prices of legally sold red sanders to Rs 9 lakh a tonne, say sources. At present, sale of old stock is permitted and the price is said to be Rs 3–5 lakhs a tonne. The asking price in China, say sources, is around Rs 20 lakhs.

III

Here is another example, a published report on a completely avoidable tragedy in which two young lives were lost in an accident in Chennai. The report contains all the answers and more and rightly so since the reader will be interested in even the most minute of details. On the negative side, the core of the report, the vital human interest element, is missing from the lead para and is buried somewhere down. The lead paragraph does not say straightaway that the two young men were dead. It was wrong to have left this fact out of the first paragraph.

The report is reproduced below, as it was published on the front page of the only daily I think to have got the news at all.

Two Youth Choke to Death[6]

CHENNAI: It must have been in a smoke-filled room that Logu (26) and Tamil Selvan (28) woke up early on Tuesday. Probably, it took them a few moments to collect their wits and wonder what was happening around them.

Both worked in a DVD shop called 'Original DVDs' on L B Road in Thiruvanmiyur and it was the shop owner Ashok that they now called on their cell phone. It was, perhaps, 4.30 am.

Logu and Tamilselvan hailed from Kancheepuram district and it was only four days ago that they took the job in the DVD shop. They were provided accommodation in a room at the back. They slept with the shutters down, little realising that their fate would be sealed behind the steel door. Outside, it was an inferno. People were running helter skelter. While some tried to rescue 20 persons staying on the other floors of the same building, Loganathan and Tamil Selvan were forgotten.

The fire started at 4.15 am due to a short circuit in the transformer junction. Within 10 minutes, it spread to the small shops and establishments around the transformer junction.

Raju, who works in a teashop opposite to the accident site, said: "Around 4.20 am, I saw sparks coming from the transformer At first, I dismissed it because it is a regular occurrence. But in 10 minutes, the fire became so big that I alerted people and we got busy dousing the fire and rescuing people. All the while we never knew that these two were stuck inside the shutters. Only when their owner came with the police at 5 am, we came to know about them."

> The police were followed by fire service personnel. Thesingu, a fireman, said: "Our first priority was to put out the fire. Once it was sufficiently down, we tried to open the shutters to bring the two boys out. But the shutter was jammed due to the fire and could not be opened easily. When we finally managed to open it, we found both of them unconscious. The fire had not reached the room, but it was smoke that snuffed out their lives."
>
> A factory, 'Welcome Fabricators,' which makes fibre doors, was also completely gutted.

Here is one way of writing the lead paragraphs of the report on this heart-rending human interest story:

> Two young men from Kancheepuram were killed in a fire inside a DVD shop on Thiruvanmiyur in the hours past midnight yesterday.
>
> The two, employed in the shop, were sleeping inside. Under an agreed arrangement, the owner locked the shop from the outside during the nights, ultimately preventing their escape. They had joined work four days ago.

It was perhaps a misjudgement to begin the report the way it has been done in the example I have cited, and speak of smoke-filled room and their taking time to collect their wits. As I had said elsewhere, it is wrong to display your writing prowess in reporting such avoidable tragedies. Besides, the lead point was that the two young men had died. This could only be guessed by the reader even after the third para.

I would also bring up the quote from the teashop assistant where he mentions another vital factor that prevented the rescue: the fact that the neighbours did not know that the two men were stuck inside the shutters. The doors were locked from outside.

IV

The following is also a press release but of a different kind, more difficult to handle. It was a statement released by the official External Affairs Ministry spokesman at the end of Prime Minister Manmohan Singh's talks in Riyadh, Saudi Arabia. As per regular practice, after distributing the statement, the spokesman will answer questions, mostly based on the text. Journalists travelling as part of the Prime Minister's entourage will be joined by local journalists at the press briefing. You can write a straight-forward report from out of the statement and the explanatory remarks that the spokesperson makes. Such high-level visits lend themselves to interpretations and senior journalists go beyond the diplomatese to try and get the big picture.

Media Briefing by Secretary (East) in Riyadh[7]

28 February 2010

Official spokesperson (Shri Vishnu Prakash): A very good evening to you and thanks for waiting. Secretary (East), Ms Latha Reddy, is here to brief you about Prime Minister's engagements today. As you know, he has had a number of important engagements, including his address at the Saudi Business Chamber. All of you were there at the chamber and you also have the text of the Prime Minister's remarks. Secretary will brief you about the other engagements of the Prime Minister that have taken place so far.

Secretary (East) (Ms Vijaya Latha Reddy): Good afternoon and thank you all for coming. I am happy to give some of you, and others who have joined us today, a briefing on the developments up to date.

As you all know, the Prime Minister and his delegation received a very warm welcome at the airport yesterday with the very unique honour that the Crown Prince himself, His Royal Highness Sultan Bin Abdul Aziz, the Defence Minister, was at the airport. This was indeed a gesture which was greatly appreciated.

Today the Prime Minister has had several meetings with several senior Ministers of the Saudi Government calling on him. He met with His Excellency Ali al-Naimi, the Minister of Oil and Mineral Resources. After that he met with His Royal Highness Prince Saud al-Faisal, the Foreign Minister, and thereafter with Mr Abdullah Zainal Alireza, the Minister for Commerce and Industry. I would like to give you a few brief points about some main issues that were touched upon during these meetings. Firstly, on the economic and commercial side both sides expressed happiness that our trade is growing and that we are now a 26 billion dollar two-way trade. But it was felt that there is vast potential yet to be tapped, particularly in the area of investments. Both sides agreed to work towards facilitating major joint ventures in investment between our countries.

Some of the areas which were identified were: petrochemicals, fertilizers and tie-ups also between institutes of technology, the healthcare sector. Overall, the Saudi dignitaries expressed confidence that there would be a substantial increase in Saudi investment in India over the coming years as India was seen as a safe and secure environment for investment.

They also expressed interest in seeing an early conclusion of the GCC Free Trade Agreement. Both sides agreed to give importance to this subject and to work towards an early conclusion of this agreement which would certainly boost trade between the two countries.

The Saudi dignitaries expressed very positive feelings about the presence of the Indian community here and the very important contribution they have made to the country. They said that through their trustworthiness and dependability they have truly become not just the largest community of foreign nationals here in Saudi Arabia but also one of the most dependable. Aramco Company informed us that they have set up a procurement office in India which is procuring up to 400 million US dollars worth of goods and services from India.

On our side, Prime Minister emphasised that we do already have in place the Double Taxation Avoidance Agreement and the Bilateral Investment Protection Agreement which would give a good safeguard and guarantee for any major investments by Saudi Arabia. It was also decided that the Joint Commission which already exists and meets on a regular basis will carry forward all the important issues on trade, investment, economic matters.

Both countries agreed that their national industrial development policies would be a useful area for mutual exchange of information since both countries have expressed interest in bringing up the share of their manufacturing industries in their respective GDPs. They also agreed to keep direct lines of communication open to resolve all issues.

On the political and foreign policy side, we exchanged views on developments in the Middle East and on the status of the peace process in the Middle East. Our Prime Minister reiterated our strong support for the Arab Peace Plan which we saw as the way forward. We also exchanged views on developments in India's neighbourhood and recent issues there and we asked for the viewpoint of Saudi Arabia on their region. This was a useful exchange of views.

After these meetings with the Ministers, as you all know, the

Prime Minister attended a brief ceremony at the Council of the Saudi Chambers of Commerce and Industry. I believe many of you were there and I am sure you were impressed by the keen interest shown in a large cross section of the top captains of Saudi business and industry. Equally on our side we had a very high level and representative and diverse business delegation which had been brought from India. The Prime Minister briefly addressed the gathering. I believe the text of the address is already available with you. We also heard brief comments from representatives of Saudi business as well as Indian business. Two agreements were also signed at the function.

That brings us to an end of what the official programmes have been today. This evening we will have some very important meetings with interaction between His Majesty the King and the Prime Minister, and we hope to be able to brief you shortly thereafter on those meetings as well.

That brings me to the end of what I have to say. I will be happy to take questions.

Question: What are the two agreements which have been signed at the business function?

Secretary (East): One is with Tatas on our side and the counterpart on the other; and the other is with the RITES, I believe the railways agency, on our side. We will give you the exact details.

Question: What are the major issues discussed with the Saudi side today and what are the agreements to be signed this evening?

Secretary (East): We will be signing some agreements on a government-to-government basis this evening, but I will give the details after they have been signed this evening. I have already described what the major issues were, during my presentation.

Question: As far as this FTA is concerned, has any timeframe been fixed?

Secretary (East): No, and I do not believe it is possible to prejudge how an FTA is going to be negotiated. As you know, it is a complex and technical procedure. We would normally have teams of official negotiators from all the countries involved, in this case all the Gulf countries representing the countries of the GCC and from our side. Normally this is coordinated through our Commerce Ministry and the counterparts in the other Gulf countries. There would be first the framework agreement and then it is followed by agreement on the text, after which there would be a lot of technical material to be exchanged and agreed to, including lists of items to be put under the free Trade Agreement. This usually does take some time.

Question: During the negotiations, has Saudi Arabia assured us anything concrete in terms of security concerns that we have in our neighbourhood?

Secretary (East): We have exchanged views on our respective security concerns in areas of interest and certainly both sides took note of each other's concerns.

Question: .... (inaudible) issues in the neighbourhood that you discussed with Saudis. Can you just elaborate on that?

Secretary (East): As you know, I believe that some of these issues are sensitive issues and these are discussed at a government-to-government level. When there are concrete developments and mechanisms set up, we would certainly make announcements. But at this stage it was more an exchange of views.

Question: There was also talk about the Saudi Aramco company getting some space in the oil refinery that was to be set up at Paradip in Orissa. Could you elaborate on that?

Secretary (East): I believe they have said that they are very interested in further exploring these possibilities both in the refinery area, as well as in joint ventures both in India and Saudi Arabia. But Aramco, as you know, is also one of the largest suppliers to us of crude. They have indicated that they would be interested in investments covering the whole value chain.

Question: Could you share with us the Saudis' stand on Pakistani situation and Af-Pak policy?

Secretary (East): I am afraid these were confidential discussions. These are not issues which I can divulge at this stage.

Official Spokesperson: Thank you.

Riyadh, 28 February 2010

The following is a straight-forward news report on the Prime Minister's visit based on the press conference. I have drafted the report.

Saudis See Boost in Mutual Trade[8]

RIYADH, 28 February: Saudi Arabia has indicated there would be a "substantial increase" in its investments in India, which it sees as a "safe and secure" destination for its funds.

This indication came at a meeting here between Saudi officials and the visiting Indian delegation led by the Prime Minister, Dr Manmohan Singh.

Dr Singh reassured Saudi Arabia that the Double Taxation Avoidance Agreement and the Bilateral Investment Protection Agreement, already in place, would safeguard and guarantee any major investments.

Ms Vijaya Latha Reddy, Secretary (East) who briefed the Press, said the two sides felt there was a vast potential to be tapped in the area of investment and identified petrochemicals, fertilizers, tie-ups between institutes of technology and healthcare as sectors for joint ventures.

The two sides wanted an early conclusion of the GCC Free Trade Agreement to boost bilateral trade which had touched $26 billion.

Aramco, one of the largest suppliers of crude to India, has set up an office which is procuring up to $400 million worth of goods and services from India. It has expressed interest in joint ventures and refinery projects.

The two countries agreed that their national industrial development policies would be a useful area for mutual exchange of information since both want to bring up the share of their manufacturing in their GDPs.

The Prime Minister reiterated India's strong support for the Arab Peace Plan as the way forward in the Middle East.

The two had "a useful exchange of views" on "developments in India's neighbourhood and recent issues" there.

Asked about the Saudi stand on the Pakistani situation, Ms Reddy said, "I am afraid these were confidential discussions. These are not issues which I can divulge at this stage."

Referring to the Indians working in Saudi Arabia, Ms Reddy said Riyadh saw the Indian community as a dependable and trustworthy people who had made "very important contributions" to this country.

Senior correspondents who go on such assignments seek to go beyond bland official statements, focussing on and interpreting the trend of high level exchanges. This Riyadh visit by Dr Manmohan Singh had aroused much expectation of improvement in bilateral relations, reflecting on Saudi pressure on Pakistan. Keeping this in view, here is another version I have drafted:

Saudis Take Note of India's Concerns[9]

RIYADH, 28 February: "We exchanged views on developments in India's neighbourhood and recent issues there," said a cryptic statement issued by India at the conclusion of substantive talks with Saudi leaders in the past two days during Prime Minister Manmohan Singh's visit.

"We asked for the viewpoint of Saudi Arabia on their region," the statement said and added, "There was a useful exchange of views."

The Ministry spokesperson who released the statement preferred to hide behind the diplomatese and declined to be drawn into a discussion on what the views of Saudi Arabia were on the role being played by its ally Pakistan in the region. "We exchanged views on our respective security concerns in areas of interest and certainly both sides took note of each other's concerns," she said in response to questions.

It was apparent that neither side could go beyond the bland reference to "useful exchange of views." No convergence of views on the regional situation was expected but India did not obviously succeed beyond stating its views and expressing its concerns.

"The issues are sensitive and ... at this stage it was more an exchange of views."

On the other area where the talks were focussed there was substantial progress. "On the economic and commercial side both sides expressed happiness that our trade is growing and that we are now a $26 billion two-day trade," the statement said.

(other details from press statement)

The two reports are based on the same statement. The first is straight and narrow reporting. The second could be attempted after the reporter gains substantial experience in covering foreign relations.

Sources and Biases

Since 'sourcing' is the building block on which the media edifice stands, the reporter has to exercise caution and be on the vigil for ever. I have earlier listed the major sources of news. I have also mentioned that reporters build their own contacts by using the information obtained judiciously, and respecting their wish to be quoted by name or designation or to remain anonymous. But my advice is not to employ this ploy: often reporters tend to hide their sources by using clichés such as 'An informed source said', 'It is reliably learnt', etc. One of my editors used to frown on such usage and his argument was that a reporter will not quote an 'uninformed' source and would not report it if it was not 'reliably learnt'.

A level of mutual trust needs to be built between the reporter and his source if it has to have value and be reliable. The reporter must be on the guard against being used by the source to plant stories and biases. Officialdom and political leaders have often used the press to fight their internal battles. No media unit worth its name should allow itself to be used by these sources. The reporter's duty is only to the readers. The reporter has to be vigilant and guard against the subjective nature of the sources. S/he should be on special alert when accepting information from a source. It would do well to keep in mind that sources may have their own perspectives and interests that may not be quite evident. The reporter has to identify these perspectives and interests before accepting any information. Political leaders, government officials and civil servants tend to project their own agendas. Information from the police is sanitised before it reaches the media.

Never on the regular reporter's 'beat,' I had opportunities to get to know sources through personal contact. But the danger always remained that sources, especially official and corporate, sometimes gave out ('planted' in our lingo) information with motives not necessarily honourable. Rarely, sources have also tried to use their contacts to 'leak' information to target their rivals. This is by now a familiar corporate phenomenon. It may not always be easy to see through their game. Here is my experience from early in my career in *Indian Express*. I had cultivated a senior official (for us, A) who became a close friend with whom I frequently had long chats over lunch and dinner. A provided useful information that I put to good use. One such was when, late evening one day, A informed me that talks to end a labour strike in a public sector undertaking had resulted in a decision by the trade union to call off its on-going protest action. This was important news for us since *Indian Express* had a large circulation in the place where the strike action was taking place. We promptly featured the decision on the front page. When copies reached the strike-bound town early next morning, workers prevented the distribution and burnt some copies, alleging this was propaganda against them especially since the rival daily had no such report. The decision to withdraw the strike, taken at the state headquarters, had apparently not been conveyed to the striking workers yet back then—the 1960s—when instant communication was unknown.

A few months earlier the same contact, A, had handed over an official circular whose contents contained some explosive information on a particular policy to be pursued by a new government that had just taken office. A senior official from Delhi was to visit the state capital to discuss the policy, it was feared, which ran counter to the national line. The circular, written by another senior official (for us, *B*), had raised the doubts that had arisen and the state's explanations. I used the contents in a front-page report which was timely since a review was to take place later that day. It created quite a stir and forced the government to explain its stand and caused much embarrassment to *B*. I attributed both reports to my success in establishing and sustaining my contact at a high level. Several years later I learnt of the inter-departmental rivalry between *A* and *B*, and that *A* might have been taking revenge through using his contact with me to embarrass his rival. No wonder, then, I stress the lesson—check and cross check your sources and your stories before giving them credence.

Lead Writing

The essence of most news stories can be stated in two or three words—for example, magistrate fines cyclist; undertrial escapes; classes begin. The objective is to capture the reader's attention and focus it on the heart of the matter.

Let us say the CAG (Comptroller and Auditor General) issues a report critically referring to scams in the issue of spectrum licences and blames the minister and the ministry for underselling a rare commodity. What is the heart of the matter? The CAG report is tabled in parliament? No. Just the tabling of the report does not make news. (It would if there had been doubts earlier whether determined opponents would try to stall its tabling.) The heart of the news here: CAG pulls up minister for spectrum scam. The lead must be built on these words. The lead will run something like this: The CAG whose report was tabled in parliament today has pulled up the government and the minister in charge of telecommunications for underselling spectrum, resulting in a loss of thousands of crores.

In the red sanders smuggling report, for example, what is the heart of the matter? Not the arrest of an individual since many have been arrested or trailed by the special task force as part of a crackdown on smuggling. The key points were the arrest of a Chinese national and the location (Chittoor) where so much action had taken place earlier in the weeks and which was the only region in the country where the red sanders trees grow. The arrest of a Chinese national grabs the reader's attention, also hinting at the possibility of an international gang being behind some of the smuggling activity. The reporter leads the report with this point and goes on to recall the events in the month and a half earlier to bring in the perspective, offers some quotations from the task force spokespersons and finally provides the background about what lures such international smuggler gangs.

If the lead captures the essence of the story in a brief manner, the reader will read on to learn the facts. The lead should contain no more than 25 to 30 words that report the essentials of the story: what, who, where, when and why or how. Associated Press news agency leads average 25 words in length. The 5Ws + 1H lead is a fundamentally important tool. Keep them at the back of the mind as you set out to the lead and the story.

The heart of the lead in most cases answers the question What happened? What is the story? And most often the answer can be in two or three key words—a subject and verb, or a subject, verb and object: Seven drown. Government bans LTTE.

Here are four variations of a lead sentence. See which is the most appropriate:

1. The peaceful routines of Taramani were disturbed today when a crude handmade bomb exploded in front of the Asian College of Journalism.
2. Violence flared in Taramani today when a crude bomb ...
3. There was an explosion in Taramani today. Many were injured when a crude bomb went off in front of the ACJ ...

4. At least three journalism students were injured when a crude bomb went off in front of the ACJ in Taramani this evening ...

The fourth example is an undoubted winner since it has all the vital newsworthy points and goes to them straight.

The importance of this needs to be stressed as one sees this rule being violated routinely. In defence of the reporter, one must say that the failure to go straight to the most newsworthy point is born of an eagerness to cram as many details as possible in the lead para. This in turn is a legacy of the pre-TV era when print journalists, not facing any competition, would weave in their interpretation of a news development as they told it. See this example: 'In a move to stop the flow of revenue to neighbouring "wet" states such as Tamil Nadu and Karnataka, the Kerala Government today decided to lift prohibition and garner the tax money for itself.' The reporter could have given the decision first–i.e. to lift prohibition–and then explained the rationale behind it, i.e. loss of tax revenue to other states. The reporter chose to interpret before reporting.

The following is a typical example from the sports pages. It must be conceded that sports reporting has some licence in the use of adjectives and colour, though this is often resorted to at the expense of reporting the news.

> NOTTINGHAM, ENGLAND: Bright sunshine and cloud cover alternated on a breezy Thursday here. Amidst nature's captivating byplay in this sleepy northern England town, arrived a dramatic piece of news from London–Andrew Symonds was in big trouble once again. Symonds's career has been a blaze of colour one moment and a sea of darkness the next–a rough ride of extreme swings in fortunes. The influential cricketer was being sent home for yet another breach of the team rules pertaining, principally, to consumption of alcohol. Ahead of ICC World Twenty20 beginning at Lord's on Friday–host England takes on Netherlands in the opener–the star-studded competition could have done without an incident of this kind.[10]

A decluttered lead suggestion would be: 'Andrew Symonds of Australia is to be sent home for breach of team rules pertaining principally to consumption of alcohol. The decision comes ahead of the ICC World Twenty20 matches beginning at Lord's on Friday.'

Tabloid Reporting

Much of what we have seen so far about news writing, including the selection of the right lead and the rigours of the bare bones style relate primarily to the broadsheet format. These tend to get diluted in the tabloid format which till recently was the sole provider catering for a very specific readership. Its style of writing, headlining and presentation of news were meant for quick reading, to serve the reader on the move-till the advent of the internet and the smart phone transformed the scene. The tabloid's handy size (27.5 cm/30 cm) was meant for the reader on the move whose cursory interest in news lasted till s/he got off the metro train. The word 'tabloid' dates back to 1901, according to the American Heritage Dictionary, when it served as a trademark for drugs and chemicals dispersed in a condensed form. By extension, it came to represent 'a newspaper of small format giving the news in condensed form, usually with illustrated, often sensational material'.

For a hundred years, the tabloid remained typecast: tabloidisation meant trivialisng news and resorting to sensationalism in preference to hard news. The display of news and photographs, governed in part by the size and shape of the page, set it apart from the broadsheet (55 cm/30 cm). The headlines were an invitation to the sensationalism in the report and reporting. One word, all-capital headlines, clipped sentences and large photographs were the hallmark of the tabloid—all aimed at ease of reading/browsing. The scene began to change two decades ago. As a measure to cut cost and economise, serious newspapers in broadsheet format began switching to the smaller format. Some of the broadsheets also adopted the tabloid layout style of letting graphics, including photographs, dominate a page. By the turn of the century, most of Europe had gone tabloid as a format. The approach to presentation of news, however, remained distinctly different.

The use of the phrase 'responsible tabloid' was once described as an oxymoron. The tabloid's choice of news made it stand apart: human foibles, titillating stories, celebrities and their lifestyle, lurid details of crimes and criminality; in effect, topics that serious broadsheets would never want to touch. Clipped sentences, even incomplete ones, a racy writing style, photographs revealing of the subject and short stories that ran no longer than 300–400 words, whatever the merit. This was the no-holds-barred approach made notorious by British tabloids. The world now knows how one more hidden tool was in full use by some of them—phone tapping.[11]

Till the internet came and transformed the media scene, forcing dramatic changes in all aspects of journalism—from writing the report to presentation of news. The sole survivor of this onslaught perhaps is the tabloid format, which is being used more and more by mainstream newspapers. Even serious business newspapers have adopted the tabloid style of allowing one photograph or graphic to dominate the page and having large, bold headlines.

Online Reporting

News gathering and writing for the new/online media are similar to print. Where online media scores is in the fact that it does not suffer the major constraint that print faces: lack of space. This in fact gives it a huge advantage over the other streams. While television and radio face the intolerable constraint of time, print has a constant battle with space. Online editions have over the years exploited this advantage to the full, introducing attractive web designs and innovative ways of grabbing the attention of the reader by utilising technology. The only hurdle it faces relates to its total dependence on the availability of the internet.

Thanks to its use of multimedia, the presentation of news in terms of content (not writing) and layout is vastly different, making special demands on the reporter and those manning the desk. Since online portals provide instant access, there is an additional demand on the reporter to update his report to keep pace with the developments and the requirements. Newspapers with online versions have resorted to continuous streaming of news developments when warranted—the British daily the *Telegraph* did this streaming successfully during the riots that hit London a few summers ago, with updates from reporters on the spot every minute. It was a pioneering effort. Additionally, the internet can secure access to invaluable archival material and expert opinion instantly, making it an educative experience. Collaborative content provision and the possibility of tracking through RSS feeds[12] and aggregators[13] are additional positive features.

An online journalist has perforce to acquire the needed additional skills, of coding copy, uploading content, web design and more; one needs to hone the skill to (a) select significant viewpoints or commentaries from a mountain of available material through social bookmarking sites such as Facebook, Twitter, Google+ and Reddit, (b) generate, share and access dispersed multimedia content through photo-sharing and video-sharing platforms, and (c) generate fairly detailed annotated maps (which tie up data and image on a map as a one-image illustration)[14] and use mashup techniques (which use more than one source to create a single new service or aid)[15] to produce content. There are many more avenues for news/views gathering. However, the challenge of gathering information online is turning often into a problem of plenty, with a number of media sites vying for attention. But with the fire hose of data also comes concerns about reliability of the sources. Popular online tools include social networking sites like Twitter and Facebook, community curated knowledge bases such as Wikipedia and Quora, government and thinktank websites, alerting services like Google Alerts and Mention, etc. In particular, Twitter can be a useful source for tracking breaking updates and conversations on relevant hashtags, and engaging directly with the source of information to get more details or research a piece. For example, much of the Arab Spring of 2011 was followed worldwide via Twitter. Twitter provided a channel for Arab protestors to bypass government censorship and organize themselves. Mainstream media turned to Twitter as a source for breaking news and engaged with protest groups to run interviews. Community curated sites like Wikipedia and Quora can be useful for identifying subject-matter experts in areas for further investigative interviews and follow-ups. This is important to ensure due diligence to uncover possible bias or conflicts of interest which may not be otherwise apparent on the public sites.

Broadcast organisations like the British Broadcasting Corporation (BBC) are also utilising Skype to connect with viewers around the world. More tools are being added. In March–April 2014, the ACJ, Chennai, participated in a collaborative programme of web streaming reports on urban poverty with news organisations in the UK and a few other countries.

Launching a new application software (i.e., an app) to support its global growth strategy on 29 May 2014, the British daily the *Guardian* gave perhaps the most graphic picture of things to come on the online media world. Describing it 'as the only way for high-quality news organisations to compete,' Andrew Miller, CEO of the Guardian Media Group, said, 'For the *Guardian* to compete and grow internationally, we have to be both excellent journalists and world-leading technologists.'[16]

The future of the media lies in online journalism, aided somewhat by the other giants of today, print and TV. In a rapidly changing environment, news gathering and news writing may no more be simple and straightforward. With media convergence rapidly becoming a reality in this country, journalists can apparently no more belong exclusively to print, TV, radio or online. More and more, reporters can be expected to collect news in multiple formats. As I had mentioned earlier, multiple cameras and audio recorders in the backpack can as well be the way to the future. This is convergence forced by the compulsions of technology and more.

Online editions are no more a luxury that some print houses permitted themselves to enjoy. A decade and half ago, at the turn of the century, only a few newspapers had an online presence; and just a cursory presence at that, more an extension of the printed newspaper without proper updating. This was starkly evident when the Kargil War (May–July 1999) broke out and I found myself at an India-Pakistan media workshop in Salzburg, Austria. We, both Indian and Pakistani journalists, had heard overnight that some planes had been shot down. Come morning we desperately searched the online portals of newspapers on both sides. There was very little enlightenment, and no hint of the brief but bitter war that was breaking out.

There is already evidence of the inroads that online is making into television, where online meets television. From the BBC and CNN at the global level to NDTV, CNN-IBN and others at home, TV channels have online versions of their programmes for readers who have neither the time nor the inclination to watch TV. What is shown on the television is simultaneously transmitted on websites, directed at smartphones, e-readers and tablets that are flooding the market.

As newspapers face declining advertising revenue, the push to go online will become irresistible. Sharing and reusing will become both inevitable and profitable as the platforms for news presentation increase. Media houses may need to move content from one platform to another simultaneously: print to TV to Internet, mobile devices and social media sites.

Converged newsrooms are the future. As we shall see in the section relating to television broadcasting, media economics dictate convergence as the only solution.

Notes

1. For answers to the reporter's sources of information and how the reporter handles them and some tips on interviewing on radio, see section Sources and Biases.
2. There is a subtle difference between the lead para and Introduction. The lead para is the first para in a report while the Introduction (or intro) can be formed by one, two or even three paras that gives the import of the entire report. But very often, they are interchangeable.
3. Prepared by faculty members at ACJ. Reproduced by permission of ACJ.
4. Prepared by the author at ACJ. Reproduced by permission of ACJ.
5. Prepared by the author for this publication.
6. Sangeetha Neeraja, 'Two Youth Choke to Death', *New Indian Express*, 27 May 2009. Reproduced by permission of *New Indian Express*.
7. Retrieved from the Ministry of External Affairs, Government of India website, http://www.mea.gov.in/outoging-visit-detail.htm?2818/Media+Briefing+by+Secretary+East+in+Riyadh (accessed 6 February 2012).
8. Prepared by the author at ACJ. Reproduced by permission of ACJ.
9. Prepared by the author at ACJ. Reproduced by permission of ACJ.
10. S. Dinakar, 'England Meets the Netherlands in the Opener', *Hindu*, 5 June 2009.
11. What began as an investigation into British tabloid *News of the World*'s journalists' listening to the voice mail messages of celebrities widened to include much more serious charges—that the tabloid paid police officers for information and even interfered with a murder investigation. The landmark Justice Lord Leveson enquiry into the cultural practice and ethics of the press has dealt with the non-legal issues of the scandal. In the trial that followed the outbreak of this scandal, Rebekah Brooks, former head of Australian press baron Rupert Murdoch's British newspaper empire, was acquitted of all charges in mid-2014.
12. Rich Site Summary (RSS) is a tool that enables the user to access websites such as those offering news and views on a regular basis. RSS feeds allow the user to retrieve content from these chosen sites, many of whom may have constantly changing content. These feeds save time and the need to visit each site individually. The number of sites offering RSS feeds has been growing rapidly and includes big names such as *Yahoo! News*. Weblogs and other online

publishers also syndicate their content as RSS feeds to whoever wants them, but the most widespread usage is in distributing news headlines on the web.

13. Aggregators: A system or organisation that gathers together or aggregates content from different sites for reuse by others.
14. An annotated map has descriptions and explanations with placement marks to facilitate reading and understanding of content. These maps can be prepared to suit specific themes and topics.
15. Mash-up technique is a web application to combine data and functionality from different sources such as a mash-up that combines *BBC* news with links to *Wikipedia* articles. The user can use this technique to include the location and photographs of a company's offices in India on one map to produce a mash-up map.
16. Wolfgang Blau, 'The Guardian Launches New Apps To Support Its Global Growth Strategy', *Guardian*, 29 May 2014.

4

Broadcast Journalism

In the Age of 24×7 TV and FM Radio

The stridency of the assertion that the printed word is supreme, and that ephemeral images of the television screen can hardly compare to it have muted over the past decade. Printed newspapers have struggled to survive and TV and online media have marched far ahead in terms of professional advancement and profitability. Arguments such as 'a picture is worth a thousand words and memory is pictorial' and 'what a picture says words cannot express in easy terms' are heard no more. There are in fact no more arguments over such statements. A couple of pictures or videos of the 2004 Indian Ocean tsunami that hit South East Asia and India told the world far more about the havoc caused than a thousand and more words could.

Television Reporting

TV's popularity today is unchallenged and the threat to the medium can come only from online which uses both the print's staple of words and the video footages of TV. I have spoken in an earlier chapter about the basic difference between print/online, where a detailed word picture needs to be presented, and the visual and audio media where economy of words is the byword and time and space are a luxury. In the previous chapter, we saw the advantages that online journalism enjoys over the printed newspapers. The broadcast media, on the other side, have advantages over the other two in terms of the presentation of visuals and audio. If in print the arrival of the computer dramatically reduced the tortuous path that news took from the field to the printing presses, technology in TV has both simplified and complicated the process by which news travels to the screen. Digital cameras and editing software have in a large measure made the task easier but instant news has thrown in huge challenges to the TV journalist.

Where the reporter today quite often doubles as photographer for a newspaper, print or online, the TV reporting team has a minimum of two, the reporter on the field and the camera person. In many cases, there are three, including one who wields the megaphone and looks after recording the needed sound bytes. More and more, multiple cameras from the same channel arrive at a scene to record a disturbance, an outbreak of violence or an accident. There are no doubt substantial similarities in the working of TV journalists and those in the other three streams. The fundamental approach to news is the same—telling it straight, telling it without frills in crisp language et al. and the criteria of news evaluation are similar. The major departure comes in the presentation of news. The cold, impersonal manner of news telling evident in print and online can be suicidal in the broadcast media of TV and radio.

'What we hear and what we see is primary and anterior to what we write about. Writing is a secondary activity,' Sashi Kumar, documentary filmmaker and chairman of the Asian College of Journalism, is fond of telling students of the TV stream. 'Remember, speech preceded writing. Keep the primacy of speech in constant focus ... writing implies absence. ... TV news is about the present, about the here and now, about the immediate.'[1]

Inverted Pyramid vs Hourglass Style

Again, the structure of news presentation is also different since the TV journalist directly addresses his viewer unlike a print colleague. In view of this interpersonal interaction, the inverted pyramid style of news writing followed by print is not favoured in TV. In the inverted pyramid, the news story begins with the most newsworthy point, or lead or lede, followed by the rest of the information in the descending order of importance, tapering to the end and offering the option to the editor to remove paras from the bottom up in case of need during pagemaking. Thanks to its time and space constraint, TV news follows a marginally different pattern of structure. It does not have the luxury of including anything but the most important so that the concluding paras often carry important information which cannot be chopped off. TV's preferred style is known by the shape the reporting takes: the hour glass, i.e. lead, middle and end. In the structuring of the news report, the lead forms the beginning as in print. Also called the teaser, it performs the same function of attempting to attract the attention of the viewer. It gives the main news point but in fewer words since visuals on the screen tell it in even more effective manner. The lead is followed by the body of the report called the 'middle' which provides the answers to the key questions relating to the main news. The end, or tag, sums up the story.

Of the 5Ws + 1H, the answers to four questions are available on the screen: What, Where, Who and When, maybe with some help from the anchor. The role of the reporter after he has captured the visuals of an event with the help of his videographer and collected the details focusses on the Why and How or So What question. I will cite one example to show the difference in approach to writing the news story for print and for TV. The following news story about the launch of a railway line connecting Kashmir Valley to the rest of the country was published in a newspaper. Later I have attempted to write the same story for TV.

Train to Kashmir Becomes Reality[2]

> JAMMU, 28 June: A 100-year-old dream became reality on Wednesday when the first train connecting Banihal in Jammu and Qazigund in Kashmir chugged through India's longest tunnel in the mighty Pir Panjal ranges.
>
> Prime Minister Manmohan Singh and UPA chairperson Sonia Gandhi flagged off the eight-coach train carrying school children and officials of IRCON from here, marking the beginning of the first rail connecting Kashmir with the rest of India.
>
> Both leaders also boarded the train and crossed the tunnel before returning to Banihal.
>
> The train reached Qazigund in 25 minutes. The Banihal–Qazigund section reduces the 35 km distance to 18 km. The section has been constructed at a cost of Rs 1691 crore. The highlight of the

section is India's longest tunnel (11.2 km) which has been drilled through the treacherous mountain terrain.

"Maharaja Pratap Singh had dreamed of this project in 1898. A project was sanctioned in 1905 but it could not be implemented so far. After Independence, Jammu got connected with the rest of India through rail. Indira Gandhi started work on the difficult Chenab section (which includes Kashmir) in 1983. Today, I am happy to announce that this project is successfully heading towards completion," Dr Singh said, after dedicating the Banihal–Qazigund line to the nation.

The tunnel has been constructed using the New Austrian Tunneling Method (NATM). It is for the first time in the country that NATM has been used on such a large scale. Under NATM the geological stress from the surrounding rock is used to stabilize the tunnel hole.

The Pir Panjal tunnel passes approximately 440 metres below the existing Jawahar Road Tunnel and its alignment crosses the Srinagar–Jammu national highway at three locations. "This is not just an engineering marvel, but an all weather link between the Valley and the rest of Jammu and Kashmir... This will usher in a new era in the development of the state," the Prime Minister said.

"As the work progresses, we will be connecting this line with other networks of the country. Work on the Katra–Udhampur section will be completed in a few months. Work on the Udhampur–Banihal line alone will then remain (to be completed). It is a challenging task. It consists of a 359 meter-high bridge, which is the world's highest railway bridge," he added. Inter-district trains are already plying within the Valley on the 118-km-long route between Qazigund and Baramulla in north Kashmir. But the Banihal-Qazigund section will connect the Valley with the Jammu division. Opening of this section promises a new beginning for the state as it will significantly ease the transportation problem faced by the people during winters when inclement weather forces closure of the Jawahar Tunnel.

Here is a possible TV version of the report, with suitable visuals on the screen:

Rail link to Kashmir Valley

Kashmir joined the national railway network when the first train from Jammu to the valley chugged through the country's longest tunnel in the Pir Panjal ranges and reached Qazigund. Travelling in the train during its inaugural run, from Banihal in Jammu, was Prime Minister Manmohan Singh. The 35 km distance through the tunnel was covered in 25 minutes. Hailing the railway line as an engineering marvel, Dr Singh said the allweather link between Jammu and the rest of the state will usher in a new era in the development of Jammu and Kashmir. Work on two other vital lines would be completed soon.

> Opening of this section of the railways promises a new beginning for the state as it will significantly ease the transportation problems faced by the people during the winter months when inclement weather shuts down road movement.

The printed version's length is a luxury that TV cannot afford. Besides, detailed reporting is not required because the visuals on the screen tell most of the story, in a more telling manner. The difference in the structure of reporting can be discerned, though not quite striking in these examples. In the print version, the lead para tells of a dream coming true of a train for the first time connecting Jammu and Kashmir regions through the Pir Panjal ranges. After this comes the point that is next in importance–the prime minister flagging off the train. These points are the most vital in the news report and can be considered the core, taking the top of the inverted pyramid. As it tapers down, the report has quotations from the prime minister's speech and details on the tunnel through the ranges that made the distance shorter. Further down, there are more quotes and more details. One can fault this report on one count. The last para, containing an important point, should have gone earlier, perhaps as an additional sentence in para four of the report. The inverted pyramid style, in which newsworthy points are reported in descending order of their importance, helped during page-making, the last of the editorial task, when the need often arose for reports to be pruned to fit the space available and edition time allowed no scope for editing changes and alteration of paras or sentences to save space. The only option at that late stage was for paras to be cut from the bottom up. The inverted pyramid method ensured that the report's value is not lost even if a few paras from the bottom are removed. In this instance, what I consider a vital point would have been lost if there was need to cut and this para had been removed.

The report prepared for TV, shorter by a third, follows the hourglass style. With visuals on the screen showing the train and its VIP passengers, the report goes straight to the vital point—Kashmir region joining the national railway network with the new train launch. The lead has all vital points and is heavy at the top. The middle portion of the report has a quote from the prime minister and his announcements. This is a part of the report but is dispensable and, perhaps, thin like the narrow middle of the hourglass. The last part, the tag, is heavy again with vital information. It has an interesting point about a solution at last to the problems of the state during winter when inclement weather halts road traffic. As you may have noticed, writing for television is also lighter since the visual gets primacy in this medium.

Relevant Terminology

Here are some key phrases relevant to TV journalism that will help to understand the processes involved.

OB Van: The Outdoor Broadcasting mobile van serves as a mini production unit, used in the early years mainly for providing TV coverage of sports and entertainment programmes from the field. The van takes signals from professional video cameras and microphones recording out in the field and helps in their instant transmission. It is in some ways a studio on wheels.

Studio: The typical studio is where the broadcasting action takes place. Equipped with professional video cameras on pedestals with wheels and headphone sets, the studio has stage lighting equipment, video monitors and a glass window for direct visual contact with the control room from where directions emanate.

Production Control Room (PCR): The control room. Much like the news room in a newspaper, the PCR is the hub. It has all the controlling devices for a TV programme. The producer who is the fulcrum around which the show revolves sits in this room and manages the show. It is here that the composition of the outgoing programme takes place. The PCR is equipped with a video monitor wall, several monitors for the ongoing programmes and control panels to select the multiple camera setup and other various sources to be recorded or seen on air.

Producer: The kingpin of a show, he is in charge of a show and takes decisions on what goes into it–and what not. The producer decides which news story goes where, at which time slot and how it must be packaged, and may also have a superior whose suggestions or directions must be incorporated in the show.

Piece To Camera: The PTC is a term used when the reporter or presenter speaks directly to the viewer through the camera. Normally there are two to three PTCs during a programme: first when the reporter introduces himself and makes the opening news report, secondly in the middle when he needs to explain a context and thirdly at the end when he concludes his report and acknowledges the contribution of the camera person and identifies the place of reporting and the channel he represents. The PTC by its very nature is couched in simple, conversational and straightforward language and is considered the equivalent of a byline for a reporter in the newspaper.

Voice Over: The voice over is a technique where a voice gives narration to a story. Also known as off camera and offstage, the voice over is not necessarily given by the reporter but spoken by someone who appears elsewhere in the production or by a

Figure 4.1 PTC during a Programme

Courtesy: Asian College of Journalism, Chennai

Figure 4.2 PCR with Control Panels, Monitors; Studio in the Background

Courtesy: Asian College of Journalism, Chennai.

specialist voice actor. It is recorded and placed over the visuals of a news story.

Anchor: The presenter of a show. He/she must use conversational language to keep the viewers engaged.

Teleprompter: A teleprompter, also known as autocue, is a visual device that helps the news or other programme readers with the script on a screen in front of them. The screen, in front of, and usually below, the lens of a professional video camera, and the words on the screen are reflected to the eyes of the presenter using a sheet of clear glass or a specially prepared beam splitter. Since the speaker does not need to look down to consult written notes, it appears as if he has the news or speech by heart and speaks without any aide. He looks directly into the camera lens and lends the operation a needed personal touch, appearing as if he is speaking to the viewer directly.

Cue: It is a signal for the anchor to speak. It comes from the producer who is in continuous contact with the anchor, passing on instructions on programmes, monitors and other details.

News Capsule: A news programme that can run for a half-hour or an hour. Often individual journalists do programmes which are news-based features, interviews and debates.

Rundown: Like the News List in print, this is a script for a news programme that has all the instructions and order of the programme.

Talkback: The intercom equipment used in the PCR for internal communication

In the TV news desk, there are two desks. The programme as recorded on the field comes into an output desk which is responsible for the script of a story. It coordinates between the field and the final programme, providing the missing links through voice overs, editing and inserting clips from archival material, and finetunes before finally delivering. The input desk has the responsibility of assigning tasks to reporters, deciding on the news developments to cover and is in charge of gathering news and news footage.

Some Dos and Don'ts for Anchors[3]

What is true for print of precise, concise writing is even more true for TV. The direct, conversational is the norm. What is delivered is delivered orally, not read, and the viewer has but one shot at hearing. Unlike in a newspaper, the viewer cannot go back and reread the text. It is for this reason that emphasis is laid on weaving the story tightly so that there is no slackening of pace or place to cut. Since this is an audiovisual medium, the journalist needs to think of all sounds—including natural sounds and sound bytes—as part of the story. Sound bytes should not be designed to break up the narration of the story or to pace it. Place the attribution at the beginning lest the viewer think you are the source. Place title, designation and descriptive qualification before the name of the person figuring in the story, not after. The reporter/anchor should be casual, engaging and where possible interactive.

The reporter should be precise in language and be sure of what he/she wants to say. The medium requires the anchor to both think on one's feet and express the thoughts in a cogent, easy flow. And as for one's own personality, the anchor must present a picture of confidence. The camera exaggerates the slightest of mannerisms. On camera, language is equally about one's own demeanour as about what one says and presents. Present a profile of yourself that immediately establishes a rapport with the viewer. An air of confidence, of ease and even a degree of casualness about you will instantly bring the viewer closer to you. Finally, when you are using a lapel mike, ensure that it is positioned correctly to capture your voice. If you are using a hand held mike, as in a stand-up report, position the mike a clenched fist below your chin.

Best Practices in Television Journalism has useful suggestions on what Sashi Kumar calls 'the Philosophy of TV'.[4] It is a structured discussion on a wide gamut of issues relating to public TV broadcasting in the South Asian region. The other participants were Syed Talat Hussain, director, news and current affairs, *Aaj TV*, Pakistan, and A. S. Panneerselvan, executive director, Panos South Asia, which groups together senior journalists from the South Asian region and conducts seminars and workshops besides producing training manuals. During the discussion, Sashi Kumar referred to the paradox that in TV, the digital medium, one gets a linear experience of viewing news since the visuals come one after the other while in print, of the analogue era, one gets a digital experience since one can have a simultaneous image of the different stories. While none of the participants ventured to predict the ultimate winner in the race between print and TV, there was agreement that each medium enjoyed its own advantages. Panneerselvan pointed out that human memory records in the picture mode and therefore TV had a more lasting impact than print. Talat Hussain spoke of how print scored when it came to doing investigative, in-depth stories.

One facet that was highlighted in the discussion was that sourcing of news has most often to be open and straightforward in TV, whereas print can hide behind camouflages like 'informed sources' and 'official sources' and publish stories from known sources which seek to remain anonymous. TV cannot also use 'off the record' remarks since it will be meaningless to quote a speaker without identifying him or her. All these are possible in print.

RADIO REPORTING

For the other broadcast media, radio, better days seem to be ahead. A much neglected medium, with a reach that no other medium has in a vast country like India, radio in its FM avatar is set to expand in a major way. If the government does allow news to be broadcast by FM radio, as has been promised, there can be a huge expansion of the network. Already, FM is popular with music lovers in urban areas as well and is the only source of entertainment in remote villages which have no cable TV network connection. Short wave stations of radio, now fully controlled by the government, can also get a reflected boost if the FM spreads and becomes popular with the broadcast of news. The medium is now a tool of government propaganda—even this is not used intelligently during times of natural calamities or outbreak of diseases. Like in Doordarshan, its TV counterpart, All India Radio's specialist broadcasts for farmers and others can also get a facelift if these are tuned to user needs.

Perhaps writing for radio is the most challenging among the four streams. All the guidelines on writing for print and on-line apply as much as the rules of writing for TV. In addition, the radio broadcast must be infused with life to grip the attention of the listener. Without the visuals or the reality of the printed paper, radio depends solely on the voice of the news reader and the attractiveness of the writing to make an impact.

Voice training is an essential prerequisite for the news reader. Besides, the first sentence should make the listener want to hear more but too many details can simultaneously be distracting and confusing. Use of short, precise words, active voice, lean sentences and the whole range of do's and don'ts for news writing are valid for radio broadcasts.

The subject-verb-object mode of telling is the most suitable. But, occasionally, clipped sentences can be effective. For easy understanding, a person's designation is preferably placed before the name. The time element should come close to the verb (last night, yesterday, etc. kept out of lead sentences). Contractions such as 'don't', 'can't' are not prohibited, with use of other contractions depending on their popularity. Rule out long quotations, using them sparingly for effect, while making it clear that they are direct quotes.

For a media student interested in radio, there are no additional lessons to learn except to operate the recorder and transmitter. Editing and reporting are much the same as for TV, without the video part of it. For editing the recorded tapes, there are enough easy-to-learn software.

A few additional tips should suffice. One relates to interviewing for radio. A good listener is a successful interviewer. This dictum applies to all streams of the media, and especially so for radio where you have to draw out the interviewee. If you choose your questions right and engage the interviewee in a conversation, you can elicit the best out of him/her. For TV, it is straightforward since both sides will be on camera. It is here that the challenge is real for the radio journalist. He has to make it conversational, lively and interesting.

How do you prepare for the radio interview? Read up about both the interviewee and the topics that will likely come up, especially to sift the new from the old from what he is saying and to ask intelligent questions and follow-up. If your guest realises you are well prepared, she/he will in all probability be more forthcoming and the session will become interactive and productive for you. More often than not, the interviews are edited for broadcast. Ensure that the excerpted part does not result in a muddled, incoherent interview. Never put words into the mouth of the person you are interviewing, clearly separating the questions and your own comments from those of the guest. Finally, if there is a need to interrupt, do so politely. You can also indicate if you are running out of time with remarks such as 'briefly, one last question'.

NOTES

1. *Best Practices in Television Journalism*, DVD, Panos South Asia, English, 2006.
2. Ishfaq-ul-Hassan, 'Train to Kashmir Becomes Reality', *DNA*, 27 June 2013. Reproduced by permission of *DNA*.
3. Much of the following in this segment is taken from the lectures given by Sashi Kumar to students at the Asian College of Journalism. Reproduced by permission of Sashi Kumar.
4. *Best Practices in Television Journalism*, 2006. The DVD is billed by the producer as a 'television training manual by experts in the field'.

5

Editing the News

The Vital Last Filter, and Timeless Values

'Doctors bury their mistakes, lawyers hang theirs, journalists print them on their front page.' Whoever coined this telling description, I heard it for the first time from Indira Gandhi, the one prime minister who did everything in her considerable power to muzzle the press and manipulate it. But who can deny the apparent aptness of the remark? Instead of 'journalists', she could as well have said 'sub-editors and copy editors'. For, more than anyone else in the newspaper, it is the editing staff who get blamed for mistakes. To some extent, justifiably so, because editing is the last stage before the printing happens and if the editorial desk (or simply the 'desk') is alert, half the mistakes in the newspapers won't occur. As one who has spent decades on the desk, I can say confidently that a newspaper that neglects the editing part can count its days. For the editing staff are the vital, final filter for a newspaper.

So what is editing? Editing is defined as the art of getting news ready for publication, broadcast or telecast. But is editing anything more than what the language teacher does in school, correcting the grammar and checking the spelling? You may also ask: Where is the need to get the news 'ready' when it is ready anyway when the reporter files the report? Yes and no. If the reporter has had some kind of professional training in a journalism school or at a news organisation, the report will not necessarily need much attention from the desk as the training involves getting the basics right. Even in this case, because of the tensions of news gathering, the reporter may err sometimes with both the content and structure of the report which can be spotted at the desk. As I will show in the following pages, there are so many pitfalls as news travels from where it happens to the pages of a newspaper or the news wires or the TV screen that you can neglect the process only at your peril. The desk is the final checkpoint or filter which ensures that the contents are correct, well written and in proper language. It is the editing desk that ultimately brings credibility to a newspaper or news portal. Copy editors forming the desk take the place of the reader or viewer and ask all the questions that the reader asks to make certain that the ultimate product has clarity and does not leave any questions unanswered. They are the reader's advocate and in that role play a vital part in ensuring quality.

I have heard this from seniors. According to a former editor of the then Bombay edition of the *Indian Express*, an Englishman, there are only two types of newspapers—a reporter's paper and a sub-editor's paper—and he would always call his paper a sub-editor's paper. I fully subscribe to this. There are subtle differences between the two. In a well edited paper, no copy or report is sacrosanct and there are no holy cows among reporters and correspondents whose report should be allowed to be published without any change. Such papers read well and are crisp.

'Strong, engaged desks are critical to the success of our file and help drive it with the news,' says Reuters news agency in its *Handbook of Journalism*, 'General' section. It adds, 'Editing stories is a highly valued skill. ... The basic task of the desk is to ensure that all stories are prioritised, that they are properly sourced, that they are presented in a way that is clear, useful and attractive, and that they are fair.' The desk 'provides an outsider's perspective that can be useful to reporters, who can sometimes become too close to a story, assume too much knowledge of the reader, or miss the regional or cross-sector implications of a news development.'[1]

In this electronic age, however, many newspapers which find themselves forced to cut staff and save on expenditure have resorted to laying off editing staff. The result can be disastrous. In the words of Deborah Howell, a columnist of the *Washington Post* (31 August 2008), 'Copy editors are the last stop before disaster at newspapers. ... They do the kind of old-fashioned nit-picking that makes for better reading and more accurate stories. ... But they may be a vanishing breed. They're leaving *The Post* and the industry in large numbers because of shrinking newspaper revenue and the immediacy of the Internet.'

Newspapers, at least in India, earned their credibility precisely through the hard, thankless work of the desk. Stating that the sub-editor's job requires 'a superhuman range of essential qualifications,' veteran editor T. J. S. George wrote in 1989, 'These are required because the news desk is where the final decisive actions take place. An inefficient reporter may get away with a badly organised story, a mis-spelt name. It is the thankless job of the sub[editor] to put it in shape, to correct the spellings. An assistant editor may write on the assumption that the day's supply of newsprint is at his sole disposal. It is the task of the sub[editor] to fit it into the available space. In this sense, the skills of the sub[editor] have a direct bearing on the quality of the paper that reaches the reader's hands.'[2]

In fact, if the desk is not alert, absurdities creep into newspapers, some of them serious and a few even hilarious. I will cite three examples. The first is a sentence from a published report. It is part of a *Hindu* report many years ago on how an intruder entered the house of a VIP via the open balcony on the first floor and was surprised by the presence of the VIP's adult daughter by name Padmavathy. The sentence read: 'The intruder hit Padmavathy, who was standing in the verandah, on her head.' It is a grammatically perfect sentence with an active verb and describes an action. But thanks to the juxtaposition of the words, it only provokes laughter. The sentence appeared on the front page of the newspaper. An alert desk should have corrected the sentence structure to make clear that Padmavathy, far from bearing the weight of her body on her head, bore the brunt of the hit on the head.

The second example is from the lead story on the front page of a major accident six years ago. Again, the original is grammatically correct but if the objective is to convey information fast to the reader it can be faulted. The original read:

> In a virtual repeat of the Vikas Marg incident nine months ago, six people, including an engineer from Gammon India, were killed when a pre-fabricated concrete segment of an under-construction Metro viaduct collapsed along with a portion of the girder launcher on Sunday morning. Fifteen people were injured in the incident

> on the Central Secretariat-Badarpur line that occurred on the intersection of Lala Lajpat Rai Path and Kalka Devi Marg, at a stone's throw from LSR College and Bluebells School.[3]

The 44-word first sentence has far too many details to make an impact at the first read. If you are patient you can read it once more and try to understand what the reporter is attempting to say. This is no way to report news, especially since the reader will simply pass on and if this type of reporting continues switch to other sources to get information.

What do we do in such cases? The desk should rewrite the sentences to make it easier for the reader to get the details. The sentences should have been split and rewritten. Read this:

> Six persons were killed when a concrete segment of a Metro viaduct under construction collapsed this morning on the Central Secretariat-Badarpur line. The accident was a virtual repeat of the one that occurred at Vikas Marg nine months ago. Among those killed was an engineer from Gammon India who are implementing the project. A portion of the girder launcher also collapsed with the pre-fab concrete segment. At least 15 people were injured. The accident occurred at the intersection of Lala Lajpat Rai Path and Kalka Devi Marg, a stone's throw from LSR College and Bluebells School.

You can fault this on only one count: it has more words than the original. As rewritten, the details are easy to grasp at first reading and without much effort.

My third and final example tells you how the desk can help reporters rephrase their own report to make it newsy and readable. A news report is more than just a collection of verifiable facts. It needs to be written cogently, with clarity, and in an attractive manner. One of my students at the ACJ landed on an excellent story for her first reporting assignment as part of the post-graduate diploma course. She filed a fairly readable report. On my suggestion on how, with the same information, she can produce a much more interesting report and with some tips, she went back and came up with the second. This is what a desk can do to a report and reporter: give life to news reports.

Surfing in Kovalam Waters

Isha Sharma[4]

Murthy, a fisherman from a small village, Kovalam, has taken to a new profession, surfing. For thousands of years, the only relationship that the villagers like Murthy shared with the sea was fishing. Now, all that is about to change.

Heavy dependency on fishing has brought harsh times upon the new generations of Kovalam village. With fewer fish and lesser catch every year, their livelihood is threatened. This has led many fishermen to take up alternative professions.

When Murthy was gifted a surfboard by a surf enthusiast 5 years back, he did not know what to do with it. With his will to learn and love for water, he learnt to surf. Since then he has been surfing. He calls it "the surf fever".

Surfing is not a famous sport in India. But his passion has inspired many Kovalam youngsters to surf. Currently Murthy coaches 25 people.

His "ultimate dream" is to open a surf school. But there are many obstacles that Murthy faces; the biggest one is the lack of surf boards and the lack of funds.

His house is full of old surf boards and he needs new ones if he wants to continue teaching surfing.

He believes he can give a new hope to youngsters of this generation if he manages to open his school. (218 words)

Here is a revised version:

Surfing in Kovalam Waters

Isha Sharma[5]

When Murthy was gifted a surfboard by an enthusiast from Israel five years ago, he did not know what to do with it. Now, he gives lessons in surfing to about 25 youngsters in Kovalam off Chennai.

A fisherman by birth from the small village of Kovalam, Murthy has a new profession now. It is surfing. It is a happy break from the thousands of years of the past when the only relationship that villagers like Murthy shared with the sea was fishing.

All that is changing, changing slowly.

Heavy dependency on fishing has brought harsh times upon the new generations of Kovalam village. With fewer fish and lesser

> catch every year, their livelihood is threatened. This has led many fishermen to take up alternative avenues to earn a living.
>
> Murthy's love for water is too deep to make him part ways with it. Without any professional training in surfing, he learnt to surf by the time-tested method of trial and error. He calls it "the surf fever".
>
> Surfing is not a famous sport in India. But Murthy's passion keeps inspiring many Kovalam youngsters to surf.
>
> His "ultimate dream" is to open a surf school. But there are many obstacles that Murthy faces; the biggest ones are the lack of surf boards and funds.
>
> His house is full of old surf boards but he needs new ones if he wants to continue teaching surfing.
>
> He believes he can give new hope to youngsters of this generation if he manages to open his school.

You can see that the second report is racy and the lead is attractive enough to induce even the casual reader to read on. The key to the success is that she picked the most interesting point in her report and placed it at the very beginning. That the young fisherman was gifted a surfboard was itself interesting and even more so was the fact that it was done by an Israeli. The immediate next point in terms of reader interest is the fact that the young man today teaches surfing to boys in his community. It is a heartwarming story and it has been highlighted in the most simple of language. This is effective writing and most readers would have read through the full report.

What has happened is that the original draft has been turned into a readable, clear and newsworthy report. This rewriting, bringing the focus on the most newsworthy element in a report, is done in the desk. This is one of the major tasks in the newsroom. An expanded report was published along with a photograph by a leading English-language daily.

All these examples must tell you that copy editing is the work that an editor (sub-editor) does to correct reports, check for facts, arrange in prescribed language, format and get ready for publication, uploading, broadcast or telecast.

Tasting Copy

Much more happens in the newsroom. Checking for facts and details—and rewriting, if needed—are the first, basic functions. For checking facts, some organisations have fact-checking staff equipped with all reference works, printed and online. Of the mountain of copy that lands on the desk each hour, each day, only five per cent or less can be used. This is true of the print medium and while online versions can accommodate much more, the broadcast media, namely TV and radio, have even greater constraints.

Today, in the paperless newsrooms, it will even be difficult to visualise a newsroom overflowing with paper. This was the scene till the computer era began. An English-language daily, for example, will have news reports being filed on a daily basis by a nationwide network of correspondents, with state capitals having a 10 or 15-person bureau and district capitals and business centres having part-timers, to make up an army of several hundreds. Where will their reports land? Till the 1980s, the network was linked by teleprinters which would work nonstop, receiving copy from all over the country, and abroad. Besides their own staffers, newspapers would subscribe to the two main national news agencies, Press Trust of India (PTI) and United News of India (UNI), which would also supply news nonstop via their printers. The bigger newspapers also had arrangements with international dailies to receive their syndicated news items and columns. All these reports will land in the newsroom and be stacked in piles according to the region. In fact, the first senior desk person who checks into the newsroom at the start of the day would confront a veritable mountain of copy. Unfortunately, the scene has now changed, newsrooms have gone paperless; they receive all their reports on the computer network. I say unfortunately because I cannot visualise a newsroom without the chaos and confusion of copy all over the place. Without the need to struggle with reams and reams of paper and paper bits, the desk's task has been made so much easier, perhaps. The task in the desk in fact begins with selection, and rejection or spiking of copy. Once the weeding out is done, copy is assigned to the different sections dealing with different aspects of news such as national, regional, international, political, business and sport. It is here that the news report is given shape, edited for clarity and correctness, given a headline and assigned to pages. It is here again that the pages are made with relevant software.

The desk also closely coordinates with the graphics section where selected photographs are checked for details and quality, and maps and news graphics are prepared. Infographics, the increasingly popular way of conveying information through graphics combined with news details, use photographs and maps as background to weave in statistical details. This news in a nutshell needs much serious attention to detail and their preparation therefore is time-consuming. A ready reckoner of sorts, the graphic designer sits with the desk (or the reporter) and designs the infographic.

Apart from these, the desk handles breaking-news stories which land at the last hour, where the sub-editor is required to write in the perspective and background since what he will get from the computer network or news agencies will only be the first reports containing just the 'flash' news. And, if the news breaks out just before the edition time, the sub-editor may have to write the story with the details that have been received and with whatever background information is available at that time.

Writing the overall intro is another aspect where the desk will be required to consolidate reports from different centres on the same topic. For example, the desk will receive reports from across the country during a Bharat bandh or weather during the pre-monsoon days when it may be called upon to give the big picture by writing the intro part of the report from the inputs available. More challenging can be a developing story such as a hijack or a terror strike where every minute the picture may change or new developments or angles emerge, necessitating changes in the lead paragraphs or sometimes altering the whole emphasis altogether.

All these tasks set the stage for the final decisions that the desk takes on an everyday basis. It is perhaps the most challenging task: to evaluate news. How does one evaluate news, what are the criteria that govern news evaluation and what role does it play for the final output?

GOALS OF EDITING

Going back to the basics, what the journalists seek to do is to tell news. Their primary goal always is to communicate. Literary flourishes, obscure terms and jargon may amuse. But to communicate clearly, journalists must rely on a vocabulary that is easily understood. The desk ensures that whatever passes through satisfies this goal of ensuring that the copy is easily understood and clear. There should never be any compromise on any of these points. One of my mentors and my first news editor would never tire of rewriting and rewriting to polish a news report and would tell us that no effort is excessive or wasteful.

The main objective of subbing or editing is to make the stories clear, accurate and cogent. There should be no loose ends and no tantalising puzzles for the reader, and no inaccuracies like wrong dates, numbers and facts which can mislead the reader. Also, today, readers are generally people in a hurry and have no patience with long winding stories. They want their information fast. So the story has to be crisp and easy flowing. For this, the desk needs to tighten stories by removing irrelevant or redundant words. It must make every word count, eliminate needless words and prefer short to long words. For example, use 'buy' instead of 'purchase', 'said' for 'commented' or 'declared' or 'averred' or 'reiterated' or 'stated'.

Sometimes editing is also required to trim a story so that it fits the space allotted for it on the printed or web page or for the broadcast media where words are a luxury. When the desk does the trimming, it should first try to tighten it by making the language leaner and stronger. Read the copy carefully and see whether in each sentence a word or phrase can be removed without affecting the meaning. Most often the tendency is to lop off from the bottom in the belief that the last few sentences or paragraphs would have no important point to make. This might affect the flow of the report and if the report is already short may leave it incomplete.

Here's a list of the tasks of the desk:

1. Spot errors in spelling, grammar and style.
2. Ensure accuracy by checking facts, names and numbers.
3. Keep the language straight and simple.
4. Cut out verbosity and eliminate repetitions.

5. Make sure the story is clear to the reader. If a question occurs to you, make sure the story answers it before you send it on.
6. Be uncompromising about fairness, good taste and legal safety.
7. Prune stories but ensure that no relevant facts are deleted.
8. See that while editing the sense is not altered and no new attributions are introduced.
9. Do not allow abbreviations without at least once giving the full version.
10. Where necessary, don't hesitate to make changes but make only changes that are essential and can be justified.
11. Ensure that the story fits the length marked on the page layout.
12. Detect potential libel, or common legal danger points. (See Chapter Six for further details)
13. Write a crisp headline and assign copy to the page indicated by the Chief Sub-editor.
14. Above all, stick to deadlines.

The use of abbreviations without giving the full version even once (point 9) is a mistake committed every other day in the media. In the report below, for example, the use of WB without the fuller version must be questioned, though everyone in Kolkata may know the answer. This mistake often occurs because journalists take it for granted that the public know the expanded version of popular acronyms like the PM, CM or the UN. As I have explained below, this habit can cause much embarrassment.

Points 8 and 10 go together. Over a period of time, some editors have tended to fall into the habit of changing everything that comes their way, rewriting for the sake of rewriting, unmindful of whether it is warranted or not. Quite often this results in the original sense of the report getting distorted or altered. The essence of editing is to make changes when necessary and essential which can be justified if challenged. Equally essential to remember is not to extrapolate, that while editing the editor does not bring in points that are non-existent in the original copy.

Points 11 and 13 come into play once the copy is edited. The next is for all practical purposes the final task of the desk and holds good for all the four streams—to fit the report for final delivery. In the case of radio, the editor keeps sharpening the cuts in the audio till it fits the time allotted for the news item in the overall schedule. For TV, the desk must ensure that the video and audio match and fit the space allotted. In the case of print, the desk has its task cut out literally by the chief sub-editor who makes the pages. The chief assigns the reports to different pages and in each page to different columns and marks out the exact length of the report that can be accommodated and the type of headline required. The desk ensures that by cutting out a few sentences and shortening some others, it sends in the exact length of copy—any more or less will revert back to the desk for refitting as the pagemaker has no editing facility.

In all the four streams, all these tasks have to be completed on a tight time schedule. Any slippage anywhere can lead to chaos. One of my editors used to say that if we fail to stick to deadlines on printing, the newspaper will reach the stands the next morning too late for distribution and come back the next day. Working to deadline in fact is the first mantra that all journalists must learn.

Let us see a simple example, of a report on a traffic accident.

Three Dead in Mishap[6]

Kolkata, 17 July: Three people were crushed to death under the front wheels and eight others injured in a bus accident near Rash Behari Avenue in south Kolkata this morning. The vehicle, belonging to the State transport corporation, apparently after its breaks had failed, mounted the pavement and was halted only by the compound wall of the post office complex on Southern Avenue which abuts the main road.

It was a gruesome accident resulting from rash driving and took place around 11 am. It is needless to say that the casualties would have been higher if the mishap had occurred during the peek hours. As the bus veered off the road, pedestrians ran helter skelter.

The 3 people who died were passersby on the road. Of the 8 injured, 3 were hurt seriously. The 3 suffered head injuries and were rushed to the nearby private hospital and admitted as in-patients. The L 9 bus was speeding to Ultadanga and it was obvious that the driver was trying to beat the automatic signal at the end of the road junction near the metro station. The bus driver jumped out of the vehicle and escaped injuries. He was later apprehended, according to the State transport minister.

It may be recalled that this road junction is accident prone and the WB Government is already implementing a project to widen the road to make it six lane. The widening is expected to ease the pressure on traffic and the pile-up of vehicles. (242 words)

Here is the checklist: the goal and result

1. Ensure accuracy by checking facts, names, etc.

   In the report, there are three proper names. Check to ensure that they are spelt out correctly.
2. Ensure that the language is straight and simple.

   Here, most sentences are simple. The only sentence which is not straight and perhaps overloaded is the last sentence in the first paragraph. Break it up and make it easy to comprehend.
3. Cut out verbosity, repetitions.

   Here, the second paragraph is an example of verbosity. Of course it is a minor crime. Correct it. Are there repetitious details? Or at least sentences that say in 20 words what can be said in 10 and need to be pruned? Look at the sentence 'It is needless to say ...' It has all the wrong things. 'It may be recalled' and 'It is needless to say' are two clichéd phrases that journalists are fond of. If it is needless to say, why say it at all. Either say it in the report or cut it out. In this case it was certainly needless to say that if the accident had happened at peak time the casualties would have been higher. Every reader knows it. Similarly, why say 'it may be recalled' at all? Are we holding a memory test for the reader? Just recall whatever background information you may want to bring to reader attention, without the prefatory phrase.
4. Make certain that the usages are correct and in keeping with the style of your publication.
5. Be uncompromising about fairness, good taste and libel (legal safety)

   Here, the first sentence of the second paragraph is dangerous. The reporter should not make an unsubstantiated judgement that the accident was the result of rash driving. If policemen or eyewitnesses say it, the remark is worded carefully and used with proper attribution. Again, paragraph four is loaded. To say the bus was 'speeding', which is itself a comment. There is the added observation that the driver was 'obviously' trying to beat the signal. Both are unfair to the driver unless the reporter has eye witnesses saying so.

Especially when reporting murder, accident or other actions involving people, the reporter needs to be extra cautious to ensure that the reader's sensibilities are not hurt. In this sense it is not at all in good taste to say 'crushed to death,' under the front wheels, etc. Leave it to the imagination of the reader. Suffice it to say that the victim was caught under the wheels of the bus. The reader can imagine what happens in such accidents. There is also no need to say that it was 'a gruesome' accident. The reader can realise that from the fact that the victims were caught under the wheels.

The report says that the driver jumped out of the bus. Without attribution to eyewitnesses or police, it becomes a statement of the reporter. Was the reporter witness to his jumping? Attribution is very important in such instances. Let the reader deduce all this from the word picture you presented. If a bus mounts the pavement, it must be either due to rash driving (by the bus driver or someone else on the road) or mechanical failure.

6. Since space is of the essence, the desk prunes stories without deleting relevant facts.
7. Ensure that the sense is not altered or new attributions or details introduced.
8. Acronyms and abbreviations should not be used without at least once giving the full version.

   Here, expand WB even if it is obvious. Abbreviations can be a veritable puzzle. I can cite at least one example where a major blunder nearly got through the desk. It was an instance involving the use of the acronym CBMs (for 'confidence building measures') without the expanded form being mentioned even once during a report on an India–Pakistan dialogue. Without a second thought, the sub-editor at the desk made it ICBMs (inter-continental ballistic missile). The error was detected before any damage could be done. And it happened because the reporter had not taken care to expand the acronym even once.
9. Where necessary, don't hesitate to make changes but be ready to substantiate whatever changes you make.

Rewrite where needed, giving background where needed. Most importantly, if the most newsworthy point is not in the lead and is buried in the fourth or fifth para of a report, rewrite to bring it up front.

10. Write a crisp headline and assign copy to the page indicated by the chief sub-editor.
11. Above all, stick to deadlines.

Keeping these points in mind, I have edited the piece in its entirety and present it here for you. One key to success in writing crisply and with precision is to keep looking for shorter alternatives, in words and phrases, and for opportunities to cut down on words to speed the delivery of news. For example, the first sentence in the accident report above says 'Three people were crushed to death ...' and the third paragraph says all three victims were passersby. I combined the two to start my first line as 'Three passersby were killed ...' The same first sentence also says 'Three people were crushed ... and eight others ...' I have cut out the 'other' since those who died cannot also be in the injured list. The use of 'the other'" has become so clichéd that you can see it every day in the newspapers. Keep looking constantly for economising on words. Every word should pull its weight, should justify its presence. Never use two words when one will do. Remember also that adjectives and all modifiers serve no purpose. Very much like the word 'very' which adds nothing of value as far as the reader is concerned. For the reader, 'beautiful' is as good as 'very beautiful'.

Three Dead in Mishap[7]

Kolkata, 17 July: Three passersby were killed and eight injured in a bus accident near Rash Behari Avenue in south Kolkata this morning. The vehicle, belonging to the State transport corporation, apparently after its brakes had failed, mounted the pavement. It was halted only by the compound wall of the post office complex on Southern Avenue which abuts the main road.

The accident took place around 11 am. As the bus veered off the road, pedestrians ran helter skelter.

Three of the eight injured have been admitted in a nearby hospital with serious injuries.

The bus was on its way to Ultadanga and it appears that the driver was trying to beat the automatic signal at the end of the road junction near the metro station. The bus driver jumped out of the vehicle and escaped injuries. He was later arrested, according to the State transport minister (Fact check: Put in minister's name).

This road junction is accident prone and the government is already implementing a project to widen the road to make it six lane. The widening is expected to ease the pressure on traffic and eliminate the pile-up of vehicles.

The following report appeared in a daily in Hyderabad. It was for the first time that the incident was being reported.

Warangal Software Engineer Shot Dead in South Africa[8]

Hyderabad: A 28-year-old software engineer from Warangal, Budde Kiran, succumbed on Tuesday to bullet injuries. His roommate, Sridhar of Rajahmundry is recuperating in a Government hospital there. Kiran sustained the injuries when unidentified assailants shot him from point blank range in Johannesburg, South Africa, last week. Sridhar was also shot at by the miscreants.

Kiran, a post graduate in computer applications, was working on an assignment with the Johannesburg Municipal Corporation and was living there for the last two years. Two assailants barged into the flat where Kiran and Sridhar were staying and snatched a laptop, wrist watches, wallets and a gold chain, according to Minister for Higher Education and NRI Affairs D. Sridhar Babu.

As the assailants were leaving the flat, Sridhar is said to have pleaded with them to return the passport and ATM card. The infuriated intruders fired four rounds at Sridhar injuring him grievously. Kiran, who came to the rescue of his friend, also sustained injuries but managed to telephone his friends living in an adjoining apartment. The duo was rushed to a Government hospital in Johannesburg, where Kiran breathed his last.

Warangal police have arranged for relevant documents for Kiran's brother B. Ganesh to secure a passport. Ganesh visited the Regional Passport Office here on Tuesday and submitted his application.

Mr. Sridhar Babu said the government had sanctioned Rs. 5 lakh ex gratia to Kiran's parents and were making arrangements for his brother's travel to South Africa at the earliest to bring back the body. Meanwhile, Indian Embassy in South Africa said it would take at least four to five days for the body to reach Hyderabad as post mortem and other legal formalities had to be completed.

Here is a reworked draft:

Techie Shot Dead in Jo'burg Robbery[9]

Hyderabad: Two software engineers from Andhra Pradesh were injured, one of them fatally, when armed intruders broke into their apartment in Johannesburg, South Africa, last week. Budde Kiran, 28, of Warangal died of gunshot wounds and Sridhar of Rajahmundry is recovering in hospital in the South African capital.

Kiran was on an assignment with the Johannesburg Municipal Corporation for the past two years.

The AP government, which announced an ex gratia of Rs 5 lakhs to Kiran's family, is helping his brother go to Johannesburg to bring the body home. This may take four to five days, according to the Indian Embassy in South Africa, since legal formalities and the post mortem examination needed to be completed.

According to AP's Minister for Higher Education and NRI Affairs, D. Sridhar Babu, the two assailants attempted to rob them of a laptop, wrist watches, wallets and a gold chain.

As the assailants were leaving, Sridhar pleaded for the return of their passports and ATM cards. This infuriated the intruders who fired four rounds at Sridhar, injuring him grievously. Kiran, who came to the rescue of his friend, also sustained injuries but managed to telephone his friends living in an adjacent apartment. They rushed the two to hospital where Kiran died.

Since the editing is for a national newspaper I prefer to say the engineers are from Andhra Pradesh. I could have identified their native place but a national readership may not relate to the names. I found it inappropriate to start with '... succumbed to bullet injuries'. It is incomplete as a lead sentence since the reader has not been told that he was injured, in the first instance. After my lead paragraphs (the first two), the following question will arise in the reader's mind: What next? More than the details of what happened in Johannesburg the reader will want to know what help will go to Kiran's family, to the surviving victim. This was why I switched to the latest news about what the AP government is doing to help the family and the victim's brother to go to Johannesburg to bring the body home. Then I have followed it with details of what happened, what the two were doing there, etc. Since the rule is to write news the way you will tell it to your friends, I have not used the Italian words duo, trio, etc. I have instead used two, three, etc. which are equally good. I have avoided archaic phrases like 'breathed his last' when 'died' would do the same service. Also, since this example predates the bifurcation of Andhra Pradesh the question of Telangana state in my edited version did not arise.

News Evaluation

Among the key tasks of the desk in the newsroom is editing. After this is completed or as it is being done, another vital task will be taken up by the desk editor–evaluating the news. This involves reading, analysing and deciding the importance of the news development in the overall picture for the newspaper. Let us consider an example. The following are two news reports of which only one can be accommodated on the front page of a newspaper.

1. A report on the brutal murder in broad daylight of an elderly couple in their farm house in a Kochi suburb, with the murderer caught by neighbours who hand him over to the Police. The couple lived there alone.
2. A report on the incursions by Chinese planes in Arunachal Pradesh and the Government's apparent eagerness to downplay their significance.

In terms of reader interest and for the residents of Kochi City, the first report will top the chart: the murder of an old couple living alone has an enormous human interest element. Ninety per cent of the readers will be able to relate to the story and will reach out to read it when given a choice. But newspapers don't use only the human interest yardstick when evaluating reports. For, the other report has deep implications for the nation's security which had once, in 1962, suffered defeat at the hands of the Chinese army. The 1962 defeat has left deep scars and even for those in distant Kochi in the south this may have greater value as a news development, going beyond the national versus local angle.

What we have just done here is news evaluation, assessing the value of news developments. This goes on continuously in newsrooms. A successful editor does this assessment fast, keeping all criteria in mind. According to a senior colleague, the Mumbai editor of a leading daily years ago excelled in news evaluation; he used to comment every day on the day's newspaper and one day had this entry about the treatment of a brief report on the movement of Chinese troops in the northern borders. The year was 1956, six years before the Sino-Indian war. He pulled up the news editor for dismissing the report as a short item in an inside page and made the written remark: 'Any report, however innocuous looking, relating to things happening on the country's northern borders should be on the front page, regardless of whether it was two paras long or 10.' This was news awareness of the highest order, from which flows news evaluation.

Analyse the paper of the past few days and see how news has been evaluated differently in different papers. Why does this happen? What are the criteria that determine these decisions? Take the front page of one day's *Hindu* and *Times of India*—dated 20 July 2011. The *Hindu* has the Murdoch drama as the lead story, along with a photograph of the father and son, and Hillary Clinton's talks as the second lead and a state story as the anchor. (While testifying in front of British parliamentarians over a phone hacking scandal involving one of his newspapers, on 19 July 2011, press baron Rupert Murdoch was attacked by a protestor who rushed at him with white foam in London. Murdoch was accompanied by his son).

But where is *Hindu*'s lead in the *Times of India*? It has been dismissed as a short report in the menu on column one middle. What does the *Times of India* lead with? The Clinton visit and her comments on the threats from Pakistan. What is new in this? In the context of the then-new terrorist attacks in Mumbai? What possible reasons could have motivated each newspaper? The *Hindu*, which had consistently devoted much news space for the phone hacking scandal and the larger issues of press freedom this raised, must have decided that the Murdoch testimony was of greater importance on that particular day than the talks of the visiting American secretary of state, Hillary Clinton. The symbolic pie attack on Murdoch added a touch of tragi-comedy to the deliberations of the British government-ordered enquiry. For the *Times of India*, on the other hand, the Murdoch testimony probably rated low since the issues involved were not of great reader interest and the news report was not featured. With the terror strike on Mumbai fresh in the memory of the public, *Times of India* rated Clinton's remarks on Pakistan as the most newsworthy for the day and featured the story as the front page lead.

These are dramatically different perceptions of the value of each news development. The process of choosing news stories and taking decisions on the degree of importance given to each is known as news evaluation. In many cases, this does not differ drastically. For example, all newspapers and news channels made a major train accident in West Bengal as the main story a few years back because of the then raging controversies over the stewardship of the railway ministry by the mercurial Mamata Banerjee. But on any given day there can be differences in perception and evaluation. This difference lends character to each newspaper/channel.

Basic Evaluation Criteria

The following are the general time-tested criteria on which news evaluation is based.

- *Proximity*: An event happening closer to home has more value than something happening in a distant land. An accident in a Delhi neighbourhood will have more value for a Delhi reader than, say, one on Airport Road in Bengaluru.
- *Prominence*: Between six persons being injured in a bus accident and one VIP breaking a leg in a fall, the latter gains in news value since a prominent person is involved. Prominence can also relate to a place or event.
- *Conflict*: Controversies, clash of interests, protests and demonstrations are all of interest to the reader and have news value. Personality clashes, wordy duels come under this. When two industrialist brothers clashed, it was front page news.
- *Consequence/Impact*: Any news development that is likely to provoke reactions is of value. The development as such might be insignificant but the fact that there can be adverse consequences flowing from it gives it news value. The most glaring in recent times has been the violent actions of the Maoists.

- *Timeliness*: This needs no explanation in this age of instant news. If till a decade ago newspapers had a lifespan of 24 hours, today there is a premium on this value of timeliness.
- *Celebrity*: Till a decade ago, conservative newspapers would not care to even mention them. Celebrities have in recent years become major newsmakers. There is increasing reader interest in the lives and lifestyles of celebrities in all walks of life and so news concerning them has great value. When, for example, Hindi film superstar Shah Rukh Khan was stopped for questioning at an American airport, or Hrithik Roshan underwent a brain surgery, the news was on the front page because celebrities are news.
- *Human interest*: Reports of human endurance, individual achievements, joy and suffering interest readers of all ages. These reports may not have great news value but are often front-paged by newspapers in preference to hard news reports.
- *Education/information*: The readers want to be informed in advance of forthcoming events of importance. News of educative value is always read with interest. In today's context, news of this genre relates to power shutdowns and protest demonstrations. At the height of the summer, the monsoon becomes news. During admission time, educational news gains value.

Changing Values and Roles

In what way is news evaluation helpful? It in fact plays a vital role: it decides where and how news reports are featured. In the print media, this assessment of value decides where the report is published–front page middle, back page bottom, city page top or not at all, and in what detail and at what length. News values are eminently unstable. Relative value should be a better description. News value changes when a more important news development takes place or when the news report under review develops into a major event or fizzles out.

How does this work? Take a plane crash, for instance. If it is an Indian plane, all the above criteria automatically come into play. Wherever the crash site, in India or abroad, all details will be of importance: detailed reports/photographs, list of passengers, flight details, possible cause of accident (natural calamity/technical defect/ sabotage). The stories acquire more poignancy if the reporters are able to collect narratives from people who've lost their loved ones. The story fulfils all the criteria listed above.

If it is not an Indian plane, what value will a crash have for Indian readers? The focus shifts to passengers. If there are Indian passengers—the criterion of proximity, in a large sense—the story gets greater value. And, reckoning with the second criterion, there will be added value if any of the Indian passengers is a prominent personality like a scientist or political leader (prominence criterion). Dr Homi Bhabha, considered father of Indian atomic science, died when the Air India plane he was travelling in crashed in France as he was on his way to Vienna to attend a meeting of the International Atomic Energy Agency. For a full 24 hours, India did not know that Dr Bhabha was on the plane and when this became known the news acquired enormously more value. Newspapers had, until then, given details of the accident prominently since it was an Indian plane and the passengers were Indian. But the next day focus shifted to Dr Bhabha and they published long obituary notes and photographs of the scientist with national leaders. Not an Indian plane, no Indian passengers; the story will have limited value as an avoidable human tragedy. The Human Interest criterion will come into play if say one passenger out of 180 had survived the crash, as happened recently.[10]

Take the case of a murder. Any murder is an uncommon event and is of interest to all readers. But its value will increase (a) if it had taken place in the neighbourhood or city, i.e., proximity; (b) if the victim is a VIP, when prominence comes into play; (c) if the victim is a political personality or controversial trader or businessman, when the criteria of consequence and even conflict come into play.

What happens when these values change? In the first instance (a), the report will contain the name of the victim and the alleged perpetrators, the possible motive, etc. and find a place on the city page. In the second case (b), the murder of the celebrity will attract more attention from people of all ages. In terms of hard news there may be nothing, but in terms of reader interest it has value. Certainly the report will be accompanied by some photograph. And it will find a top of the column spot on the city page. In the third case (c), the news value depends on the consequences of the event—whether there will be retaliatory violence, trade and business sabotage activity, etc. Most often, what starts as an innocuous quarrel leads to much violence and destruction. While the desk must weigh these, it must also see if the ramifications could be felt beyond the city and state. If it has national level interest, the value goes up and the report may as well be taken out of the 'regional' page and taken to the front page or any of the 'national' pages. (What is the difference: Regional pages appear only in the regional edition circulating in particular areas while national pages—like editorial pages—appear in all editions.)

Contrast the death of two men in recent times: the assassination of Rajiv Gandhi and the elimination of LTTE (Liberation Tigers of Tamil Eelam) chief Prabhakaran. Reflect on how these two happenings had played out as news developments. The first shook the nation and the world whereas the second was a denouement everyone was waiting for. The approach to both was different.

1. What is newsworthy: what interests readers/viewers is newsworthy.
2. Death is more newsworthy than injury, injuries carry more weight than monetary loss. For example: (a) A bank is robbed and huge amounts of cash and jewels are stolen from the locker. (b) A drug store is broken open, some cash taken away and the watchman is murdered. Which has more news value between (a) and (b)? Why? The second, since a life has been lost against cash and valuables which can always be replaced.
3. Firsts, largests and leasts often make news.
4. A fatal accident close to home typically will trump a plane crash far away.
5. The unusual, the unseasonal and controversial all make news.
6. Today's story may be dead tomorrow. Timely is news.

Tackling Developing Stories

'Priority', 'Top Priority', 'Urgent', 'Flash' and 'Flash Flash' are some of the key slugs that newswires use to alert desks about an emerging story of importance. In the past half a century, there have been many instances of such developing stories which have rattled the world. The assassination of American President John F. Kennedy and the sudden death of Prime Minister Lal Bahadur Shastri stand out for their shock element. Developing stories, as you can guess, are news developments that have not reached their conclusion at the time of going to press, in many instances often with unknown consequences.

Very often a story breaks out at an inconvenient time. In the pre-computer age, when the media meant mostly the printed newspapers in this country, any outbreak of news after 10:00 PM for the morning dailies was an emergency. It is a time one edition had just been put to sleep and the next is in the making. All calculations go awry. For example, it was noon in India when Kennedy was shot and newspapers—no television or online then (this was the pre-satellite era of the 1960s)—had time enough to get details, photographs, etc. for the next morning. In contrast, Lal Bahadur Shastri died past midnight Indian time when most newspapers had put their latest editions to sleep and printing had started; it was a logistical nightmare. The assassination of Indira Gandhi and killing of the entire family of King Birendra of Nepal and other leaders in neighbouring countries were equally shocking. But, the death of Shastri was more shocking because it was poignant. He died in the hour of his triumph, soon after signing a historic agreement with Pakistan's Ayub Khan in the then Soviet city of Tashkent. The agreement, worked out under the Kremlin's good offices, ended the second of three wars with Pakistan shortly after Shastri had assumed office as Prime Minister succeeding Jawaharlal Nehru. The signing had taken place around 10:00 PM and Indian newspapers were filled with the details. Most newspapers had also placed a photograph of Shastri, Ayub and Soviet Premier Kosygin shaking hands, on the front page. It was around 2:00 AM when the editors and news editors received urgent calls from news agencies to say that Shastri had died of a heart attack in his sleep. In this case journalists just got the flash news and did not have the time to wait for agencies to file complete stories. Journalists wrote the intro, provided all the missing links, the context. Such emergencies don't happen every day and when they break out it is an experience of a lifetime for journalists.

The murder of Sri Lankan Tamil leader Amirthalingam was another instance. The Tamil Tiger rebels were holding talks with him, ostensibly to forge unity among the ethnic minority. Around 8:30 PM on the third day of the talks, our contacts phoned from

Colombo to say that the leader had been killed. There was no more information and the first edition at 10:00 PM went with just the news that Amirthalingam was dead, without any perspective. Later editions had more details about the presumed perpetrators and their motives. Again, the desk had to write the story since Sri Lanka's emergency regulations threw a blanket on all information flow.

The Indian Ocean tsunami of 2004 and the Qom earthquake in Iran are other examples of developing stories which test the alertness of the desk. Reports on both these natural calamities spoke of a few deaths in each case and they later turned out to be devastating in their impact. What must have been published on an inside page got full play as the tragedy unfolded in full measure.

The Truant Cyclone[11]

Following are reports of a cyclone which played hide and seek with the eastern coast near Chennai for a week.

Day 1: Bay depression forms and the civic authorities take prescribed precautionary measures, initiating steps to issue alerts to fishermen and people living close to the coastline, evacuate low lying areas and clear public buildings where rain-affected people can be accommodated, alert people for preparation of food packets, etc. After decades of total unpreparedness, the authorities have learnt the lessons and are ready.

Day 2: Bay depression intensifies and moves closer to the coastline. This means the previous day's overcast sky has opened up. You have rain accompanied by high velocity winds which can be disconcerting. Roads which are never in good shape give way and traffic becomes more unmanageable.

Day 3: Depression remains stationary and continues to disrupt normal life as rain and wind continue. Educational institutions are closed—also to free up space for accommodating the increasing number of people dislocated from their living spaces. The city's canals begin to swell posing yet more danger to people living on the banks.

Day 4: Depression shows no signs of appreciable movement during the early morning. Met authorities say it had moved away from the coastline but remained centred in the bay still to the south of the city. Since cyclones in this region move west towards the land masses there was no way that the city could let down its guard. By afternoon, the depression moves east and away. If it moves north or north-west, the city will escape its fury.

The Met authorities begin to issue hourly bulletins on the truant cyclone as the city groans under the weight of the water and wind and the continuing, nerve-wracking threat of the cyclone hitting. The press recalls that in the early 1970s a similar cyclone had caused incalculable damage—even forcing a Greek cargo ship aground off Chennai. (It was stuck in the sands of Marina Beach for a number of years. The *Stematis* soon became a tourist attraction on the beach.)

Around midnight, the Met office puts out the following bulletin: The depression in the Bay is centred at 11:00 PM about 100 km northeast of the city and is expected to move in a north-westerly direction and cross the coast early in the morning. The rain and winds will intensify when the cyclone makes landfall.'

What are the implications of this bulletin? After having been buffeted around for nearly a week the city will wake up to the news in a few hours. What does the news mean to the residents?

What do you do? Your edition deadline is 1:30 AM. By the time the night duty reporter hands you over the report/copy, it will be 12:30 AM and you have hardly half an hour to close the edition.

At least one city daily interpreted the weather bulletin to mean that Chennai had this time escaped the fury of the cyclone since the system had moved up north and was forecast to cross the coast in Andhra Pradesh. This was important for the cyclone-weary residents. The daily was right and the city was spared the wrath of the cyclone as the sky cleared by the next morning. The desk, as the veteran reporter did, could have played safe and quoted the Met forecast, reporting where the cyclone was centred and heading. It took the initiative to inform the readers that their week-long suffering may be at an end. It did an excellent job by writing the story in and headlining that the cyclone may have spared Chennai.

Example One[12]

The following factfile is a reconstruction of the helicopter accident in which the then chief minister of Andhra Pradesh, Y. S. Rajasekhara Reddy, was killed in 2009.

I present it as a sequence of happenings relating to Dr Reddy, on 3 and 4 September 2009. The desk was required to prepare a news report each for release at 6:00 PM on 3 September and 06:00 AM and 10:00 AM on 4 September.[13] The word limit permitted was 200 words each.

3 September 2009

- **8:38 AM:** CM leaves Hyderabad by helicopter for Chittoor district, about 500 km south. He is with his principal secretary and his chief security officer. There is a pilot and copilot. Copter has enough fuel to cover the distance of 500 km.
- **9:10 AM:** Pilot reports to Chennai control, which takes over from Hyderabad, that he is near Rollapenta, entering Nallamala forests and climbing 5,500 feet. Two minutes after this, contact breaks off.
- **9:45 AM:** In the absence of any more contact in Chennai, copter is declared missing, as per regulations.
- **10:15 AM:** Private search parties take out sorties but find the weather conditions hostile, with very heavy rain and high velocity winds reducing visibility.
- **12:00 noon:** As concern deepens, Union Home Minister P. Chidambaram calls high level meeting and seeks Defence rescue teams to join the effort to locate the missing chief minister. Chidambaram briefs the Prime Minister and Congress party president Sonia Gandhi.
- **1:30 PM:** Defence ministry's Chetak helicopters join the search operation. Dornier unmanned aircraft and Avro called in.
- **2:30 PM:** Chidambaram expresses concern in public for the first time. He is asked about Naxalite groups being active in the region. PM calls high level meeting in Delhi. Panic grips Hyderabad and Congressmen gather at the party office and Secretariat.
- **5:30 PM:** Five companies of Central Reserve Police Force enter Nallamala forest with night vision devices. Even as visibility decreases, 20 teams of the army and state police, including anti-Naxalite squad, and officials enter the 1,000 sq. km forest area.
- **6:30 PM:** Aerial search called off due to poor light and bad weather conditions.
- **7:00 PM:** Sonia Gandhi dispatches two senior party leaders to Hyderabad to help organise rescue and deal with an emerging crisis.

- **8:00 PM:** PM orders full-scale rescue effort. Air Force's Sukhoi-30 aircraft join the effort, with their thermal imaging devices.
- **9:00 PM:** Chidambaram refuses to speculate whether the Naxalites could have targeted the helicopter or taken the CM prisoner. A former CM, Chandrababu Naidu, had come under a daring attack in the same area (in the temple town of Tirupati, part of Chittoor district).

4 September 2009

- **06:00 AM:** No trace of YSR and his chopper. Aerial search resumes in the wake of dawn to trace the CM as Andhra Pradesh begins to come to terms with an unfolding tragedy.
- **8:30 AM:** Chopper located atop a hill. No word on its condition or the fate of the five occupants.
- **8:50 AM:** Inaccessible by road, Air Force drops men on the site. Five charred bodies are recovered. Chopper is broken and burnt. Bodies lifted off and taken to Cuddapah.
- **9:15 AM:** State government confirms in an official communication that the helicopter crashed into the hill and burst into flames. It had veered off the flight path into thick clouds due to near zero visibility.

Three Different Versions

My version of the three reports follows with explanations on my decisions.

Here is the first report prepared for the 6:00 PM broadcast:

CM's Copter Goes Missing

Hyderabad, 3 September: A helicopter with Andhra Pradesh Chief Minister Y. Rajasekhara Reddy, which left here this morning for Chittoor, has gone missing. Nearly nine hours after it lost contact with ground control, there is no word yet.

Aerial and ground search parties have launched intensive combing operations. The region where the helicopter has gone missing is considered a naxalite stronghold. The weather conditions in the area were hostile, with heavy rain and high velocity winds.

The helicopter had enough fuel to fly to Chittoor 500 km down south, where the Chief Minister was headed. It was climbing 5,500 ft near Rollapenta and entering Nallamala forests when the pilot lost contact.

As concerns deepened in the state capital and the authorities officially declared the helicopter missing in the absence of any contact for more than an hour, Union Home Minister P. Chidambaram called a high level meeting in Delhi to review the emerging situation. He met the Prime Minister, Manmohan Singh, and the Congress president, Sonia Gandhi, to brief them.

The defence ministry's Chetak helicopters, unmanned Dorniers and Avro were called in to join the aerial search by the afternoon. As evening approached, ground searches have been intensified. Five companies of the Central Reserve Police Force with night vision devices and 20 teams of the army and state police, including the anti-naxalite squad, have entered the 1,000 sq km forest area. (235 words)

Rationale for the 6:00 PM report: In para one, I mention 'nearly nine hours' straightaway to indicate to the reader the seriousness of the development, that there is no trace yet in the past nine long hours. With this I avoid mentioning the time he left, etc. In the second para I indicate the scale of the search and the two possible causes for the copter missing. No speculation, just a mention of the fact that the forest where it disappeared has seen naxalite activity and also that it was raining heavily.

Here is the second report prepared for the deadline of 3:00 AM for the morning daily:

Copter Search Intensified

Hyderabad, 3 September: The Air Force's Sukhoi-30 aircraft, with thermal imaging devices, joined the search effort tonight as no clue has emerged yet on the whereabouts of the helicopter of the Andhra Pradesh Chief Minister, Rajasekhara Reddy, which went missing 14 hours ago.

Reddy left here for Chittoor, 500 km down south, at 8:30 AM and the helicopter lost contact with the ground control within an hour. The pilot reported flying at 5,000 ft near Rollapenta and entering the Nallamala forests. The weather conditions in the area were hostile, with heavy rain and high velocity winds.

The forest is a naxalite stronghold, but speaking to newspersons in Delhi in the afternoon, Union Home Minister P. Chidambaram refused to be drawn into speculation on whether the rebels may have targeted the helicopter. A former Chief Minister, Chandrababu Naidu of the Telugu Desam Party, had come under a daring attack by the naxalites in the temple town of Tirupati which is part of Chittoor district.

The defence ministry's Chetak helicopters, unmanned Dorniers and Avro were called in to join the aerial search by the afternoon. As evening approached, ground searches were intensified. Five companies of the Central Reserve Police Force with night vision devices and 20 teams of the army and State police, including the anti-naxalite squad, have entered the 1,000 sq. km forest area.

Tension has gripped Hyderabad as Congressmen gathered at the party headquarters for information on the whereabouts of the Chief Minister. The party's president, Sonia Gandhi, has dispatched two senior central leaders to assist in the search operations and to manage the emerging political situation. (270 words)

Rationale for the 3:00 AM report: From the deadline of 3:00 AM, it is apparent the report is for the morning dailies. So, in the lead para I have mentioned the details about when the copter left Hyderabad. The lead point should of course be the Air Force joining the strike, indicating immediately the seriousness of the development and the element of desperation. In the second para I also tell the reader about the concern in Delhi.

Here is the third report prepared for the radio broadcast at 10:00 AM:

Chief Minister Dead in Copter Crash

Hyderabad, 4 September: The Andhra Pradesh Chief Minister, Dr Y. Rajasekhara Reddy, is dead. Search teams dropped into the inaccessible Nallamala forest region have recovered the body of Dr Reddy and airlifted it to Cuddapah.

As the State comes to grips with the death of its Chief Minister, an official communication confirmed that the helicopter crashed into a hill and burst into flames. It had veered off the flight path into thick clouds with heavy rain and near zero visibility.

Aerial searches, which resumed at six in the morning, spotted the wreckage of the helicopter around 8:30 AM, nearly 23 hours after it went missing. With the forested region inaccessible by road,

Air Force dropped its personnel on to the site. Rescuers located five charred bodies, those of Dr Reddy, his principal secretary and chief security officer along with the two pilots.

The helicopter was a total wreck, broken into pieces and burnt.

Dr Reddy had left here yesterday morning for Chittoor 500 km down south. Within an hour of flight, the helicopter lost contact with ground control. The pilot had radioed in two minutes earlier that he was climbing 5,000 ft and was near Rollapenta and entering Nallamala forests. The weather conditions were hostile, with heavy rain and high velocity winds.

Aerial search operations were hampered by rain and were given up as evening fell. Focus shifted to ground search and five companies of the Central Reserve Police Force with night vision devices and 20 teams of the army and state police, including the anti-naxalite squad, entered the 1,000 sq. km forest area for combing operations. (270 words)

Rationale for the 10:00 AM report: After nearly 24 hours of speculation on the whereabouts of the copter, the foremost news point was that the CM was dead and immediately the fact that the copter had got caught in blinding rain; also, that the body had been recovered. After the lead para, I have included the details on what exactly happened and when the body would reach Hyderabad.

Example Two

The following is a reconstruction of the story of the hijack of an Indian Airlines plane soon after it took off from Kathmandu, Nepal, to Delhi. The hijack-hostage drama held the country's attention for a week before coming to a relatively happy ending with the release of all but one of the passengers held hostage by the hijackers. The key events have been included in a fact file where the whole episode begins in the forenoon and ends by the evening.

Write three reports for different media units using the details, which are terse messages as they came into the newsroom from reporters at different centres. This is how the initial reports are received before the reporters or the desk write the story in a comprehensive manner.

- **10:00 AM:** Flash: An Indian Airlines (IA) Airbus with 120 passengers has been hijacked while on a flight from Kathmandu to Delhi. Reports in Delhi say that the pilot has radioed ground control that there are four armed hijackers who have demanded to be taken to Karachi.

- **10:30 AM**: The IA plane was hijacked 20 minutes after it took off from the Nepalese capital. It has enough fuel to fly up to Amritsar. The special committee on emergency operations is currently gathering at the PMO in Delhi. Government sources rule out yielding to the demand of the hijackers to fly the plane to Karachi. The hijackers have not made any other demands and their identity is yet to be known.
- **11:00 AM**: An anonymous caller tells Reuters news agency in Islamabad that the Lashkar is responsible for the hijack. Sources in Delhi say the hijackers are demanding the release of some militant leaders held in Indian jails. It is apparent that jihadi elements are behind the hijack.
- **12:00 noon**: Hijackers are told that there is enough fuel only to go to Amritsar, agree to the plane refuelling there and taking off. They warn against commando action to stop the plane taking off again. Hijackers claim to have shot dead one of the passengers who began an argument and was soon supported by other passengers.
- **12:30 PM**: Plane lands at Amritsar. Hijackers throw out the body of the passenger they had shot dead. What is their motive? Pressure builds up in Delhi as relatives gather at the airport demanding action to get the passengers released. Government spokesman says no yielding to hijackers' demands which are now known—they want the release from prison of Hafiz, the jihadi leader who had trained in Pakistan and had masterminded several terrorist strikes in India, including the vicious attack on the Indian parliament.

Write a report without leaving out details for a 1:00 PM edition. Reporters on the field from various centres keep filing copy. They have no time to coordinate/give context.

- **1:00 PM**: Plane takes off from Amritsar after refuelling and instead of heading for Karachi flies out to Kandahar across the border in Afghanistan.

- **1:30 PM:** Amid screams for action from relatives, Cabinet ministers present in Delhi meet under Deputy Prime Minister L. K. Advani. Mr Advani has often opposed yielding to terrorists and favours a hard line. Hijackers present a list of names of detainees they want released from different Indian prisons. Hafiz heads the list and he is in a high security prison outside Srinagar. Hijackers also threaten to kill more passengers if there is delay.
- **2:00 PM:** Plane lands in Kandahar amid scenes of pistol waving and jihadi slogans from the ground. Kandahar is the stronghold of the Taliban who are in control of Afghanistan. There are reports of a division within government over the response to the threat from the hijackers. Jaswant Singh, foreign minister, urges some action to get the passengers back. There are reports that Washington does not want the government to yield by releasing terrorist-prisoners. The airport scene in Delhi continues to be tense as relatives step up pressure for the safe return of the passengers. They urge the government to meet the demands of the hijackers.
- **2:30 PM:** Hijackers release women and children and they decline the offer and prefer to remain within the plane instead of going into what must be considered hostile territory.

Prepare a report for an edition at 4:00 PM.

- **4:00 PM:** Amid signs that the government is bringing some of the terrorist-prisoners to Delhi the government reiterates it will not yield to their demands. This provokes huge protests at the Delhi airport and elsewhere.
- **5:00 PM:** A special plane with Mr Jaswant Singh, foreign minister, and six of the terrorist-prisoners leaves Delhi for Kandahar as the government announces it is yielding to the hijackers' demand since more than 120 lives are involved.
- **6:00 PM:** Special plane lands in Kandahar, the released prisoners leave in jeeps in a visible show of triumph and amid firing in the air and other signs of celebration. Simultaneously, Mr Jaswant Singh and party get into the Indian Airlines plane which leaves Kandahar.
- **6:45 PM:** The hijacked plane returns to Delhi nearly 12 hours

after it was seized in the air. There is relief at Delhi airport but no celebration.

Write a comprehensive report for the edition at 9:00 PM. Is there a human interest story? Highlights of the first report are: An Indian Airlines plane from Kabul seized mid-air, hijackers want terrorists freed, Delhi says no. For the second report, the highlights are: Plane lands in Kandahar, Taliban stronghold, Delhi ponders as pressure mounts, passenger shot in cold blood.

Since the first and second reports deal with a developing, fast evolving story, care should be taken in writing, especially use of the tenses. Here is how I would write the third report, when the action has ended. Assume you are writing the report for All India Radio's prime news broadcast at 9 pm or the TV channels' news hour.

IA Plane Back, All Safe[14]

An Indian Airlines Airbus with 119 passengers, hijacked by four armed men to Kandahar, returned to Delhi this evening, ending nine hours of national trauma. The release of the passengers and plane was secured in exchange for six terrorist leaders freed from Indian prisons.

The hijackers seized the plane 20 minutes after it took off from Kathmandu, Nepal, on its way to Delhi. They demanded to be taken to Karachi, stopped over at Amritsar for refuelling and then diverted the plane to Kandahar in Taliban-controlled Afghanistan. They soon demanded the release of six terrorists undergoing long prison terms.

Initially refusing to yield to the demands, the Government gave in late in the evening and sent the External Affairs Minister, Jaswant Singh, in a special plane with the released prisoners. Singh returned with the Indian passengers in the hijacked plane.

An anonymous caller at the Reuters news agency in Islamabad had claimed that the Laskhar-e-Toiba was behind the hijack.

In a brutal demonstration of their terror tactics, the armed men had killed a passenger and threw out his body at Amritsar.

As relatives of the hostages gathered at Delhi airport, opinion appeared divided within the Government. While the Deputy Prime Minister, L K Advani, was said to be opposed to surrendering to the terrorists, Jaswant Singh was keen on some steps to get the passengers back home safe.

> Every hour of indecision added to the tension at the airport as the relatives stepped up pressure for action to get the hostages back.

Before we move away from news evaluation, here is another kind of news break that is rare and certainly new to the Indian media when it first happened. The assassination of Mahatma Gandhi shocked the nation, and its aftermath was an outpouring of grief. A tested leadership at the national level ensured that there was no outbreak of revenge-seeking violence. The second assassination that the country witnessed had a different impact. The killing of Indira Gandhi in 1984 created a political vacuum which was exploited by some vested interests and resulted in an unprecedented massacre of Sikhs. The pogrom began within hours of the assassination which occurred at around 10:00 in the morning. By nightfall, there were reports from several parts of the country that Sikhs were being targeted; there was rioting in the streets. Both the assassination and the riots were certain to have a lasting impact on the nation. How did a newspaper report the two which, in terms of the evaluation criteria, had equal news value? Leading dailies attempted to strike a balance, giving equal coverage to both on the front page. Of course the assassination was the natural lead story which was accompanied by photographs but the riots were also given top of the page prominence. Not many details were available on the riots and the casualties but there were enough to warrant the display. As I had said earlier while describing the situation around the death of Lal Bahadur Shastri, news judgements are relative. What goes today on the front page may another day get only an inside-page mention if there are relatively more important news developments. It is a continuously evolving value. But, news that is 24×7, with its 'breaking news' and news flashes on online portals, has perhaps blunted the issue for the print media in the past decade.

Writing Overall Intros

Intro and lead are often interchanged and, are perhaps, interchangeable. But a crucial difference is as follows: Lead writing is to write the lead para for a specific story. Intro writing, on the other hand, is to write an introduction, often involving different strands of news and is mostly done at the desk. For example, for the Delhi Assembly elections, the intro for the story–also called overall intro–is written by the Delhi bureau chief or at the desk, whereas reporters file many reports. Almost always, each centre of reporting will file its own report written in such a way that it can stand alone. So the desk merges them in the overall intro and ensures that there is no repetition.

Example One

Let us look at an overall intro of about four to six paragraphs for a national daily on the Bharat bandh called by the two main non-Congress opposition parties, the BJP and the Left Front, on 31 May 2011, to protest against an unprecedented increase in petrol prices. There are reports from various centres. The half-day strike affected normal life in some parts of the country. The intro paragraphs should bring out the key points of the bandh and attempt to give the big picture.

Reports from different centres

In New Delhi, with several autorickshaw unions joining the bandh, nearly 55,000 autos and 15,000 taxis stayed off the roads. BJP leaders blocked 100 traffic intersections in the capital as part of the forced shutdown. The Delhi Metro bore the brunt of the crowds, with several lines choked with harried commuters. 'Autos are not plying. After struggling for an hour I managed to find one which demanded an exorbitant fare,' said Richa Srivastav, a commuter in Central Delhi's Mandir Marg.

In BJP-ruled Karnataka, bandh supporters set three buses on fire and stoned about a dozen others, forcing the authorities to suspend bus services in the capital Bangalore. According to initial reports, the bandh evoked a good response in several districts of Karnataka. Public transport was hit and shops and business establishments shut in several parts of the state. Schools and colleges had declared a holiday.

The shutdown passed off relatively without tension in Mumbai. There were sporadic incidents of violence in Thane and Pune, officials said. There were at least four incidents of government buses being stoned in the two cities, considered stronghold of the BJP's ally the Shiv Sena. The bandh was supported by anti-corruption crusader Anna Hazare. Mumbai's dabbawalas suspended their tiffin delivery for the day.

The movement of trains and commercial vehicles was hit in several parts of Odisha. The ruling Biju Janata Dal supported the shutdown. Protesters blocked roads and highways in several areas and disrupted traffic in and around the capital Bhubaneswar. Train services were also hit as protesters squatted on the track at Cuttack and Bhubaneswar stations.

Protesters set fire to a bus, put up roadblocks and disrupted train movement at least at one place in Left Front ruled West Bengal. Fewer private vehicles and taxis were seen on the roads, markets were closed in a few pockets but most people in Kolkata and the districts went about their daily routine, police said. In neighbouring Howrah, supporters of the shutdown torched a stationary government bus, but there were no injuries. Train services were disrupted for some time in the Sealdah section of Eastern Railway after protesters squatted on the track. Heavy security arrangements had been made with a large posse of police personnel deployed on the roads to maintain peace.

The shutdown impacted life across Bihar, ruled by the JD(U)-BJP alliance, with sporadic violence reported from some areas. Hundreds of workers of the ruling alliance forced shops and commercial establishments to close down. JD(U) chief Sharad Yadav was reportedly detained in Saharsa district for leading a protest march. Protesters damaged a number of vehicles in Patna, Gaya, Bhagalpur, Muzaffarpur and Darbhanga to force the shutdown, police said.

What are the takeaways from these reports? The key points are that the bandh was 'successful' in the areas where the sponsors were politically strong. In other states, there was lukewarm or no response, though this has not been mentioned in the example.

Here is a sample introduction:

Opposition States Observe Bandh

A Bharat bandh sponsored by the opposition BJP and the Left Front affected normal life in at least four states, ruled by them and their allies. The half-day bandh had been called to protest against an "unprecedented" increase in petrol prices.

There were reports of sporadic violence in Mumbai, stronghold of the BJP ally Shiv Sena, and Bangalore, capital of BJP-ruled Karnataka where the shutdown was reportedly widespread. Supporters of the bandh belonging to the Biju Janata Dal and the Janata Dal (United), both allies of the BJP, disrupted train traffic in Odisha and Bihar. In Left Front ruled West Bengal, life was disrupted but there were no reports of violence. (More reports are taken from other centres and suitably added here)

Style and Stylesheets

All publishing houses, media organisations in particular, have stylebooks of their own that govern all aspects of writing. These have evolved as comprehensive reference works over the past few decades after starting as nothing more than manuals for the journalists in the organisation to follow. Apart from ensuring uniformity and continuity, they also demonstrate the respect the organisation has for its readers and viewers.

For every question relating to grammar, punctuation, spelling and usage, the stylebook has a clear answer. Capitalisation (should 'g' in government be in capital or lower case?, for example), prefixes (Mr, Mrs or Ms, etc), honorifics, abbreviations (govt or gov?), designations (of officials, government leaders, judicial officers, military top brass) and a score of other usage issues crop up on a daily basis in a newspaper office. Besides the general news, other specialist sections such as sports and business have their own quota of doubt-raising instances. For all these journalists, the stylebook provides a ready-reckoner. The stylebook also has advice on legal issues, libel, articles of the Constitution, important legislative measures, handling crime and courts.

Many of the well-known stylesheets are a veritable mine of information and advice for young journalists, both reporters and editors. The stylesheet has guidance on some of the fundamentals of writing that are not too well known. One is that Indian media in English use the British language, not its American version in spelling. In my early years in the profession, I had an opportunity to work with a senior to try and put together a stylebook for the Madras (now, Chennai) edition of *Indian Express*. We had for guidance the daily review/comments of the English editor of the paper in its Bombay (now, Mumbai) office. Several months of poring over the notes and jotting down points proved fruitless in the end since the project was terminated halfway. But the lessons I learnt in editing and reporting have stood by me, proving their timeless value. Here is one such comment on a report which said that the speaker at a meeting made a 'concrete suggestion'. Nothing unusual in the usage till you read the comment–is the 'suggestion' made of some heavy stuff? Such clichés should be cut out, my editor said. For, 'suggestion' would have meant the same thing as 'concrete suggestion' to the reader. Followed diligently, the stylesheet will bring about a welcome uniformity in usage in a newspaper that the reader will value.

Writing Headlines

As important as editing is headline writing. The headline is the main entry into any story–whether it is a news report, feature, business or sports report. It is through this that the reader or viewer perceives the story at the start. The headline is the advertisement that sells the story. In a major way, through its type, size and shape, the headline is a window on the paper. Headline writing in fact is the toughest part of editing, though newspapers often disagree about what is the most important element of their features. Some newspapers have seniors whose only job is to write the front page headlines and other important headlines. Like many other journalism practices, headline writing looks ever so simple but takes years of experience to master. One key aspect is to know the story in full detail.

Headlines can make or mar a news report. A good headline is concise. The news headline should always give information. Giving the crucial information quickly and intelligibly within the confines of a column is headline writing skill. All good news headlines follow certain rules in what they say and how they say it. What they say is the single most important news point and it should be said accurately, intelligibly and impartially.

What role (or function) does a headline play?

1. It miniaturises the report or encapsulates it.

2. It highlights the main point in the report.
3. It packages the news and the newspaper.
4. It also grades the news through the use of (point) size and (column) width (single, double, banner, etc.).

What are the attributes of a headline? It identifies the underlying theme and expresses the central news point using as few words as possible. And it makes use of active voice and active verbs, which lend immediacy to a story. This is because use of the passive voice is an invitation to boredom; active verbs breathe life into a headline and story. For example, 'Condemned convict asks for pardon' is perfectly fine. It has a verb in the active voice. However, when we use an active verb the difference is striking: 'Condemned convict pleads for pardon'. One can avoid the use of adjectives through the use of active verbs.

Headlines without verbs are label headlines which are a mark of lazy, irresponsible work. For example a news report that states: 'The High Court rules that a college principal had been sacked on mala fide grounds and wants him reinstated.' A label headline will say: 'High Court ruling on principal's sacking'. This is correct but unattractive and fails in its role of trying to capture the attention of the reader. A better headline would be: 'Principal's sacking male fide: Court' or 'Take back sacked principal: Court'.

The headline is usually in the present tense even if the event had taken place the previous day since this lends it more credibility. This licence applies only for writing headlines. 'CM appeals for calm' is fine in the headline even though the chief minister may have made the appeal the previous day. A headline is kept simple and is not verbose. A headline is a short, direct sentence without extra adjectives or adverbs (The only exceptions to this will be the sports pages). Words like 'as', 'during' and 'about' are usually avoided as they tend to slow down the headline. A verbose headline will be: 'CM exhorts people to be patriotic' (on a day when the CM may have appealed to people to avoid generating a lot of waste for the national good.).

Enough information is provided in the headline to give the casual reader an impression of the story. All comments, as in editorialising, are kept out of a news headline. However, this is often violated. For example, when the minister admits failure of his agricultural policies the editor may be tempted to give the headline 'Agriculture minister eats his words' but this is a comment and must be reserved for the editorial pages. 'Agriculture minister admits mistakes' or 'Agriculture minister retracts' will be more appropriate. For example, if a headline says, 'Maharashtra Jains included' when the state government decided to extend reservation in jobs to the Jain community, it is ambiguous in the absence of any indication of where the community has been included. A label headline falls in the same category; it does not say anything and just mentions the subject of the report. A label headline is the result of failure to apply the mind.

Headlines are not overtly witty. There are places where wit can be employed; for example, in human interest stories where the objective should be not to give information but to tempt the reader. A contrived attempt at wit can put off the reader. Here is an example from the 1960s. The report in question related to the death of a postman on a rainy day when he was electrocuted as he tried to cross a puddle of water near a pavement. There was leakage of electricity around a lamppost and the postal worker with his bag of letters and parcels came in fatal contact with it. The newspaper had the human interest story on the front page with the headline: 'His Last Post'. The editorial office was flooded the next day with protests from readers over the headline.

The main headline should stand on its own, in the sense that it should convey a sense fully and should be complete and not depend on an extra line or word to make sense. In the era gone by, fitting the headline would always pose problems as there was little flexibility with headline types which were made of metal and had only some sizes—unlike now when size does not matter for the computer. Today we have arrived at a situation where we write headlines for a reader who may have no time or inclination to read the report and wants to be spoon fed. It is in response to this demand that newspapers are resorting more and more to blurbs, straplines and shoulder lines.

On Design and Layout

While the past decade has witnessed breathtaking changes in the way news is handled and where it is made available, digital media and the software revolution are simultaneously transforming the approach to layout and design, particularly for print and the web. In the past decade, newspapers have copied some of the features of the tabloid and morphed into racier versions, in the main acknowledging the importance of design and layout. The eight-column layout formula of the broadsheet has given way to differing column widths and numbers. In a competitive world, design has become a tool to attract readers, and to supplement the words, we have the infographics that tell it all in the most telling manner.

While online layouts have their own parameters and principles, print continues to be governed by the Reverse 6 principle for page layout. The idea is that the reader's eye goes first to the left hand top of the page, travels to the right top, comes down to the bottom and then moves up to the middle, tracing a path in the shape of a mirror image of number 6.

In the digital world, design has acquired its own life. Phones and tablets have created new ways for audiences to get their news, making it much harder to design a website that works for all readers. A site that looks great on a laptop might be illegible on a phone, while a sleek design on a tablet might look simplistic on a desktop monitor. To make sure everyone has a good experience, building different sites—one for phones, another for tablets, and a third for laptop and desktop users—was an option. But this might have worked when there were just a few mobile-device sizes. Today's oversized phones, shrunken tablets and everything in between have made it a daunting prospect.

DESK JARGON

Before we move on, let us see some of the desk's own jargon.

subbing: Another name for editing; derived from 'sub-editor'

copy: This is the collective noun for the reports flowing into the newsroom. It includes all reports, those filed by staff reporters/correspondents and those sent by wire services. Unedited copy is raw copy.

intro: The first para in a report is the Intro or Lead or Lede.

byline: Credit for the author of the report, given variously as Staff

Reporter, Special Correspondent in the anonymous mode and for seniors with their names.

dateline: The place of origin of the report and the date, given at the very beginning.

body matter: The text of the copy that substantiates the lead

body type: The size and group of fonts in which the body matter is printed

indent: the blank space at the beginning of the para or in the margins of the columns

drop: The first letter of an article printed in large size

subhead, headline: Set in smaller type, main headline

headline type: The size and shape of a headline

strapline, shoulder: Secondary headlines that support the main headline

slug: Applicable in print and online, the slug is the tag or identity of a page of news report. These slugs which read like 'fire one', 'fire two', etc. are especially helpful when corrections or additions are needed to be carried out.

rule: The line that separates columns and boxes, etc

wire services: News agencies that supply news to subscribers.

caption, photo credit: The explanatory lines accompanying a photograph and the name of the photographer or agency supplying the photograph.

For all the four media streams, the main role of the complementary acts of reporting and editing is to convey information of current interest in as easy a manner for the reader or viewer as possible. So what does one look for in the reports given in chapters 3 and 5 and in the exercises in the appendices of this volume? If the journalist knows the answer, s/he can frame the report appropriately. For example, in the report on idol recovery, the core or key was that the idols were found hidden under a bed in a lodge and that six persons were arrested, straightaway alerting one to the possibility of an idol lifting gang in operation. In the report on the death due to suffocation of two young men in a fire, the heart of the matter was the fact that the two had been locked inside the building and could not come out despite their desperate efforts and so were choked to death. Who was culpable? Partially the owner of the DVD shop perhaps but this was an avoidable tragedy. Another human interest story, but ending on a happy note, was the one on how the gift of a surf board transformed the life of a young fisherman: this was the core of the report and came out in the revised version. In the Mumbai report on the near-collision of two aircraft, in the absence of an official version, the key was the different versions put out by the two airlines involved. The lead emphasised that a collision was averted at the nick of time and then went on to give both versions, without the report itself saying what had happened or speculating on it.

NOTES

1. Reuters, *Handbook of Journalism: Guide to Operations*, 94. Available at http://handbook.reuters.com/extensions/docs/pdf/handbookofjournalism.pdf (accessed March 2015),
2. T. J. S. George, *Editing: A Handbook for Journalists*, New Delhi: Indian Institute of Mass Communications, 1989, 18.
3. TNN, 'Delhi Metro bridge crash kills 6: Cracks in pillar had been reported, but given all-clear by engineers', *Times of India*, 13 July 2009.
4. Reproduced by permission of Isha Sharma and ACJ.
5. Reproduced by permission of Isha Sharma and ACJ.
6. Prepared by faculty members at ACJ. Reproduced by permission of ACJ.
7. Prepared by faculty members at ACJ. Reproduced by permission of ACJ.
8. *Hindu*, 'Warangal Software Engineer Shot Dead in South Africa', 8 July 2009, Andhra Pradesh edition. Reproduced by permission of the *Hindu*.
9. Prepared by faculty members at ACJ. Reproduced by permission of ACJ.
10. The reference here is to the Yemen Airbus crash on 30 June 2009. The plane was carrying 153 people and plunged into the Indian Ocean around 2:00 AM. A teenage girl who did not know how to swim survived.
11. Written by the author for this publication.
12. Written by the author for this publication.
13. The 6:00 PM deadline was for the radio news broadcast, the 3:00 AM for the newspapers that would hit the stands next morning and the 10:00 AM was for the special news bulletin on the flash news.
14. Written by the author for this publication.

6

Media Ethics

Professional Code and Gender Issues

Journalists have certain rights and privileges that accompany their profession, but with those privileges comes a responsibility to act ethically and to always report the truth.[1]

Nothing illustrates the continuous need for the media to introspect better than two recent cases involving the media, one in Britain and the other in India. Both focus on the ethical practices of the press, and both reflect poorly on the record of the press. The latter instance, under investigation, has through obviously authenticated taped conversations thrown light on alleged ties involving politicians and sections of the media and of business houses. The media has ridden the storm without a known thought to remedial measures. The first instance, under more intense and much more transparent investigation, relates to one single act which provoked nationwide revulsion in Britain—the alleged hacking of the mobile phone of a murdered teenager. In the words of the senior judge who conducted a government-ordered enquiry, 'From that beginning, [the enquiry] has expanded to cover the culture, practices and ethics of the press and its conduct in relation to the public, the police and politicians.'[2] No party comes out with flying colours.

The two cases are a wake-up call and must be taken seriously by the media if it is to retain its hard won credibility. As the media in India enters a new phase of expansion, there need to be in place codes of conduct, professionally organised self-regulatory mechanisms, and a proactive complaints commission besides the Press Commission.

The trust of the public should be maintained at whatever cost in the media's role as purveyor of information and watchdog on the wielders of power. Later in this chapter we will also look at two recent developments impacting the media. One is a major triumph for those campaigning for a more transparent society through the RTI (Right to Information). In the other case, the country, especially the media, may have to wait longer for the enactment of the legislative measure to grant protection to whistleblowers, who are the media's collaborators in its effort to expose corruption and malpractices in public. The legislation has a few more hurdles to cross before it becomes a reality.

The RTI Act and the proposed legislation on protection to whistleblowers are two measures that the media should embrace as its own and protect against attempts at dilution of news. There have been several attempts by different groups to take themselves out of the purview of the RTI Act and most of these have been thwarted by an active, alert civil society. As for the whistleblower legislation, which has crossed the parliamentary hurdle half way, several interested groups have opposed it but without avail. The vital importance of both legislation to the media and a free society where information flows without hindrance cannot be overemphasised but does the media care? That in the past five years and more, a number of RTI activists and whistleblowers have been murdered and silenced through other means should alert the media to the vested interests opposed to transparency, ready to adopt any means to safeguard their turf. Brian Leveson, member of the British House of Lords, who enquired into the phone hacking scandal in his country, has placed issues in clear perspective and I offer no apologies for quoting him at some length. He has said, 'The [British] press, operating freely and in the public interest, is one of the true safeguards of our democracy. As a result, it holds a privileged and powerful place in our society. But this power and influence carries with it responsibilities to the public interest in whose name it exercises these privileges. Unfortunately, as the evidence has shown beyond doubt, on too many occasions, those responsibilities have simply been ignored. This has damaged the public interest, caused real hardship and, also on occasion, wreaked havoc in the lives of innocent people.'[3]

Leveson's report on his enquiry into 'the culture, practices and ethics of the Press', had some damaging, revealing statements to offer: '... senior politicians across the spectrum have accepted that in a number of respects the relationship between politics and the press has been "too close". I agree.'[4]

'A free press in a democracy holds power to account. But, with a few honourable exceptions, the UK press has not performed that vital role in the case of its own power,' Leveson says in his report, adding: 'None of this, however, is to conclude that press freedom in Britain, hard won over 300 years ago, should be jeopardised. On the contrary, it should not. I remain firmly of the belief that the British press – I repeat, all of it, – serves the country very well for the vast majority of the time. There are truly countless examples of great journalism, great investigations and great campaigns. Not that it is necessary or appropriate for the press always to be pursuing serious stories for it to be working in the public interest. Some of its most important functions are to inform, educate and entertain and, when doing so, to be irreverent, unruly and opinionated.'[5]

Concerning Individual Privacy

The two instances cited earlier are symptomatic of the state of the media at the present time in India and around the globe. The biggest casualty as media organisations compete fiercely with one another is privacy. The one cardinal principle of recognising and respecting the individual's right to a certain degree of privacy is ignored. For private people have a greater right to control information about themselves than officials and others in public life. Only an overriding public need can justify intrusion into anyone's privacy.

The respect for the privacy of individuals is observed more in the breach, particularly when the media reports high profile murders, cases of corruption, sex-related offences and mud-slinging matches. Arising from this lack of respect for privacy is the peril of libel which we will see later in this chapter. In this era of rampant politicisation of issues, allegations fly around but the media needs extra caution while reporting these. The political person can get away with making wild allegations against his opponent but the media can be charged with libel for reporting them.

Before we move on to the laws that the media must be familiar with, let us look at some of the ideals and principles that must govern the profession of journalism and those practising it. The profession has over the past century and more set its own rules to suit the socio-political times but there was for long no universal standard. For the first time, in 1997, a professional body in the US set out some guiding principles, extraordinary in their range and sweep. In the following paragraphs, we look at the set of principles evolved by the American professionals. We will also see the evolution of a code of conduct for journalists that needs to be followed.

In 1997 the Committee of Concerned Journalists, administered by the US-based Project for Excellence in Journalism, identified nine principles that should govern professional journalism. The committee spent four years on the research, holding 20 public forums around the US, organising a reading of journalism history and a national survey of journalists, and released the Statement of Shared Purpose.[6]

In a 'statement of purpose', the committee offered nine principles flowing from its 'understanding of what defines our work'. These comprised what the committee described as the 'theory of journalism'. Heading the list is the universally accepted principle that journalism's first obligation is to the truth. It said that journalists should be as transparent as possible about their sources and methods so that the readers can make their own assessment of the information being provided. Journalists, said the second principle, should maintain their 'allegiance to ... the larger public interest'. It was a 'commitment to citizens-first' an 'implied covenant that tells the audience the coverage is not slanted for friends or advertisers'. Calling the third principle 'a discipline of verification', the committee suggested ways that could prevent personal and cultural biases from undermining the accuracy of a journalist's work. The method—and not the journalist—needed to be objective, it said and suggested that the journalist seek multiple witnesses and disclose as much as possible about sources. 'This discipline of verification is what separates journalism from other modes of communication, such as propaganda, fiction or entertainment'. In an indirect indictment of resort to sensationalism, the committee advised journalists to 'keep the news comprehensive and proportional'. It added: 'Journalism is a form of cartography: it creates a map for citizens to navigate society. Inflating events for sensation, neglecting others, stereotyping or being disproportionately negative all make a less reliable map'. Other principles listed included the need for journalists to: (a) maintain an independence (not neutrality) from those they cover for professional purposes: 'Independence is an underlying requirement of journalism, a cornerstone of its reliability', (b) serve as a monitor of power, 'a watchdog over those whose power and position most affect citizens', (c) provide a forum for public criticism and compromise, and (d) make what is significant to be interesting and relevant.

LIBEL AND DEFAMATION

In the discharge of their duties, journalists need to be conversant with some of the laws of the land whose provisions will crop up on a regular basis in news reporting and editing. Libel and defamation laws top the priority list. Among others the reporter must be familiar with are key provisions of articles of the Constitution relating to civil and political rights, socio-economic rights flowing from the Directive Principles and freedom of speech and expression and details of at least four legislative measures: the Parliamentary Proceedings (Protection of Publication) Act of 1977, the Press Council Act of 1978, the Copyright Act of 1957 and the Right to Information Act of 2005. There are also sections in other Acts such as the Police Act and Evidence Act which come up regularly in news reports and about which they have to be familiar. Public Interest Litigation is an additional area where the courts have turned proactive. The media has in general been lax in respecting the individual's rights and privacy and got away with impunity thanks to a lack of awareness among the public. Whatever defamation action the media has faced has arisen mostly for political and personal reasons. Even today, there is much disregard on this count. How often have we not seen in an accident report a bus driver being straightaway described as 'rash and negligent'? The driver apparently has no means of taking the media to court or perhaps is not aware that he is being maligned in public.

Defamation is defined thus: 'Whoever, by words either spoken or intended to be read, or by signs or by visible representations, makes or publishes any imputation concerning any person intending to harm, or knowing, or having reason to believe that such imputation will harm, the reputation of such person, is said, except in cases (listed in the statute), to defame that person.'[7] Crime/accident/court reporting are areas where both the reporter and the editor need to exercise extra caution since the risk of defamation is higher, whether the victim takes them to court or not. Fairness in reporting is a given, but not observed rigorously. The media also needs to show restraint and swear by 100 per cent accuracy. In the context of criminal law, two principles have evolved: (a) that the accused is innocent unless and until proven guilty (legal terminology) and (b) guilt must be proved beyond reasonable doubt. The following is a broad listing of guidelines regarding what constitutes defamation.[8]

- The publication or re-publication (telecast/broadcast) of any material, including quotations, that causes injury to a person's reputation involves defamation. Reporters should constantly watch out for such dangers which can render the media vulnerable to legal proceedings.
- In reports relating to crimes, an unproven action is not to be taken as a fact. The axiom that a person is deemed to be innocent until proven guilty should be a constant guide. An accusation remains an accusation till a court of law, after due process, reaches a conclusion regarding the culpability or otherwise of the person accused. It is a violation of the person's rights to put the label of criminal till the court judgment is delivered.
- It is wrong to report 'three robbers were arrested' or 'thieves caught' when in reality what is being reported is that a robbery or theft has taken place and police have detained or arrested (the two are, obviously, different) a few persons for questioning as part of their investigation. Calling them 'criminals', even if the police describe them as such, is to pronounce judgment straightaway and is defamatory.
- In the case of arrests made, reporters should ensure that they do not prejudge. When arrests are made, the sections under which this has been done and the action that they relate to such as murder, forgery and cheating must be specified. It must also be mentioned if the police have filed a chargesheet. The registration of a First Information Report (FIR) does not constitute even a prima facie indication that the charge may be true. An FIR sets a police 'investigation' (as against an 'enquiry') into motion. The words 'investigation' and 'inquiry' must not be used lightly; they

are not variations of the same process. A Preliminary Enquiry (PE) by the Central Bureau of Investigation (CBI) or another police organisation does not amount to an investigation. If the police make allegations, make that clear so that these are not taken as forming part of the reporter's copy. The attribution should be repeated in all later references to the allegations, even when they occur multiple times in the same paragraph.

- The use of the word 'alleged' does not absolve the reporter. In a criminal case, there is no need to mention any previous record of indictments of the person. In a classic case, the editor of the *Times*, London, had to tender an apology in court for publishing a report that mentioned that someone who had been arrested for a crime had had 'six previous convictions'. He might have been guilty in those six instances but was innocent in the latest one. The reasoning was that such references to earlier records might create prejudice against an accused.
- While reporting and commenting on court judgments, fair comment is permissible but not attribution of motives or mala fide with regard to the court.
- There is potential for defamation even in the use of photographs and other illustrations and their captions.[9]

Legislators, members of the two houses of parliament and of state assemblies enjoy certain privileges which you cannot breach. The freedom of expression that they enjoy is absolute. If a member says something against another in the House, he is protected under the privileges of the House but the media can face defamation if it reports it. The media can be hauled up before the Bar of the House if it infringes any of the privileges of the House or its members. Proceedings expunged from the records by the Chair cannot be published or broadcast. Parliament or a state assembly gives you the privilege to cover its proceedings in the media but it is not a right and the privilege can be withdrawn.

Copyright laws are observed more in the breach in India but awareness of intellectual property rights is increasing. You cannot use copyrighted material without the permission of the author. Infringement of ideas cannot happen either but there is no infringement of copyright over news because no one holds a monopoly on it. Copyright in India expires 60 years after the death of the author for books and periodicals. These come into the public domain after this period. In the case of a photograph, it is 50 years from the time it is printed or comes into existence. For broadcasts, it is 50 years from the time a programme is telecast.

Right to Information

One of the most serious dangers to a country's security and ultimate survival stems from a diminishing degree of trust between the government and the governed, and this governance deficit is the result of a dangerous absence of transparency. More open governance is the answer to much of the internal problems. One tool to make governance more transparent is the grant of the right to information to the people. This is a tool that India gave itself in 2005. It has begun to reap the benefits. There are of course some fundamental requirements to make this right work for the people. The first is a bureaucracy that works by the rules. Second, an active media and civil society that use the tool to ferret out information that the rulers want to keep under wraps. Third, a civil society that ensures that there are no restrictions imposed on this right through the back door. Finally, a judiciary that acts as the guardian of the people's rights.

It was in Rajasthan that the movement gained momentum, with civil society groups organising a pioneering social audit. These early steps ultimately resulted in the movement for the introduction of the right to information legislation that has the potential to strike a vital blow against official corruption. It was in 2005 that parliament enacted the Right to Information Act (RTI Act). Attempts were made by sections of the bureaucracy and the political leadership to dilute some provisions but these were defeated by a combination of the media and civil society.

The passing of the legislation is an unqualified triumph for civil society. The then government headed by the Bharatiya Janata Party introduced the legislative measure in fulfilment of the party's electoral promise but no action was forthcoming after the introduction of the measure in parliament. The successor government, formed by the Congress-led National Democratic Alliance, made good the promise and helped pass the legislation in parliament. The salient features of the legislation include a clear definition of what constitutes 'information', the establishment of 'information commissioners' in different regions who are responsible for responding to queries from the public and a time schedule within which the answers have to be supplied by the bureaucracy. The areas which needed to be kept out of the purview of the public domain for security and other considerations were also well defined.

The aims and objectives as enunciated in the legislation were explicit. Of the imperative need to provide 'information' to the public in a successful democracy, the legislation said, 'Democracy requires an informed citizenry and transparency of information which are vital to its functioning and also to contain corruption and to hold governments and their instrumentalities accountable to the governed ...'[10] Set against this need to provide 'information' was the fact that 'revelation of information in actual practice is likely to conflict with other public interests including efficient operations of the governments, optimum use of limited fiscal resources and the preservation of confidentiality of sensitive information.'[11] The legislation sought to harmonise these conflicting interests 'while preserving the paramountcy of the democratic ideal' in 'An Act to provide for setting up the practical regime of right to information for citizens to secure access to information under the control of public authorities, in order to promote transparency and accountability in the working of every public authority, the constitution of a Central Information Commission and State Information Commissions and for matters connected therewith or incidental thereto.'[12]

Every citizen has a right to know how the government is functioning. Right to information empowers the citizen to seek any information from the government, inspect any government document and seek certified photocopies thereof. Some laws on right to information also empower citizens to inspect any government work or to take samples of material used in any work. The right to information includes the right to: inspect works, documents, records, take notes, extracts or certified copies of documents or records, take certified samples of material, obtain information in the form of printouts, diskettes, floppies, tapes, video, cassettes or in any other electronic mode or through printouts. This is an invaluable right which, if exercised in the right spirit, can end a major source of corruption in government building works where quality is often sacrificed by private contractors by bribing their way through regulations.

Various time-limits and deadlines have been prescribed for responses to be given under the RTI Act. Any bureaucratic failure gives the applicant the right to approach appropriate authorities for relief. Officials face penalties and even short jail terms if they fail to comply with the request for information.

Origins of the RTI Act

The RTI Act is a powerful weapon in the hands of the purveyors of information and the following is an interview with the activist-pioneer and Magsaysay awardee Aruna Roy on how the campaign originated in Rajasthan.[13]

> The campaign in Rajasthan was born from an agitation for minimum wage by a workers and peasants union in the late 1980s. According to Roy, government officials regularly denied poor, illiterate workers their rightful wages, claiming that according to their records, these people had not worked. Because the records in question were kept classified, most illiterate people felt that making government records accessible to public scrutiny would solve the problem of contradictory claims.
>
> Their argument was bolstered when the disclosure of an official enquiry report revealed that a bogus company had received illegal payments for labour that had never been done. The enquiry traced the company to government employees from Bhim, a small town in Rajasthan. Denied wages, one worker demanded access to records covering the entire period of his employment.
>
> The government's efforts to stifle the grassroots campaign set the stage for the first public hearing in December, 1994. From this the next step was the demand for social audit of public expenditure which led ultimately to the nationwide campaign for the right of people to information.

The struggle in Rajasthan by poor people was symbolised by a slogan, which had brought the issue alive with a fresh perspective: 'The Right to Know, the Right to Live'. It was clear, therefore, that the right to information had to be included as part of the fundamental right to life and liberty under Article 21 of the Constitution. The campaign to empower the people with information was fully on, and successfully culminated in 2005.

Whistleblower Act

Another legislation aimed at ensuring transparency by exposing corruption at different levels was introduced in the Lok Sabha and passed in 2011 and is currently with the Rajya Sabha. The main objective of the Public Interest Disclosure and Protection to Persons Making the Disclosures Bill is to safeguard those exposing corruption or malpractice by public servants. The broader goal is to initiate public participation to help keep corruption in check.

Who is a whistleblower? A whistleblower exposes corruption in an organisation with the objective of serving the public good for which the person will have statutory protection from prosecution. A whistleblower can be a government or corporate employee, a contractor or an official; can expose deeds which are sought to be concealed in the affairs of government, the corporate world or in projects of public utility. Whistleblowers are a relatively new phenomenon in India. But their importance in a democracy with a free press–for whom the whistleblower can be a lethal weapon–is yet to be recognised at the national level. Western democracies have vibrant whistleblower protection legislation and conscientious whistleblowers have done great service to their nation by exposing corrupt acts. The exposure of the Pentagon papers in the 1970s at the height of the Vietnam war and the Watergate scandal were shining examples of how honest individuals stood up to the might of the state and exposed the misdeeds and lies of government leaders.[14] We also have a number of examples in the recent past.

Parliament has been debating the legislation that gives the whistleblower protection from prosecution for some years. In the absence of the legislation, in fact, the few brave persons who have defied all odds to expose corruption in public life have had to pay a heavy price. In recent years, incidents of harassment, intimidation and violence against whistleblowers have been reported across the country, deterring members of the public from speaking out against wrongdoing in the public sector. In 2003, a young engineer was shot dead by unknown persons after he denounced unlawful dealings in a national highways project in Bihar. Satyendra Dubey, the project engineer at the National Highways Authority of India's Golden Quadrilateral Corridor Project in Bihar, wrote to then prime minister Atal Behari Vajpayee complaining of corruption in the project and gave details of how private contractors were siphoning off funds. Apparently for this bold act, this 30-year-old engineer was murdered by unknown assailants. In May 2012, an official in Karnataka was fatally attacked by unknown assailants in the heart of Bengaluru. S. P. Mahantesh, 48, was known as an honest officer in a department plagued by allegations of corruption and land scams. Mahantesh, a Karnataka Administrative Service officer and Deputy Director of Cooperative Audit, was a crucial source for some of the exposés published by the *Hindu* on irregularities in housing societies.

If implemented, the Bill would create a legal framework to investigate and prosecute cases of corruption involving government officials. On top of that, the Bill would empower the Central Vigilance Commission (CVC), an autonomous body appointed to check corruption, to guarantee police protection to whistleblowers if deemed necessary. Under the provisions of the bill, anyone who fears retaliation can seek protection. The Bill seeks to replace a 2004 resolution which empowers the CVC to receive, investigate and act on complaints filed by whistleblowers. The absence of a protection clause must have worked as a dampener and discouraged many from acting against officials. A protection clause would certainly encourage citizens to speak out against the bureaucracy.

'Paid News' and 'Fake News'

One malaise that hit the media and continues to pose an existential threat has been dubbed 'paid news', itself a contradiction in terms. Paid 'news' or paid content are articles in newspapers, magazines and the electronic media, which hail the master who has paid for them. The 'news' is much like an advertisement but without the warning of the ad tag. It is a serious malpractice since it deceives the reader, not letting him know that the 'news' is, in fact, an advertisement. The editors guild and some vigilant journalists have woken up to the danger, have raised the flag of protest and initiated legal action. The election commission is taking steps to counter the adverse effects of the virus on the poll process, significant especially since the virus is manifest in its most virulent form during times of election. If accepted without even a whimper of protest, the acceptance of paid news will signal the negation of all that the media has achieved in the past century and a half—the media has indeed achieved extraordinary degrees of freedom, integrity and reliability. The tragedy is that barring the protests by some senior journalists, there has been no response otherwise. There is unfortunately very little awareness among the readers, who will be affected the most.

The malaise is symptomatic of a deeper disease afflicting the media. The larger trend began more than a decade ago with the blurring of the distinction between the editorial and advertisement departments, when managers (with the apparent authority of the proprietors or under their instigation) began to run the editorial, superseding the editor with impunity. This was in striking contrast to the the 1950s and 1960s when at least one conservative newspaper had banned its reporters from receiving gifts and compliments at press conferences, asking them not wait for the lunch that often followed such meets. It was perhaps in the 1970s that the practice began of corporate houses giving expensive gifts or gift vouchers to correspondents at press meets; from there to the era of 'paid news' was, apparently, a logical extension.

The virus has struck at a time of flux in the media industry and, unless removed from the body, it can kill the freedom of the press. Newspaper and TV are both admittedly businesses in some sense but till recent times an impregnable wall had separated the business from journalism. The wall apparently is no more impregnable. With industrial houses entering the business of media in a big way, there needs to be redoubled vigilance to ensure that the two aspects are kept apart and the sanctity of the editorial side is maintained if media freedom is to survive in a meaningful way.

The obnoxious practice of paid news came to light during the 15th Lok Sabha elections in April–May 2009. To ensure free and fair coverage by the media during the 2009 elections, the Press Council of India had issued guidelines applicable to both the government functionaries and the press. The disturbing trend of 'paid news' came to light after the elections when other sections of the media highlighted the payment of money by candidates to representatives of media companies for favourable coverage.

The fraud takes place at three levels. What should concern the journalist is the first of the three, with the other two unrelated to the media. At the first level, the readers or viewers are deceived into believing that they are reading/watching independently-produced news content while it is essentially an advertisement. All kinds of arguments have been put forward by managements to justify what is nothing more and nothing less than sale of news space. It is a negation of journalism. At a second level, by not officially declaring the expenditure incurred on planting 'paid news' items, the candidate standing for election violates the Conduct of Election Rules, 1961, which is meant to be enforced by the election commission under the Representation of the People Act, 1951. Finally, by not accounting for the money received from candidates, the media company violates provisions of the Companies Act, 1956 as well as the Income Tax Act, 1961. The phenomenon of 'paid news' goes beyond the corruption of individual journalists and media companies. It has become pervasive, structured and highly organised and, in the process, is undermining democracy.

On 6 June 2009, the Press Council of India expressed serious concern over the phenomenon of 'paid news' that doubly jeopardised the functioning of an independent media and the working of democracy by influencing free and fair elections. The council noted that the press provided a service akin to a public utility–it exercised its right to inform because the public had a right to know. The press thus functioned as a repository of public trust and had the obligation to provide truthful and correct information to the best of its ability when such information was being presented as news content. 'Such news content is distinct from opinions that are conveyed through articles and editorials in which writers express their views,' it said.[15]

The editors guild took up the issue with the election commission, urging strong action against both candidates and media persons. It deplored the growing trend in some quarters for political advertisements to be purveyed as news. A delegation from the guild submitted a memorandum to the commission, expressing the guild's grave concern over the 'paid news' phenomenon. It cited several investigative reports which highlighted the prevalence of the pernicious practice. Chief Election Commissioner Navin Chawla said that while the commission did not have the mechanism to monitor the candidates in all 543 constituencies, some random samples could be examined closely. If a few candidates were made an example of, it would serve as a warning to others.

Election Commissioner S. Y. Qureshi said that the manner in which the election commission handled the complaints against then Maharashtra Chief Minister Ashok Chavan in the Maharashtra assembly election would serve as a test case to demonstrate the commission's commitment to tackling the growing malaise of 'paid news'. That 'test case' was in the final stages of its journey at the time of writing this book. Following up on the issue, the election commission sought the advice of the Supreme Court on the scope of its authority. On 5 May 2014, the Supreme Court gave the go-ahead and said that the election commission was empowered to inquire into the allegation of 'paid news' if the expenses for the same are not reflected in the election returns filed by the candidate.

The apex court bench of Justices Surinder Singh Nijjar and Fakkir Mohamed Ibrahim Kalifulla said this while dismissing an appeal by Ashok Chavan, who had challenged a Delhi High Court order that held that the commission can inquire if the payment for the paid news was not disclosed by the candidate in his election expenses returns. The issue arose when Chavan's opponent for the Bhokar seat in Nanded, Maharashtra in the 2009 assembly election filed a complaint with the election commission, accusing him of hiding expenses on a 'paid' supplement titled *Ashok Parva* (The Era of Ashok) in a leading Marathi daily. Chavan and the daily's management denied the allegation, saying that the supplement was not a paid one.

Whatever the final outcome of the case, the spotlight on this pernicious practice must help in the fight against it. I can say that if the protagonists stand by their principles, journalism can only emerge stronger. In the early post-Independence era—the one that built up the media as it is today—journalists were the pioneers, fired by the ideals of the profession. They were also the wall that separated the editorial from the commercial and stopped errors of slants and campaign journalism.

Faking news, fake news, satire news are the latest entrants in the social media scene in India, fast gaining readership especially on

Twitter. Satirical writing is no stranger to this country; the foremost publication devoted to political-social satire was *Shankar's Weekly* which I had cited earlier in another context here in this book.

This genre of writing is a parody presented in a format typical of mainstream journalism, and called a satire because of its content, according to Wikipedia. It adds: 'News satire has been around almost as long as journalism itself, but it is particularly popular on the web, where it is relatively easy to mimic a credible news source and stories may achieve wide distribution from nearly any site. News satire relies heavily on irony and deadpan humour.'[16] If the irony or serious indirect comment on social problems stirs you, the satire would have served its purpose. If the humour provokes laughter, some good has come. But it is only the gullible, the thin-skinned and the over-faithful who will take fake news as real and get agitated over the contents. Though there is no flagging of the 'fake' content, readers can discern the hyperbole without much difficulty. In the US, fake news is part of television comedy, aired late in the evening. Like all parody, such writing is meant to sting but not hurt. 'The UnReal Times' and 'Faking News' are among this genre of writing popular in India.

ACCOUNTABILITY WITHIN

The Ombudsman or Readers' Editor

The idea of an independent ombudsman who hears complaints from the public against public bodies that deliver consumer services is well established in Britain where the different streams of the media have their own pointsman. There is also an Ombudsman for the advertisement services. For radio and television, the Office of Communications (Ofcom) is the regulator. It covers UK's communications industries, with responsibilities across television, radio, telecommunications and wireless communications services. The idea of an independent agency to hear complaints from members of the public against the media, especially about the fairness of its services, has not yet taken off in India. In a pioneering effort, the *Hindu* was the first newspaper group to set up a Readers' Editor. The office was launched on 14 January 2006. Then editor-in-chief N. Ram, in a statement, spoke of the social responsibility of the press, 'which must begin with interaction with and accountability to readers'. He added, announcing the terms of reference of the Ombudsman, 'For a daily newspaper, this must happen on a daily basis.'[17]

Ram said the key objectives of the appointment 'are to institutionalise the practice of self-regulation, accountability, and transparency; to create a new visible framework to improve accuracy, verification, and standards in the newspaper; and to strengthen bonds between the newspaper and its millions of print platform and online readers.' He acknowledged that the *Hindu* had 'been inspired to do this by the exemplary practice and experience of the *Guardian*, UK, over the past decade in a crucial area of newspaper performance.' The preamble[18] set out the terms and conditions, which I give in full since this path-breaking effort at accountability in the media should be of interest to journalists and journalism students.

The terms of reference were

> To collect, consider, investigate, respond to, and where appropriate come to a conclusion about readers' comments, concerns, and complaints in a prompt and timely manner, from a position of independence within the paper.
>
> To seek to ensure the maintenance of high standards of accuracy, fairness, and balance in our reporting and writing.
>
> To create new channels of communication with and greater responsiveness to readers, whether by email, telephone, the Internet, surface mail, or through the columns of the paper.
>
> To seek the views and, where appropriate, the written comments, of journalists whose work is the focus of readers' concerns: to take these views into account when responding to readers, and to make critical appraisals, if judged necessary, on an objective and fully-informed basis.
>
> To look for ways of improving the paper's work and performance, in the broadest sense, by collating and analysing readers' concerns, ideas, and suggestions and identifying possible new or alternative courses of action and ways to develop the paper for the benefit of its readers and the paper itself.
>
> To write a regular column addressing one or several aspects of readers' concerns, suggestions, and complaints, the content to be determined independently and not subject to prior approval by the Editor-in-Chief or others on the staff, other than in respect of matters of fact and style.

To use this column as a platform and forum for readers' views.

To require of the Editor-in-Chief that he or she take steps to ensure that his or her staff co-operate fully and promptly with the Readers' Editor should they be requested to provide assistance in responding to readers' concerns and complaints. Similarly, the management and marketing departments of the newspaper insofar as their activities relate to readers' concerns about editorial content.

In consultation with the Editor-in-Chief and/or his or her nominee, to decide whether and when a correction should be published and/or apologies tendered, when deemed necessary, insofar as any correction/apology is not the subject of, or may be prejudicial to, a current complaint to the Press Council of India, or defence of an actual or possible legal action against the paper, or actual or possible legal or other action by the affected journalist(s).

In order to keep fully in touch with the workings of the paper, the Readers' Editor shall have an established right of access to the Editor-in-Chief, to heads of department meetings, to planning and review meetings, to daily editorial and news conferences, and to other relevant forums. The Readers' Editor should be available to report, on an ad hoc basis, to the Editor-in-Chief and to these other groupings. The existence of the Readers' Editor, and how to contact him or her, should be advertised fairly prominently on a daily basis in the paper.

Sexual Violence at the Workplace

'The news media worldwide are not free and representative without the equal voice of women.'[19] The sessions court judge in Mumbai said the following in a case of rape of a young woman journalist-intern: 'Exemplary and rarest of rare punishment is required in the case and such crime violates all rights of the survivor.'[20] The incident had shocked the media world and underlined the uncertain environ in which women journalists work. In fact, the year 2013 was perhaps the worst for women journalists as it was for the female workforce itself across the country. The violence against women journalists was not confined to the field. The work place was equally hostile, the hostility obviously unseen and unreported. Another sorry episode, the *Tehelka* reporter's case stands out as an example and a warning, whatever the truth and whatever the verdict in the ongoing legal proceedings be. That such an allegation was even made is a sad commentary on the conditions of work of women journalists. In a country where the working woman is at a disadvantage, women journalists have often faced hostility and explicit sexual harassment at the workplace and in the field. Cultural constraints and plain chauvinism ensure that women journalists are kept out of the newsrooms. I remember in the late 1960s and early 1970s, the *Indian Express* in Chennai (then Madras) permitted women staff in the editorial department to stay on till the late editions—women journalists were themselves a novelty in those days and the *Indian Express* move caused quite a stir among the conservative journalistic community in the city. They were the honourable exceptions.

Today the scene is changing but only slowly. Women have succeeded in breaking the wall only in the broadcast media; it is heartening to see a young woman reporter sitting inside a crowded, tension-filled hut and talking to a crowd of villagers about the horrendous rape of two teenagers that had taken place a few days earlier. Around the globe, the scene has changed totally. Women reporters are covering the most vital and challenging stories of the day, and are putting their personal safety on the line to detail corruption, socio-economic divisions, politics and war. They do so in a variety of environments, each of which produces a separate set of risks. But in India there is little doubt that even today most often women reporters are still confined to 'soft' stories and weekend features.

In such a scenario, the rape of the journalist-intern inside the dilapidated mill premises in Mumbai came as a double shock. Mercifully, the case has been fast-tracked and the convictions handed out in quick time. Three of the main offenders have been awarded the death sentence by the sessions court. Awarding the death penalty, the court said, '[The] Mumbai gang-rape accused have least respect for law. They don't have potential for reformation as per [the] facts of [the] case.'[21] The suffering that the gang-rape survivor and her family has undergone is unparalleled, the court said. '[The] Mumbai gang-rape accused were emboldened since law enforcing agencies hadn't caught them. ... If this is not the case where death sentence prescribed by law is not valid, then which is?' the judge is reported to have asked.[22] The three men sentenced to death had already been convicted for a gang rape of a telephone operator on the same premises in July 2013, a month before the photojournalist was brutalised on 22 August.

The rape incident, when the criminals took advantage of the desolate mill premises and the fading light of the evening, and the *Tehelka* case have brought the focus on an issue that has hardly been addressed by any professional body of journalists in this country. We do have on the statute book a mandatory provision for an internal mechanism to check sexual harassment in the workplace but this has hardly been implemented. In a time of crisis, activists raise the issue and protest the absence of this statutory provision but then all is forgotten.

Supreme court guidelines on sexual harassment

The fight for equality and protection against sexual harassment received a major boost in 2013 when country-wide demonstrations forced the Union government to take follow-up legislative steps on the historic judgment in the *Vishaka vs State of Rajasthan* case (1997) by the Supreme Court. It was a case where Vishaka and other women's groups filed a PIL against the State of Rajasthan and the Union of India to enforce the fundamental rights of working women under Articles 14, 19 and 21 of the Constitution. The petition was filed after Bhanwari Devi, a social worker in Rajasthan, was gang-raped for stopping a child marriage. The court decided that the consideration of 'international conventions and norms are significant for the purpose of interpretation of the guarantee of gender equality, right to work with human dignity in Articles 14, 15 19(1)(g) and 21 of the Constitution and the safeguards against sexual harassment implicit therein.'[23] The petition resulted in what are popularly known as the Vishaka Guidelines. The judgment of August 1997 given by a bench of Chief Justice J. S. Verma and Justices Sujata Manohar and B. N. Kirpal provided the basic definitions of sexual harassment at the workplace and listed the guidelines to deal with it.[24]

It was a significant legal victory for working women in the country. For the first time, the court laid down the requirements for employers in dealing with complaints of sexual assault and harassment. The judgment was unprecedented for several reasons: the Supreme Court provided the first authoritative definition of 'sexual harassment'. Confronted with a statutory vacuum, it went creative and proposed the route of 'judicial legislation'. Here are some general observations from the judgment:[25]

The judgment recommended a Complaints Committee at all

workplaces, headed by a woman employee, with not less than half of its members being women. All complaints of sexual harassment by any woman employee would be directed to this committee. This is significant because an immediate supervisor may also be the perpetrator. The committee advises the victim on further course of action and recommends to the management the course of action against the man accused of harassment.

How does the judgment define sexual harassment at the workplace? 'Anything at work that can place the working woman at disadvantage compared to male employees in her official career just because she is a woman can be termed as sexual harassment. Unwelcome sexually determined behaviour and demands from male employees at the workplace such as: any physical contacts and advances, sexually coloured remarks, showing pornography, passing lewd comments or making lewd gestures, sexual demands by any means, any rumours/talk at work place with sexually coloured remarks about a working woman, or spreading rumours about a woman's sexual relationship with anybody.'[26]

What are the constraints? Because of the nature of the offence, reporting a sexual crime depends on whether or not the victim—or survivor, whichever is more appropriate—is able to speak about it and report it. For various reasons, the crime is shockingly under-reported. Social stigmatisation, traumatising legal procedures, the hostile attitude of public officials, discouragement from families and friends who want to protect the survivor from the toll that fighting a case may impose on her, are some of the often compelling factors that impose silence. This, in effect, works to the benefit of the perpetrator of the crime, comments Brinda Karat in an article in the *Hindu*. In the case of a working woman, almost always the victim is an employee subordinate to the man who has sexually assaulted her, and reporting the crime becomes all the more difficult because of the apprehension that it would involve, in addition to everything else, the loss of livelihood. In case after case this is what happens: the woman who dares to complain of sexual harassment against her boss loses her job, the former member of parliament says. She adds, 'The young woman journalist in the Tehelka case showed exemplary courage in reporting the crime to the second-in-command... But she was let down again by those she had trusted.'[27]

In the West there have been quite a few studies undertaken on the subject by professional bodies. The prevalence of sexual harassment in newsrooms across the globe is well-documented. In India, Ammu Joseph's 2005 research with Indian women journalists chronicled widespread harassment that ranged from gossip and character assassination to touching and demands for sexual favours.[28] While some newsrooms adopt anti-harassment policies, the personal and professional implications of workplace harassment mean some victims never report the abuse.

Here is what the International Women's Media Foundation (http://www.iwmf.org), set up in 1990 by a group of American women journalists dedicated to strengthening the role of women professionals worldwide, said, 'While threats, abuse and violence are part of many journalists' experiences, a number of these types of incidents take on a gender or sexual component when directed at women. The perpetrators of violence, threats and abusive behaviour toward women journalists range from government authorities and criminal gangs to their co-workers, bosses, sources and subjects.'[29]

The foundation released the findings of a global survey on harassment and violence against women media workers. The survey was launched in August 2013 and completed by almost a thousand women from around the world. Nearly two-thirds of survey respondents said they had experienced some form of intimidation, threats or abuse in relation to their work, ranging in severity from name-calling to death threats.

The survey found that the majority of threats, intimidation and abuse directed toward respondents occurred in the workplace and was perpetrated most often by male bosses, supervisors and co-workers. It also found that most incidents of harassment and violence were never reported, even though a majority of women who experienced them said they were psychologically affected. In addition, the survey gathered data regarding sexual violence, physical violence, sexual harassment, and information security threats experienced by women journalists as well as what measures have been taken for prevention, protection and preparedness within news organisations.

The survey was conducted jointly by the London-based International News Safety Institute and the Washington-based International

Women's Media Foundation (IWMF). The foundation put together a set of recommendations based on suggestions from experts, women journalists and a security and management consultant. It is meant as advice and may not be appropriate to all situations in which the journalist finds herself, but should be regarded as providing a starting point for safety considerations. Under the heading 'Preparation' it said: 'All journalists are inexperienced at some stage in their careers, but inexperience should not equal insecurity. Journalists must ensure they are well-prepared to understand and mitigate the risks they may face in the course of their work'.

Such preparation includes considering whether or not reporting a story might compromise a journalist's safety. If a story requires travel to a new environment, the journalist should research the location, language, culture and customs in advance and make informed decisions about how she will conduct her work. When appropriate, she should establish local contacts vetted by her news organisation, colleagues, or other reliable sources in advance of her departure. Journalists should be clear about their travel arrangements and schedules, even when field reporting locally. They should leave contact details with a trusted person and have the appropriate documents with them, including relevant permits, press passes and insurance. They should carry out a risk assessment, have the appropriate training and equipment when possible and ensure they have a contingency plan to get out of trouble if the situation deteriorates.

The organisation has listed several practical recommendations under various heads, including cultural norms and clothing (purely in terms of the journalists' own safety against violent protests by different groups), situational awareness and emotional response, logistical precautions and staying safe, communications and networks, health and first aid, different landscapes and changing needs and harassment, attack and sexual violence (in which suggestions have been made on ways to fend off possible offenders among colleagues in the office, seeking safety when you find yourself alone in a strange crowd and your reaction when subjected to sexual assault or violence when you should seek medical help as quickly as possible as well as emotional support since you can go through a range of emotions.

LEVESON ON ETHICS AND ACCOUNTABILITY

Let me conclude this chapter on ethics and accountability in the media with some very relevant observations of Lord Leveson in his final report presented to the British Government in late-2012.[30] He offered important suggestions on self-regulation for the media. As Indian media enters what appears to be a turbulent phase, his prescription will be of great interest.

Lord Leveson proposed the passing of legislation for a new, independent self-regulatory system for the media and repeatedly emphasised that he was not suggesting a body to regulate the press: 'that is for the press itself to do,' he said. 'Guaranteed independence, long-term stability and genuine benefits for the (media) industry cannot be realised with legislation.'

The legislation, Lord Leveson said, would achieve three things: enshrine, for the first time, a legal duty on the Government to protect the freedom of the press, provide an independent process to recognise the new self-regulatory body and thereby reassure the public of its independence and efficacy and bring new and tangible benefits for the press. He proposed independent regulation of the press, organised by the press itself with a statutory process to support press freedom, and provide stability and guarantee for the public that this new body is independent and effective. Speaking in the context of the phone tapping scandal and alleged press-police-political nexus which ultimately led to the appointment of his enquiry, Lord Leveson said the press had an important part to play in promoting police-public relations. As for the press and politicians—another issue thrown up by the scandal—he said the overwhelming evidence was that relations on a day-to-day basis were in robust good health and performing the vital public interest functions of a free press in a vigorous democracy.

Lord Leveson said he was more concerned about lobbying conducted out of the public eye, 'through the relationships of policy makers and those in the media who stand to gain or lose from the policy being considered'. This gave rise to the perception that the power of the press to affect political fortunes may be used to influence that policy. This was a long-standing issue, he said, adding significantly, 'and one which, over the years and across the political spectrum, has repeatedly resulted in opportunities being missed to respond appropriately to legitimate public concern about press behaviour.'

NOTES

1. This quote, from the University of Richmond's web page on its journalism undergraduate course (http://journalism.richmond.edu/courses/index.html; accessed 6 February 2015), perhaps best illustrates the link between the privileges and responsibilities of the press.
2. Lord Justice Leveson, 'A Report into the Culture, Practices and Ethics of the Press Remarks by Lord Justice Leveson: Thursday 29 November 2012', *The Leveson Inquiry: Culture, Practices and Ethics of the Press*, available at http://webarchive.nationalarchives.gov.uk/20140122145147/http:/www.levesoninquiry.org.uk/wp-content/uploads/2012/11/Remarks-by-Lord-Justice-Leveson-29-November-2012.pdf (accessed May 2014).
3. Ibid.
4. Ibid.
5. Ibid.
6. Committee of Concerned Journalists, ''Statement of Shared Purpose', Pew Project of Excellence in Journalism, available at http://www.journalism.org/resources/principles-of-journalism/ (accessed March 2015).
7. Section 499, Indian Penal Code
8. Material in this section on libel and defamation are based on advice from a senior journalist.
9. At times, wrong photographs have been added to reports. Once in an obituary report a newspaper published the wrong photograph, not that of the man who had died but of another with the same name who was alive. In another instance, instead of the profile photograph of a minister, that of a local leader with an unsavoury reputation was published. In both cases, the newspapers prominently published an apology and carried also the correct photograph in each instance. This goes as well for illustrations, maps in particular. Extra caution needs to be taken when maps of the border region are used.
10. Government of India, 2005, 'The Right to Information Act, 2005', available at http://cic.gov.in/rti-act.htm (accessed May 2014).
11. Ibid.
12. Ibid.
13. The following is an abridged version of the interview by Deepak Mahaan. Deepak Mahaan, 'Transparency and Poverty in India', An interview with Aruna Roy and Nikhil Dey, available at http://www.worldpress.org/article_model.cfm?article_id=1123&dont=yes (accessed May 2014).
14. *New York Times* and *Washington Post* scored historic victories for the freedom of the press in the late 60s and early 70s when they overcame insurmountable obstacles to establish their right to expose official misdemeanours which their governments did everything to keep secret. The first—which came to be known as Pentagon Papers—exposed the reality that in the conduct of the Vietnam War (1955–75) truth and transparency were at a premium when governments pursued controversial policies. The second—resulting in effect from the first, was dubbed the Watergate Scandal—showed the extent to which aides went to

suppress information and keep a President in office. Both dailies published excerpted details of documents which for the first time revealed, among other things, continuous, unacknowledged efforts by the American government to prevent Communist takeover of South Vietnam and undermine the regime in the North. In both instances, the press demonstrated extraordinary vitality and single mindedness of purpose: to expose the truth. Whistleblowers proved a vital tool. Both episodes, in particular the extraordinary care for authenticity and caution that the *NYT* editors and *Post* professionals took are now part of journalistic lore. For details, see Douglas Martin, 'Gerald Gold, Editor on the Pentagon Papers, Dies at 85', *New York Times*, 3 August 2012; *Encyclopædia Britannica* Online, 'Watergate Scandal', available at http://www.britannica.com/EBchecked/topic/637431/Watergate-scandal (accessed 27 April 2015).

15. Press Council, '"Paid News": How Corruption in the Indian Media Undermines Democracy', Sub-committee report available at http://presscouncil.nic.in/OldWebsite/Sub-CommitteeReport.pdf (accessed March 2015), p. 2.
16. *Wikipedia*, 'News satire', available at http://en.wikipedia.org/wiki/News_satire (accessed May 2014).
17. *Hindu*, 'Readers' Editor, The Hindu: Terms of Reference', available at http://www.thehindu.com/news/resources/article482493.ece (accessed May 2014)
18. Ibid.
19. IWMF, 'About Us', available at http://www.iwmf.org/about-us/ (accessed March 2015).
20. Philip Varghese, 'Death Well Deserved!', *Afternoon Despatch & Courier*, available at http://www.afternoondc.in/city-news/death-well-deserved/article_106916 (accessed March 2015).
21. Ibid.
22. Ibid.
23. J. S. Verma, Sujata Manohar and B. N. Kirpal, 'Vishaka & Ors Vs State of Rajasthan & Ors on 13 August, 1997', available at http://indiankanoon.org/doc/1031794/ (accessed March 2015)
24. http://en.wikipedia.org/wiki/Vishaka_Guidelines (accessed March 2015)
25. Verma, Manohar and Kirpal, 'Vishaka Vs State of Rajasthan'.
26. Ibid.
27. Brinda Karat, 'Issues of Sexual Assault: The Tehelka Case', *Hindu*, 25 November 2013.
28. Ammu Joseph, *Making News: Women in Journalism*, New Delhi: Penguin, 2005, 101–09.
29. http://www.iwmf.org/introduction/ (accessed March 2015)
30. All quotes in this section are from Justice Lord Leveson, 'A Report into the Culture, Practices and Ethics of the Press'.

7

The Future and the Past

Can Indian Media Buck the Trend?

I began this book with a statement in the introduction about the media scene today being completely and comprehensively different from what it was when I entered it four decades ago. The theme has remained the same through the book and I can do no better than to begin this final chapter with observations on the media today by an English judge who has studied the scene intensely in the past few months. 'There is no doubt that the mainstream, professional media is in the process of evolving, that it is moving towards a business model based around the Internet. It is also likely that in the not-too-distant future a large percentage, if not the majority, of the print media will be entirely online: that it will no longer be a print media.' This was Justice Lord Leveson, member of the British House of Lords, at a lecture at the Melbourne University, Australia, on 12 December 2012. Leveson, who conducted a government-ordered enquiry into 'the culture, practices and ethics' of the British Press following a phone hacking scandal involving a popular daily, made the comment while discussing the future of the Press. He invited attention to two aspects of the media scene: how 'news gathering is taking place against a changing, if not a rapidly and dramatically changing, background' he was referring to the Internet and secondly, and for him more importantly, 'the law and the place that it occupies in relation to story gathering and reporting.'[1] The developments he spoke about are happening sooner and faster than professionals in the media thought likely or feared, as evidenced by the fact that in the past year more American newspapers have embraced convergence and taken the digital route as a measure of survival, consigning the long-standing print edition to memory.

Professional journalists and others had for the past decade no doubt been predicting the demise of the newspaper and migrating to the digital world, blogs being the most prominent and productive outcome of the switch. Doubts about the state of the media had begun to be raised even earlier. Writing in the late-1980s, a BBC journalist Stephen Smith asked the following questions about the impact of the computer: 'Should we consider these new media merely as extensions of the newspaper form? Are they simply new publishers (and old) moving into a new form of competition with the newspaper? Are they a threat to the newspaper or to any other information medium? Are they news media at all, or rather some new kind of reference medium? Will they remain forever locked into specialist forms of information, thereby stripping the newspaper of some range of material but leaving the bulk of information paperbound as in the last several centuries?'

Smith's questions have been answered: the internet has transformed the media scene in a way no technology had done earlier. One immediate consequence is that we have online-only newspapers and journals such as *Huffington Post.* These are proliferating and creating a new kind of journalism which is freed from many of the rules and practices of the old profession. The old regulations are not the only casualties. Lost on the way is also the credibility that the print media had built up over decades. It is this widening credibility gap that may in fact have already brought home the value of the time-honoured practices of good journalism, evolved over the past several decades. In the battle between speed and accuracy, the former has in recent years won the short distance race but is already losing out in the marathon. Today, the most sought after and trusted online news portals are those run by newspaper houses like *New York Times* and *Guardian* in the UK. One factor favouring such standard daily newspapers is that in the avalanche of information and data available on the Internet, the reader may be at a loss to find credible information. The reader's choice falls on the credibility provided by the online versions of the national newspapers. I feel that the dire prediction that print will vanish from the earth is also unlikely to apply to India and some of the other developing countries. The Indian newspaper industry is certainly bucking the global trend for now and witnessing signs of renewal of the print media after a sluggish few years. Moreover, all print publications are opening their own online versions which are becoming increasingly popular with the tech savvy younger readers and the diaspora. This may prove ultimately to be the winner. I for one see the print media marching ahead hand in hand with the digital.

Penetration of the Internet

Two realities, unpleasant but real, will ensure that print continues to thrive in this country for at least the next generation. The shamefully high levels of illiteracy and the lack of penetration of the Internet will ensure that the digital media remains second—a distant second—to print. As poverty lifts and awareness increases, the demand for newspapers, especially in the regional languages, will only increase. The rapid increase in the circulation of Hindi language newspapers and magazines is testimony to this. As I see it, in the ultimate analysis it is only the print media which is prepared for the task of giving reliable information. For, it has built up the resources and established facilities to send reporters to the spot to report on news developments. For those who cannot or do not care to access the print version, the online versions of print are an alternative. The trend more and more will be for this formula to emerge. Whether it is paid online or partially free appears to be the question. There is as yet no business model.

Brian Leveson cited one consequence flowing from this. In his address in Melbourne he pointed out how the closure of local newspapers in recent years in the US and the UK has resulted 'in a reduction in the extent to which local services, whether government, health, education or transport can be held to account.' He added, 'When I started at the bar, there was a local reporter in every court: that is no longer the case. Society will be less well served as a result.'[2] Another consequence has been the intense search for a business model to tackle the problem of generating a monetary return. Leveson referred to the creation of pay walls, a model which appears to be successful for specialist newspapers such as the *Financial Times* but not for all. Pay walls are an in-built system by which organisations prevent their websites being accessed without payment of a prescribed fee. Two versions of this have emerged in recent months. One is a soft pay wall where organisations such as *New York Times* allow users to access some content free of charge—say, for example, five articles a month—and ask for payment of a fee if the user exceeds this limit. Some also allow free access to certain sections of the newspaper such as opinion. A hard pay wall offers none of this concession.

Lack of Awareness

But these existentialist challenges that the media industry is facing are hardly known outside the industry. There is surprising lack of awareness of the financial challenges facing the media, according to a survey during the summer of 2013 done by the Pew Research Centre. It asked Americans whether they had heard much about the financial challenges that the news industry faced, like the steep decline in newspaper advertising revenue. Sixty per cent of the respondents said they had heard little or nothing, indicating that 'awareness of the industry's financial struggles is limited.'[3]

Digital news sources are now used daily by 50 per cent of Americans, according to Pew's survey, making the Internet nearly as important a source as television. Mobile phones and tablets were mostly responsible for the surge in digital news consumption. Computers and mobile phones, of course, redistribute news from television, radio and newspapers. But cutbacks at many of these traditional sources continued in 2012, Pew found. With shorter stories and scarce coverage of politics and government, local television newscasts in the US, like local newspapers before them, were suffering from 'shrinking pains'. The report describes cutbacks in the reporting ranks of newspapers and television networks and a surge in efforts by politicians, corporations and others to tell their own stories. 'This adds up to a news industry that is more undermanned and unprepared to uncover stories, dig deep into emerging ones or to question information put into its hands,'[4] the report's main author, Amy Mitchell, wrote in an introduction. As for India, the picture is perhaps not as desperate. The likely pattern even as online journalism picks up is for the major newspapers in different languages to go digital as an insurance and provide their own online version. The two will complement each other, not compete. What can happen in the near future in India is that at each major urban centre, one newspaper will take a predominant position, with local news being covered by free circulation community weeklies. This is a pattern seen in Australia a decade ago before the online revolution swept all print media off.

I began the book with a reference to Justice Katju's remarks on the prescription of a basic minimum qualification for those entering journalism. I conclude with a history of the Indian media.

The Long Predigital Era

The Internet revolution signalled the end of a long era which began in the mid-nineteenth century. The newspaper as the twentieth century knew it came from the pamphlets which carried royal edicts and proclamations. Advances in printing technology rendered the process less expensive and the product affordable for the common man. The romance with the printing press began then, to be followed nearly a century later by the broadcast media, first the radio and then television. It is how we learnt what was happening at both the national and international level. The radio made some inroads and then television but the print continued its dominance even in the age of 24×7 news when newspapers no longer broke the news. The world wide web and the Internet altered the scene but ever so gently that we did not realise it in the first half of the decade; until news was taken over by technology, as it today is.

The progress of newspapers in India had one fascinating aspect: the country's Independence movement and the spread of the newspaper reading culture ran simultaneously. The nationalist movement was fully complemented by the fledgling newspapers. The story is told in the following paras excerpted from two lectures I had given at the ACJ. Here then, in two parts, is the story of the Indian media, led by print.

EARLY YEARS OF THE PRESS

The story of the newspaper in India is the story of the freedom struggle and, as Independence neared, the story of its separate evolution. The two had certainly run together during the freedom movement when many leaders were also journalists, editing their own publications in different languages–Gandhi, Dadabhai Naoroji, Mahadev Ranade. On the other side, many founders and editors of leading newspapers took a leading part in the first session of the Indian National Congress: among them, Narendranath Sen, editor of *Indian Mirror*, Calcutta, and G. Subramania Iyer, editor of the *Hindu*, Madras, were prominent. Present were also editors of *Mahratta* and *Kesari* of Poona, *Hindustan* and *Tribune*.

If the story of the Indian media was the overlapping story of the freedom struggle, a quarter century into Independence, this role in June 1975 morphed into a struggle to retain the freedom of the press when the press learnt the validity of the saying 'Eternal Vigilance is the Price of Liberty'. In a country without recorded history, it is no wonder that there were no 'newspapers' till late into the eighteenth century. News gathering perhaps was an avocation during the Mughal period. Who would have performed this function and how noble was this profession then? The practitioners were actually spies and officials working for the rulers. They prepared manuscripts on the activities of the citizens and sent the reports to the King. Newspapers in the modern sense came to be published during British rule. The British, in fact, gave India the printing press and paved their own exit route. But for their sham attempts to prevent the spread of the newspapers, there might not have developed in a short period a freedom movement that ultimately drove them out. For, the early newspapers were vigorous campaigners for social reform. It was partly the attempts by the authorities to prevent free expression of opinion that kindled an interest that had hitherto not been felt by the Indians. They wanted to throw off the colonial yoke.

Under the long colonial rule, there were two major assaults on the freedom of the press, as we know it today. The first was aimed at protecting the East India Company from its former employees and the second assault, half a century later, sought to stifle nationalistic writings in Indian language newspapers. Again, the first moves to produce an independent newspaper were initiated by Britons. They had their own reasons: most of them were disgruntled Britons who had lost their jobs with the East India Company for practising 'private trade' which went against the company's interests. Also, surprisingly, the printing press preceded the advent of the printed news by a hundred years. It was in 1674 that the first printing apparatus was established in Bombay, with the Company providing a generous supply of types and paper. A second was installed in Madras in 1772—nearly 100 years later—and an official press in Calcutta in 1779.

The first attempt to start an Indian newspaper was made in 1776 by William Bolts. He had resigned from the Company but the notice of his intention—he had, he said, manuscripts which most intimately concerned every individual—proved his undoing. Company officials got scared that all their secrets might come out and Bolt was directed to leave Bengal and proceed to Madras and thence take his passage to Europe. The first newspaper, *Calcutta General Advertise*, also known as the *Hickey's Bengal Gazette*, came out in January 1780. It was started by James Augustus Hickey. With no pretensions to literary attainments, he filled his two-sheet newspaper with scurrilous attacks on the private lives of servants of the Company, including the Governor-General. He was deprived of the privilege of circulating his newspaper through the channel of the General Post Office. He soon landed himself in libel action and jail from where he continued to edit his newspaper. But the fines imposed on him reduced him to penury. The Company was too powerful for one man, even a white man.

Other newspapers soon came into existence in Calcutta and Madras: *Calcutta Gazette*, *Bengal Journal*, *Oriental Magazine*, *Madras Courier* and *Indian Gazette*. Surprisingly, Bombay was late in catching up—the first Hindi daily, *Samachar Sudha Varshan*, began in 1854. The second and third decades of the nineteenth century saw nationalism strike a chord among Indians and begin to grow as a concept. There were nationalist echoes from other linguistic regional provinces like Gujarat and Punjab. Raja Rammohan Roy, one of the giants responsible for infusion of new ideas, launched the first of his many nationalist newspapers—*Mirat ul Akhbar*. This was the time when a British personality, James Silk Buckingham, joined hands with Raja Rammohan Roy in the fight for freedom for the press. They became close friends and their association was in striking contrast to the background of the Indian-owned press and the British-owned press which functioned in exclusive compartments. Each in his own sphere took up the struggle for the freedom of the press and has left his mark. Buckingham's *Calcutta Journal* became a pioneer in exposing misdeeds in the British administration. He soon paid the price for this and was deported.

The Buckingham episode resulted in the first press ordinance in March 1823 and more restrictions and stringent punishment for transgression. Deportation was the threat to English editors. Indian citizens were coerced as well and Raja Rammohan Roy, who had launched a number of newspapers and vigorously campaigned for social reforms, fought a major legal battle against the ordinance which sought to introduce a licensing system and penalties for defaulters. The infamous Vernacular Press Act was the second major assault on the freedom of the press. Passed in 1878, it sought to impose severe restrictions on Indian language newspapers. Its chief object was believed to be to cripple and kill *Amrita Bazaar Patrika*, then a Bengali weekly. There were 35 papers in Indian languages in Bengal at the time. The colonial rulers picked out *Patrika*, which had no base yet in Calcutta, and offered inducements to the proprietors to support their policies. Or else, the Act would be used to subvert and suppress the Bengali weekly which would come under its purview. *Patrika*, which already printed English pages with the Bengali version, overnight switched to an all-English publication, which kept it out of the clutches of the Vernacular Press Act. The attempt to muzzle the press failed and the ordinance was repealed. This mindless colonial ruthlessness had one beneficial consequence: patriotic sentiments grew in proportion. The vehicle of information dissemination became a tool for the freedom struggle.

Even as these battles for press freedom were being fought, more newspapers in different languages were launched. In Bombay, four newspapers merged under the new name *Times of India* in 1861. Three other Anglo-Indian newspapers, *Pioneer* in Allahabad, *Civil and Military Gazette* in Lahore and *Statesman* in Calcutta were established during this period. A fourth, *Madras Mail*, became the first evening newspaper in the country. The *Hindu* followed soon after in 1878. The *Tribune* in Lahore and *Leader* in Allahabad were marching forward. There were no newspapers only in Punjabi, Oriya and Assamese. The press by then had begun to play a dual role: professional and nationalistic. Most of the English newspapers like *Statesman* in Calcutta, *Madras Mail* in Madras and *Times of India* in Bombay—all started by Englishmen—echoed the English rulers' voice. Indian language newspapers and in English only the *Hindu* in Madras, *Patrika* in Calcutta and a few others took on the colonial rulers. The *Hindu* in fact became a beacon of patriotism in the south. The first five decades of the twentieth century witnessed mainly consolidation, with the press facing and overcoming obstacles to progress erected by the colonial rulers. There were also some significant additions to the industry, most notably *Hindustan Times* in Delhi and *Indian Express*, originally headquartered in the then Madras (now Chennai). The regional language press saw some expansion. Today, the media scene has undergone a metamorphosis. The explosion of magazines in different languages in the 1960s and the advent of television and the new or digital media have dramatically altered the media scene. 'Today India's press is a metaphor for its advancement in the globalised world.'[5]

The Coming of Age and After

It is widely acknowledged that India's newspaper evolution is nearly unmatched in world press history. In terms of diversity and the varied nature of the audience, it has no parallel. The achievement is matched only by the impossible hurdles it has faced and continues to face: illiteracy, poverty, economic and social inequities. In the early years, the press began to take shape and be given shape by the nationalist movement, by the urge to be free of the colonial yoke. The press became both the cause and the effect of this. During the 1880s, the press was assiduously nurtured by the leaders of the coeval movement for political independence. We saw the birth of several newspapers in English and Indian languages. The turn of the century and the arrival of Mahatma Gandhi on Indian soil speeded the process. The independence movement picked up momentum while on the other side the newspapers began to gain muscle. By the middle of the 1920s, the press had acquired an independent status as an autonomous institution in its own right. Writes N. S. Jagannathan in his excellent narrative, *Independence and the Indian Press*:

> Still drawing its sustenance from the fount of nationalist sentiment, it had now acquired a life of its own, with wider concerns and greater diversity of views and interests. And when in 1937 the Congress assumed for the first time responsibility for governance in some of the provinces of India, it had its first taste of the traditional adversarial role of the Press in all democracies. By then, the Indian

Press had come of age, even if total independence itself was still in the future.[6]

Independence had two sides for the press. During the freedom struggle, launching a newspaper and providing a source for dissemination of nationalist opinion and information was an act of patriotism. No more was this true as we moved into the 1930s. It was time businessmen began recouping their investment in the press. Most British proprietors of the English language newspapers planned to either shut down or sell their establishments to Indian buyers. By 1947, there were leading newspapers in most regions and most languages. In the capital, *Hindustan Times* group, coming under the Birlas, began to make its presence felt. In the west, *Times of India* faced competition from newspapers like *Indian Express* and *Free Press Journal*. The south was happy with the *Hindu* which faced a degree of competition from *Madras Mail* and *Indian Express*. The press in Hindi and the regional languages had begun to find their feet. It was a time when freedom of the press was a given. No one doubted the efficacy of this belief or the commitment of the ruling parties to this. Nehru famously said, 'I would rather have a completely free press with all the dangers involved in the wrong use of that freedom than a suppressed or regulated press.'[7]

Like in most other walks of life, this was an underdeveloped industry that struggled along. The professional scene was anything but encouraging and in the absence of the zeal for freedom which motivated the press till 1947, there was little to cheer. But there was nothing to fear in those years of the 1950s and the early 1960s. In fact, the government appointed a press commission in 1952 to look at the state of the Indian press, its printing presses, the freedom it enjoyed and the working conditions of journalists. It created a press council to oversee ethics and hear complaints from the reading public. There were no obstacles to progress and no overt or covert interference. Nehru and his government trusted the press to prepare its own self-regulatory mechanism. Then came a step that shook the nation and shook the press out of its slumber. To call it a turning point is a misnomer. The internal Emergency that Indira Gandhi imposed in mid-1975 was a chilling shock treatment for the nation and threw the press into a coma. When it recovered—thanks entirely to outside, fortuitous circumstances–it was a new version. If Nehru was an ardent supporter of the freedom of the press, his daughter showed no inclination to the contrary in her early years as prime minister. The nation reposed enormous faith in her democratic credentials. However, she was soon to have other ideas. Faced with turmoil on several fronts, Gandhi imposed Emergency on an unsuspecting nation on 26 June 1975, suspending all rights and liberties. Her sweep of arrests covered political opponents, trade union leaders and more than 250 journalists. Newspaper editors were required to adhere to a set of written guidelines issued by the government on what should and should not be published. Three ordinances were issued, banning the publication of 'objectionable' material, abolishing the press council and withdrawing the right to report the proceedings of both houses of parliament.

Indira Gandhi used draconian measures to silence the press and was ready to use any tool. Newsprint allocation was one: in a situation of severe shortages worldwide this was an effective weapon. The government had full control of import of newsprint and of release from factories owned by it. It is still difficult to visualise the situation. Newspapers had no option since newsprint was not available in the open market and they had no licence to import. Most publishing houses submitted to the rigours. Newspapers were required to submit their reports to local officials acting as censors, get their stamp of approval and then only publish them. Those who infringed this censorship rule were punished with fines and threat of closure. Most newspapers would take copies of their reports to the censor office and get them stamped. For late stories, the censor office decided it would post one of its men at the newspaper office itself. Gandhi also tried other means to gain control over the press. She merged the four news agencies functioning at that time in the country, two English and two Hindi, under the name of Samachar. Few newspaper organisations resisted these draconian measures, obviously more keen to save their businesses and investments. Gandhi also used time-tested tactics to bribe and win over journalists. Supply of newsprint was one such tactic. There were other bonanzas: favourites received more advertisements, more opportunities. There was one champion of freedom who defied the government for whatever reason. Ramnath Goenka of *Indian Express* group in fact faced the biggest challenges. Politically opposed to her, he challenged government regulations at every step. Gandhi gave him trouble in many ways: the government even cut off electricity to his offices in Delhi and prevented the newspaper being printed and brought out the next day. They stopped water supply and got the owners of his buildings to evict him. His headquarters in Chennai was even more vulnerable. Some newspapers and magazines tried to beat the censor in novel ways. A few who left blank spaces where reports had been censored were called in and warned against such tactics.

Punjab Kesari, another brave newspaper which was to defy the diktats of the terrorists in the 1980s during the militant Khalistan agitation, switched to publishing soft stories on the front page. It would run cultural and other reports on the front page, pushing politics to the inside pages. The censors of course had no answer to this. Some journalists also campaigned against the censorship vigorously by travelling to different capitals and speaking out. But overall it was compliance of the most shameful sort. L. K. Advani, who became information minister after the Emergency was lifted and elections held, said it most succinctly: journalists were asked to bend and they chose to crawl. The Janata government which came in after the elections in February 1977 lifted all restrictions on the press and appointed a commission to enquire into the abuses of the newspaper industry during the emergency. In two years Gandhi was back in power–ironically it was during her term in the 1980s that there was a spectacular growth in the number of newspapers and magazines. It was also the first time that the Hindi daily *Dainik Bhaskar* overtook an English newspaper to become national number one in terms of circulation. The newspaper revolution, more precisely media revolution was on.

There was a magazine boom covering English, Hindi and all regional languages, spurred on by the greater advertising budgets of the consumer goods industry: these included *Sunday*, *India Today*, *Week*, *Business India*, *Business Week*, *Sports Star*, *Sports Week*, *Sports World*, *Debonair*, *Savvy*, *Inside Outside*, *Stardust*, which blazed a new trail, and specialist magazines. The growing number of middle class was dictating the growth. It was in this milieu that private television broadcasters came on the scene. Today the pioneer in the field, NDTV, faces competition from a multitude of channels in all the regional languages of the country. The media scene has in recent years become more complex with the arrival of the online editions.

NOTES

1. Excerpts in this paragraph are from Justice Lord Leveson, 'Hold the Front Page: News-Gathering in a Time of Change,' public lecture, University of Melbourne, Melbourne, Australia, 12 December 2012 (available at http://www.judiciary.gov.uk/wp-content/uploads/JCO/Documents/Speeches/lj-leveson-speech-hold-the-front-page-melbourne-12122012.pdf; accessed May 2014)
2. Lord Leveson, 'Hold the Front Page'.
3. Pew Research Centre, 'The State of the News Media 2013'.
4. Ibid.
5. http://www.pressreference.com/Gu-Ku/India.html (accessed March 2015)
6. N. S. Jagannathan, *Independence and the Indian Press: Heirs to a Great Tradition*, Delhi: Konark Publishers, 1999, 133.
7. http://www.pressreference.com/Gu-Ku/India.html#ixzz3QwCSSGCE (accessed May 2014)

Appendices

Examples, Exercises and Recommended Reading

Appendix 1

Basic Newswriting Exercises

Exercise One: On 5Ws + 1H

Identify the 5Ws + 1H in these news reports[1]:

1. BEIJING: At least five persons were killed in flash floods in a channel of the mighty Yangtze river in a remote northwestern region of China on Friday, according to delayed reports reaching here on Sunday. The full extent of the loss of life and property is not yet known but officials discounted reports that the flash floods had been caused by dam construction nearby.
2. MUMBAI: The Maharashtra government has strongly defended its decision to have reservations for Muslims and denied that the measure had been taken with an eye on the coming State Assembly elections. "Our party is genuinely supportive of the minorities," said the Chief Minister in the state assembly on Saturday.

Exercise Two: On Removing Clutter[2]

Cluttered sentences are the result of unclear thinking or a desire to pack too many details into a sentence. The reporter who writes such sentences must make it a point to revise them carefully so that the confusion is cleared at the beginning. In the following sentences cut the clutter and bring clarity.

1. In the cellar there are four wooden-type crates with nothing in them that might perhaps be used by us for storing paint cans inside.
2. This morning at 6:30 a.m., I woke up out of sleep to hear my alarm go off, but the alarm was turned off by me, and I returned back to a sleeping state.
3. Some sort of identification that would show how old we were was requested of us by the man that collects tickets from people at the movie theatre.
4. Spain, the European football champion, won the final of the World Cup Football, defeating Holland by a solitary goal scored in the extra time after the two teams remained scoreless at the end of the scheduled 90 minutes to final whistle in an exciting duel played at the Nelson Mandela stadium in the bustling South African capital of Johannesburg today.
5. Over 80 passengers of a stationary train were killed when some bogeys of the train were thrown out of the rails in an accident caused by an express train coming in the opposition which rammed into it and the two trains collided.

Decluttered, the sentences can read like this:

1. Paint cans can be stored in the four crates in the cellar. (Crates are always made of wood, if they are to be used for storing they must be empty with 'nothing in them' and storing is always 'inside')
2. I turned off the alarm at 6.30 and went back to sleep. ("returned back" is a very Indian usage).
3. The usher at the movie theatre asked us for age proof.
4. European champion Spain won the World Cup football final against Holland by a solitary goal scored during extra time.
5. Over 80 passengers of a stationary train were killed when some bogeys were thrown off the rails when an express train crashed into it. (It is a collision only when both objects are moving and moving in opposite direction).

Exercise Three: Writing a Report

I

The following published report is on a rarest of rare solar eclipse happening before dawn and partially visible in Chennai. The eclipse was a major global event and the main report was carried in the newspaper on the front page. The scene in Chennai was what was sought to be caught in the report. It falls short on several counts, with the reader not getting a feel of the atmosphere on the scene at the planetarium in the pre-dawn hours. The focus should have been on how the young and old who had gathered at the planetarium reacted to the spectacle, not the spectacle itself. Rewrite the report keeping the guidelines in mind.

Thousands throng Birla Planetarium[3]

CHENNAI: The 'partial solar eclipse' was witnessed by thousands at the Birla Planetarium on Gandhi Mandapam Road on Wednesday. Some visitors came in as early as 4 a.m. to watch the "eclipse of the century." Their eyes were glued to the skies to watch the once-in-a-lifetime opportunity of viewing a rising eclipsed sun by 5.52 a.m. Many were apprehensive about clouds playing spoilsport. But they were in for a surprise when the sun, which was in and out of clouds till 6.15 a.m., presented itself brightly towing the moon which had already bit 60 per cent out of it.

There was a lot of action immediately. It elicited cries of excitement among the crowd. Solar filters had been provided by the Planetarium, as it is not safe to watch the event with the naked eye. Many waited with bated breath to have a glimpse of the rising star through telescopes that were installed at various places at the Planetarium.

S. Vivek, treasurer of the Photography Society of Madras, was excited about shooting the event with his camera. "I wanted to capture the eclipsed (2-3 per cent) rising sun and so I hastened to the terrace of the Planetarium as early as 5.15 a.m. But I saw it only by 6.15 a.m.," he said.

Mahalakshmi, a homemaker, was present on the campus by 4 a.m. "I wanted to be the first one in the queue to watch this phenomenon," she said.

By 6.30 a.m., the moon's shadow began to recede. Still with the welder's glass and the filters, the celestial pair was a sight to behold.

Radhakrishnan, a scientist from Kalpakkam, said solar eclipses are educative. The element Helium was discovered in 1869 during a solar eclipse. It has a lot of applications in various fields. "The view was really a breathtaking one. The awareness created regarding these celestial events also raises the expectations about them, he added.

"The awareness has helped dispel superstitious beliefs about eclipses," said Uthra, head of the Physics Department of D.G. Vaishnav College. Some schoolchildren who had come along with their teachers were, however, disappointed that they could not watch a solar blackout or see planets such as Jupiter and Venus.

"This happens only during a total solar eclipse," said P. Iyamperumal, Executive Director, Birla Planetarium.

II[4]

Here is a story of instant reader interest, gripping in all its details. An everyday activity in today's paperless world turns such a deadly exercise to a citizen.

ATM[5]

BENGALURU: Even by Bengaluru's appalling standards, this was a shocking incident and it happened at an ATM on a busy road in the early morning hours. A machete wielding man attacked a woman inside the ATM as she was drawing money.

The victim Jyothi Ramesh is a bank officer in a public sector bank and received serious injuries on her head and shoulder and has been admitted in hospital. She will need multiple surgeries and doctors said a fracture in the skull may lead to a paralysis on the right side. Jyothi is conscious and has given her version of what happened to police.

The ATM was at that time unguarded, like so many in this city which have no watchmen to ensure safety of machine and men. The violent incident was captured on the CCTV inside the ATM and police said they had a fairly clear picture of the assailant. The search for him has taken police to the neighbouring state of Andhra Pradesh.

Reacting to the incident, which was the ninth such attempt to loot ATMs in the past two months, the Karnataka Home Minister said ATMs without security will be shut down. The banks have been given three days to provide security at their vending machines which now dot the city.

The incident happened 10 minutes past 7 am in the morning at the Corporation Bank's ATM on JC Road. According to police, as Jyothi, a Corporation Bank manager, entered the ATM, her assailant pushed his way in and pulled down the shutters so that no one could see what was happening inside.

The CCTV footage, which was released to the media and has caused widespread outrage, has given a vivid picture of the incident. It shows the assailant asking the victim to withdraw cash. She refuses and pleads with him to leave her. Angered by her refusal, he hits her viciously with the machete and, leaving her bleeding profusely, escapes.

Police said they were alerted by passersby who saw blood stain at the entrance to the ATM. They found Jyothi in an unconscious state and shifted her to hospital.

Police commissioner Raghavendra Auradkar said they had definite clues about the accused. He recalled that police had recently arrested two people who had killed a security guard and said there was a two-hour gap between the latest incident and the time police got the alert. He said his force was alert and efficient and had successfully cracked different varieties of crimes.

Doctors at the hospital said the victim's skull was fractured and a small piece of bone had gone into the brain, causing a "penetrating injury". This has led to partial paralysis on the right side. But there is no danger to her life.

Jyothi's bank colleagues, who were unaware of what happened to her for more than four hours, said she had gone to the ATM to fetch money to celebrate her daughter's birthday, which fell today.

What are the key points here? Attempts to loot Automatic Teller Machines (ATMs) are no more an uncommon occurrence and have ceased to make headline news. Attackers snatching briefcases overflowing with currency notes from persons emerging out of banks and ATMs are not a new phenomenon either. In Bengaluru, as the report states, assailants have neutralised armed guards and looted money from ATMs. There was even an attempt to cart away an ATM, which had been temporarily installed and yet to be secured. But here is apparently a rare instance of a well-planned attempt at robbery which turned violent. A man, waiting for a victim, slips into the ATM even as the customer moves to the slot machine to withdraw cash, unaware of the armed intruder following her. Her pleading with the man, her brave refusal to take out money and the attacker's mad act of wielding the machete are not everyday happenings. The most newsworthy element in this story is the fact that the woman customer was savagely attacked inside an ATM by an armed intruder, beside the very relevant fact that there was no armed guard posted outside.

As I have stated earlier, go to the heart of the matter straightaway and not waste words such as "Even by Bengaluru's standards, this was a shocking ...". Keep these observations, if you must, to later paragraphs. I would cut the first sentence and start the story with the second. Two additional points would also find a place in the first para: that she was seriously injured and secondly that the ATM was unguarded. My first para will read: "A machete wielding man attacked a woman inside an unguarded ATM this morning, seriously injuring her, and escaped. Passersby spotted blood oozing out of the shuttered ATM and alerted police, who rushed the victim to hospital."

I will follow this up in the next para with the vital fact that the whole incident has been captured by the CCTV camera inside the ATM. Police said the armed man, who sneaked into the ATM behind Jyothi, threatened her and asked her to withdraw money. When she refused, he hit her on her head and shoulder and escaped. He had pulled down the shutters when he followed her into the ATMs.

In the third para will come the remarks of police on the woman's injuries and her condition and the doctors' observations.

My fourth para will report the police statement that they have a fair picture of the assailant from the CCTV camera and that their hunt has taken them to neighbouring Andhra Pradesh.

After these vital details have been reported, we can revert to the deleted first sentence in the first para and say that this was shocking even by Bengaluru's poor safety standards and go on to recall earlier attempts at looting ATM.

III[6]

Fact file

For a morning daily dated August 20, write a 300-word news report from the following fact sheet on the Mumbai railway motormen's strike. The key to writing this story is to see where the most newsworthy point is. The strike is not the lead point since this would have been noted by that morning's newspapers. Look for the lead point and bring it up front and suitably weave the other points into the report. You have my version, too.

Mumbai, Thursday, 18 August: As Mumbaikars got ready to go home after work, they were in for a shock on Thursday afternoon. Motormen belonging to the Central and Western Railways went on a sudden strike demanding a pay hike and, among other things, the filling up of vacancies immediately since they were getting "overworked and stressed". The motormen were agitated that they had to do overtime and forgo weekly offs to maintain services to make up for an acute shortage of staff. The agitation started around noon. Most of the stations were affected on the Central, Western and Harbour lines. Central Railway Mazdoor Sangh president RP Bhatnagar said the motormen were agitating against the lack of action by the railway ministry in responding to their "just demands" for a pay increase and more recruitment to end staff shortage. Central Railway Public Relations Officer S Mudgerikar said the situation would be brought under control soon. Officials have been in constant touch with the unions. In the evening 20 striking motormen were dismissed for refusing to report for work.

Mumbai, Friday, 19 August: The motormen's strike continued on the second day (August 19) in Mumbai. The agitation by over 600 motormen on the Western Railway (WR) and Central Railway (CR) compelled the railways to issue a rare advisory on Friday morning. "People may undertake (train) journey only if it's very important," said a bulk SMS with a helpline number 10721 to assist stranded commuters. Apparently only 15-20 per cent of the local trains were running today, resulting in overcrowding and commuter anger and frustration at stations across Mumbai. While hundreds of commuters managed to reach their homes late on Thursday, the situation was worse on Friday morning with the railways announcing the cancellation of nearly 80 per cent of the total 2,000 daily services which cater to approximately seven million passengers. The BEST and MSRTC came to the rescue of stranded commuters by deploying additional services in the city and elsewhere. The motormen's agitation has had a devastating effect on Mumbai's roads and highways which have been plagued by traffic chaos since Thursday evening. Shiv Sena chief Bal Thackeray announced that he would fight for the genuine demands of motormen and asked them to resume work immediately. Maharashtra Navnirman Sena (MNS) chief Raj Thackeray also urged the motormen to call off the strike. Otherwise, he added the warning, they would face his party's wrath. "The motormen should withdraw the strike by afternoon, else my party would oppose the strike," he said. Incidentally the MNS party poll symbol is the railway engine. The state government planned to invoke the Essential Services Maintenance Act (ESMA) against the motormen, but realising that this might not help solve the problem decided against resorting to the draconian Act. Late in the afternoon on August 19 (Friday), the motormen decided to call off their agitation on the basis of an assurance from the state government that it would mediate between them and the railway ministry. "The government took the lead to resolve the crisis as normal life was thrown out of gear due to the strike and people were facing a lot of hardships," home minister RR Patil said after a meeting with the motormen's representatives.

Example report

Motormen Call Off Strike

MUMBAI, 20 August: Motormen of the Central and Western Railways called off their two-day-old strike tonight, ending the paralysis into which the metro's commuter life had been thrown. The flash strike began around noon yesterday.

The decision to call off the strike came after the State Government promised to mediate between the motormen and the Railway Minister.

"The (state) government took the lead to resolve the crisis as normal life was thrown out of gear due to the strike and people were facing a lot of hardship," Home Minister R R Patil said after a meeting with the motormen's representatives.

Commuters' nightmare, which began yesterday afternoon, turned worse today with the railways running only 15-20 per cent of the local trains. An advisory from the Railways said tersely, "People may undertake (train) journey only if it is very important," said a bulk SMS.

The motormen have been demanding a pay rise and recruitment of additional staff to fill vacancies. Their union complained that the motormen were being asked to forego offs and work for long hours to make up for a shortage of staff.

The strike saw two local political outfits take up positions. The Shiv Sena chief came out in support of the striking men but appealed to them to call off their work stoppage since it hit Mumbaikars hard. His nephew's MSN on the other hand asked the workers to resume and warned that if they failed they would face the wrath of his supporters.

IV[7]

Write a 300-350 word report based on the following details.

Fact file

Calcutta, 19 July: A speeding train rear-ended another train at the Sainthia station in West Bengal's Birbhum district, 190 km from Kolkata on Monday, July 19. Both trains were bizarrely on the same track. Railway authorities said the accident, near the Jharkhand border, was probably caused due to human error. The Uttarbanga driver most likely overshot a critical signal near the station at around 2 am on July 19. Witnesses said they shouted at him to stop, but he was going so fast that he could not brake in time. He hit the Vananchal Express that was pulling out of Platform 4. The Uttarbanga Express driver is dead.

Railway Board Chairman Vivek Sahay said the driver was experienced and could not have committed such mistake. "We do not know whether the signal was given. Even if the signal was given, the train has to stop at Sainthia," Sahay said. Sixty passengers have been killed and about 93 injured in the accident. The toll will most likely go up as the rescue effort intensifies. The collision was so severe that the roof and sides of one of the compartments of the Vananchal Express were slammed onto an overhead bridge for pedestrians. A part of another compartment of the Vananchal Express split and fell on the road along the tracks after being thrown over the bridge. The Army was sent in for rescue operations. Bodies were rescued from the wreckage with equipment like gas cutters. Villagers in the area were the first to try and rescue passengers.

Railways Minister Mamata Banerjee who inspected the site of the accident said the accident raised suspicion, implying that there may have been some sort of sabotage. "Human life is very important," she said. Two months ago, another major accident in West Bengal near Jhargram saw the Gyaneshwari Express derails—48 people were killed. Ms Banerjee had rejected claims of sabotage by Naxalites in the area, blaming the accident on "a political conspiracy." Ms Banerjee has been attacked by a series of politicians including former Railways Minister Lalu Prasad Yadav, who said the tragedy proved "carelessness." Ram Vilas Paswan of the LJP raised a point that Ms Banerjee's opponents have been pushing for a few months—that she spends too much time handling the politics in her home state of West Bengal, and not enough on managing the Railways. "Full-time involvement is needed there. The Railways Minister should take a decision on whether she wants to continue as a minister or do politics in Bengal. The two cannot go on at the same time. We are not going to tolerate her playing with hundreds of innocent lives once in every three months anymore," said Paswan.

The Railways also does not rule out sabotage. "As the chairman of the Railway Board, I can tell you I am more worried about the fact that most of the train accidents are now involving Mail Express trains, and in many of them we find there has been some willful interference. We have had five cases of sabotage this year." said Vivek Sahay, adding the the railways " will investigate all angles." Eastern Railway CPRO, Samir Goswami said a few trains—the Kanchenjunga Express, the Sealdah bound Darjeeling mail and the Kanchankanya Express were diverted.

The following are a few points to note:

1. Lead the report with the casualties. The facts have been put down as they came in, which is perhaps why the casualties are noted lower down the paras.
2. A collision occurs when two bodies move in opposite direction. In this case this is not a collision since both trains were moving in the same direction. 'Rear-ending' is a fairly correct way of reporting. 'Rammed' also implies hitting from behind.
3. When you mention possible causes of the accident, there must

be extreme caution, with attribution of the source of such comments clearly mentioned.

4. Keep facts separate from speculation and politicking.

V[8]

Write a 300-word report for a Delhi edition newspaper dated 3 September from the following factsheet. First note down the sequence of events, the actors and the plan and then proceed by giving the latest information first and then following up. The action spans three days. Make that clear in your report.

Fact file

31 August: One and a half year old Ishaan goes missing. The housemaid Seema alias Savita Karketa had taken him to a neighbourhood park. The two do not come home. Parents complain to the police

2 September: Police announce that they have traced the boy in Faridabad. Five persons, including Seema and a former maid Pratima, are arrested. The others arrested are Pratima's friend Ashok Kiro, and Krishan Dev and Shanti alias Anu Begum who runs a placement agency in southeast Delhi. Police Commissioner B K Gupta said the accused planned to call the family for a ransom demand of Rs 2 crores. They had planned to contact the family for ransom once the latter had lost hope of finding the child. 'Krishan Dev is the mastermind behind the kidnapping. Fifteen teams of senior police officials were formed and pressed into service to nab the culprits.' Mr Gupta added, 'On September 1 late in the night police arrested three women in this connection and rescued the boy following a tip-off.'

2 September, Police press release: The police in a press release on September 2 gave these details: As per the plan of the culprits, Seema waits with the baby in the park around noon when Krishan and Anu Begum arrive in a car. The trio then escape with the boy. That night the accused keep the boy at a rented accommodation in neighbouring Sarai Kale Khan. They had arranged the room, booked in advance, mainly to give the police the slip and mislead them. To mislead the

landlord, the accused tell him that Ishaan is suffering from cancer in the leg and is being taken home after treatment and needs to rest for the night. Krishan poses as the boy's father, Anu Begum as the mother and Seema as his maternal aunt. On September 1, the accused move the boy to a rented house in Tilpat village in Harkesh Nagar area of Faridabad. They hire the house for Rs 1,000. It is here that the police catch up with the culprits and trace the boy on September 1 late night and arrest three accused. A senior police official said that though they had known that the kidnappers were first-timers, they were prepared for a gun battle. 'Police were ready to face them if the accused were to use firearms. Luckily they did not have any such weapons as they are not professional kidnappers.' Police later in the night of September 1 arrest Ashok Kiro from south Delhi and Krishan Dev from Maharani Bagh.

VI

Fact file

Pipeline: Rajiv Gandhi Gramin LPG Vitrak Yojana

Who launched: Hans Raj Bhardwaj, Governor of Karnataka dedicates to nation

Where: at Indian Oil Corporation's Devanagonthi oil terminal near Bangalore

When: 2 July

Other dignitaries: Pipeline launched in the presence of M. Veerappa Moily, Union Minister for Law and Justice; Murli Deora, Minister of Petroleum and Natural Gas; B. N. Bache Gowda, Minister of Labour, Government of Karnataka; K. H. Muniyappa, Minister of State for Railways; S. Sundareshan, Secretary (Petroleum); B. M. Bansal, Chairman, IndianOil; and other dignitaries.

Purpose of the pipeline: To ensure uninterrupted, reliable and economical transportation of petroleum products to meet the growing demand in and around the city of Bengaluru; to cater to the demand of petroleum products of Bengaluru and surrounding areas

Impact: Ease pressure on Railways, roads and also help in decongestion of traffic in the city. Prior to the launch of the pipeline, these products were transported by rail/road, which was time consuming and costly.

Project cost: Rs. 273 Crore

Length of pipeline: 290-km

Nature of pipeline: Underground

Origin of pipeline: Chennai Petroleum Corporation's Manali refinery near Chennai Destination: Devanagonthi terminal of IndianOil on the outskirts of Bengaluru.

Unique feature: The pipeline crosses national and state highways, railway lines, Krishna main canal and six rivers and about 50 district and village roads in its journey through three states—Tamil Nadu, Andhra Pradesh and Karnataka.

Statistical update of Indian Oil's network: With the commissioning of this pipeline, the network of Indian Oil's crude oil and product pipelines is now 10,652 km in length and 75.26 million tonnes per annum in capacity. The Corporation is currently implementing new pipeline projects of over 2,000 km in length, worth approximately Rs. 6,000 crore.

What the petroleum minister said: Petroleum products plays an important role in the economy of the country while stressing that Oil Marketing Companies (OMCs) are performing the mammoth task of supplying petroleum products to every nook and corner of the country round the clock. "With the addition of Chennai–Bengaluru pipeline, the availability of products would be further augmented," Deora said

Published report

Bangalore-Chennai Oil Pipeline Launched[9]

BANGALORE, 3 July: A pipeline commissioned on Friday at the Indian Oil Corporation (IOC) terminal in Devanagonthi near Hosakote to bring petroleum products from Chennai to Bangalore might help meet the City's need for speedy and uninterrupted fuel supply.

Petroleum products are traditionally being transported by freight trains or by road. The new pipeline is the second one to be constructed to supply oil to Bangalore. The first pipeline, transporting fuel from Mangalore via Hassan to Bangalore, was launched a few years ago.

The 290-km underground pipeline, commissioned on Friday by Governor H R Bhardwaj, was completed at a cost of Rs 273 crore, three months ahead of schedule. It has an installed capacity to transport 1.45 million tonnes of white fuel (petrol, diesel, kerosene and aviation turbine fuel) per annum from the Chennai Petroleum Corporation Manali refinery to Bangalore via Chittoor.

About 96 km of the pipeline traverses through Tamil Nadu, 111 km through Chittoor district of Andhra Pradesh.

The remaining 83 km of it passes through Karnataka. The IOC already has a 36-km-long pipeline connecting the Devanagonthi terminal to Bangalore International Airport at Devanahalli to supply aviation turbine fuel.

Union Minister for Petroleum and Natural Gas, Murli Deora, who spoke at the pipeline's inauguration, said the Opposition parties should have introspected before calling for a nationwide stir on July 5 to protest against rise in fuel prices.

'Consumption Increasing'

In his address, Petroleum Secretary S Sundareshan said that the consumption of petrol and diesel was increasing at 15 and 10 per cent, respectively, per annum and the state-run oil companies were prepared to meet the increased demand.

"The Gas Authority of India Limited (GAIL) will build a pipeline from Dabhol in Maharashtra to Bangalore and another from Kochi in Kerala to Chennai via Mangalore and Bangalore at a cost of Rs 5,000 crore by 2012.

"Reliance Petroleum is also building a pipeline from Chennai to Bangalore to supply gas for power projects and other industrial users, while the Mangalore Refinery Petroleum Limited (MRPL) is investing Rs 15,000 crore to increase its refining capacity," Sundareshan said.

Gramin LPG Scheme

Earlier, Governor Hans Raj Bhardwaj also launched Rajiv Gandhi Gramin LPG Vitarak Yojana, a Central scheme that aims to establish small, low-cost LPG distributor units in rural areas.

Four beneficiaries were allotted distributorship after random selection. An additional 124 dealers will be soon appointed across the State.

This is a well-written report, with the proper lead and providing answers to all the questions. I only wish the report had been supplemented with a map or drawing showing the alignment of the pipeline which straddles three states.

VII

Press Note

The following is a press release from the police department received at the newspaper offices in Delhi late in the evening on 9 March 2010. It has been reproduced as it was received at the newspaper offices. This is a veritable puzzle–and an everyday reality at the newspaper offices. Prepare a news report based on the information in the press release for publication in the next morning's edition. A "blind murder" is one without apparent clues. There are some discrepancies in the press release. If the reporter has the time (deadline could be close) and the inclination, he calls up the police station to seek clarification. In the press release, two figures have been given for the age of the victim. See my version and published versions from two newspapers the next morning.

Press Release, dated 9.3.2000, North West District

Sensational Blind Murder Cum Robbery Case of Old Lady Solved

Introduction

With the arrest of a lady aged 24 years namely Smt. Dolly @ Hema, W/O Sh. Gopal Aggarwal R/O R/o I-1/65, Budh Vihar phase 1, Delhi, Police Station Rani Bagh, North West District, has solved a blind murder case of Smt. Manjeet Kaur W/O Sh. Amarjeet Singh R/o H No. 1789, Mulatni, Rani Bagh, Delhi. The Police team also recovered the mobile phone of deceased and certain other articles stolen from her house after the murder of deceased.

Incident and Police Team

On 23.2.2000 at 10.28 PM, a PCR call was received at P. S. Rani Bagh that a dead body of female is lying in her house at H No. 1789, Multani Mohalla, Rani Bagh, Delhi. Immediately, a Police team rushed to the spot and found that a dead body of a female was lying in the pocl of blood on the bed of her house and the throat and left wrist were slit by a sharp weapon. One almirah in other room was found ransacked. Accordingly a case FIR No. 60/2010 U/S 302 IPC was registered and investigation was taken up by a Police team comprising of Inspector Narendra Kumar SHO/Rani Bagh, SI Ram Prakash, SI Ramaraj, HC Sushil under close supervision of Sh. G.S. Nana ACP/Saraswati Vihar. Later on after checking the belongings, sons of deceased told to the police team that both the mobile phones of deceased, some clothes, cash and jewellery were missing from the house.

Investigation

The Police team started its investigation without any clue. All the relatives and acquaintances of deceased were interrogated at length but all the efforts proved futile. Finally the police team was able to zero on accused lady Smt. Dolly @ Hema, aged 21 years W/O Gopal Aggarwal R/O I-1/65, Budh Vihar phase 1, Delhi.

Interrogation

During the course of sustained interrogation accused Dolly revealed that she had known the deceased lady since earlier and was in continuous contact with her because the deceased lady was running a Marriage Bureau. On the fateful day the accused lady had gone to the deceased lady with her husband on the pretext of marriage of her brother-in-law. Accused was familiar with the topography of the house and also knew it that the deceased was staying alone. Since, the accused couple was under heavy debt, she thought that she along with her husband shall be able to steal jewellery articles, cash from the house of the victim being a lonely lady. When the duo overpowered the victim in order to conduct robbery she started shouting. This made the husband to get hold of her along with his wife Hema and using a kitchen knife they slit her wrist and neck which lead to her death. After that they took away the cash, jewellery articles, documents, mobile phones from the house of the victim. After reaching home she found that the most of the jewellery articles were artificial. She threw the artificial jewellery into MCD's garbage Dalao in Mangolpuri which could not be recovered.

Accused Arrested

Dolly @ Hema W/O Gopal Aggarwal, R/O I-1/65, Budh Vihar phase-1, Delhi.

Profile of Accused

Accused arrested belongs to lower middle class of society with education upto Matriculation.

Recovery

1. One mobile phone of deceased
2. A ladies suit in transparent polythene bag with blood on it.
3. Some jewellery of deceased in blood stained purse
4. Some receipts showing use of stolen money.

All out efforts are afoot to arrest the remaining accused in the case and more recoveries are expected.

XXX IPS,
Dy. Commissioner of Police
North West District, Delhi

Example report

Woman Held for Rani Bagh Murder[10]

NEW DELHI, 9 March: Dolly, 24, has been arrested for the murder of an elderly woman in Rani Bagh a fortnight ago. Police said they were on the lookout for Dolly's husband.

Manjeet Kaur, who ran a marriage bureau in Rani Bagh and lived alone, was found in a pool of blood, with her wrist and neck slit, at her residence on Feb 23.

Police began without clues and following the interrogation of neighbours and friends, zeroed in on Dolly who confessed to have committed the murder, according to a press note from the North West district police chief.

Police said Dolly told them that she used to visit Manjeet Kaur and knew that she was estranged from her husband. Dolly said she and her husband planned to rob Manjeet and visited her on the day of the murder under the pretext of discussing a marriage proposal for her brother-in-law. When she and her husband, Gopal Aggarwal tried to steal things in her house, Manjeet raised an alarm. In panic, Gopal used a kitchen knife to slit her throat and left wrist and let her bleed to death. The two picked up some valuables and fled.

Police said they had recovered the murdered woman's cellphone and some other personal belongings.

The Delhi police press release lacks clarity. Note the divergence even with regard to the age of one of the accused in reports published the next morning by two newspapers in Delhi.[11]

Exercise Four: On Lead Writing

Write the following into crisp, easy to read leads which can be just one sentence or a few. Your objective should be to capture the most newsworthy point and bring it out. The first has many redundancies. It has been edited and converted for you, from a long-winding 39-word lead into a 20-word lead. Attempt the rest of the exercise. The latter groups some of the more difficult examples. But the more variations you attempt the better since you will come across news developments like these on an everyday basis. While the first example has been generated, all the exercises are taken from printed newspapers.

1. HYDERABAD: Suburban police, not well known for the prevention of crime on the outskirts of the capital, arrested four persons on Thursday in connection with many burglaries reported in suburban areas and recovered gold jewels weighing 150 sovereigns from the accused. (42 words)

   Suggested lead: Hyderabad: Suburban police arrested four persons on Thursday in connection with many burglaries and recovered jewels weighing 150 sovereigns from them. (20 words)
2. CHENNAI: A 22-year-old woman, identified as Vaidehi, was found dead under mysterious circumstances in suburban Chathirapatti near Oomachikulam on Thursday. Police said the victim had stab injuries and cut marks around the neck. The motive of the crime is being investigated. Preliminary inquiries revealed that she might have been murdered as the result of an illicit affair. Chathirapatti police have registered a case of murder. Further investigation is on. (68 words)[12]
3. CHANDIGARH: Advice from the Prime Minister Manmohan Singh that Sikhs should forget the "painful events of 1984" notwithstanding, radical political outfit Dal Khalsa has decided to mobilise its activists for the "Genocide Remembrance March"

along the lanes and streets of the holy city of Amritsar, on June 3 this year to observe the 25th anniversary of the launching of the army action "Operation Bluestar" at Harmandar Sahib (Golden Temple complex). (69 words)[13]

4. CHENNAI: As the Triumph of Labour statue on the Marina stood in stately repose, a rainbow group of Lesbian, Gay, Bisexual and Transgenders gathered near it to take up a solidarity march, the first of its kind in Tamil Nadu, demanding the revoking of section 377 of the Indian Penal Code which criminalises homosexuality. Nearly 700 persons marched the four km stretch till the Gandhi Statue, with at least half of the crowd comprising supporters of the LGBT community like family members, friends and NGO workers. (85 words)[14]
5. CHENNAI: On June 27, when 73-year-old Lakshmikutti Ammal was found murdered in her Tiruvallur Nagar house in Kodungaiyur, the police were surprised that nothing more than a cell phone was missing from the scene of crime. Twelve days later, on Friday, many others were surprised when the police took into custody three teenagers for the murder. (55 words)[15]
6. NEW DELHI: A day after she allegedly made up stories about her husband's murder by four robbers, 29-year-old Sumit Kaur's friend Puneet alias Arsh Deep (30) is claimed to have confessed to having killed Jagmohan Singh Kohli. Sharad Aggarwal, DCP (West) said Puneet, a Class XII dropout, broke down and confessed to the crime, after which the police extracted a confession from Sumit. (61 words)[16]

EXERCISE FIVE: ON FEATURE WRITING

Here are two exercises which can train you in writing news features.

I

You can write the following features and analyses on the Tsunami that struck the Indian Ocean on the morning of 26 December 2004. Just to recall, it was almost the first time in living memory that the eastern coast of India experienced the devastating effect of the natural phenomenon. It left the coastal areas of the southern districts in Tamil Nadu in total destruction, killing an unknown number of people and displacing thousands more. The livelihood of the majority of the people living along the coast, including fisherfolk, was destroyed. Hundreds of boats and fishing nets were lost.

You can write features on the following, as supplement to the main news story:

1. First person accounts of people who had gone through the nightmare on that day. For example, one man said that as he was sitting on the parapet of a viaduct near the coast he was sucked into the sea by a giant wave. It was impossible to shout for help or to swim across as the waves were too strong and high.
2. What is a tsunami? Explain in simple terms the scientific reasons for why and how it happens, and where the 2004 tsunami originated and the devastating path it took to reach the east coast of India and go beyond to hit Kerala and travel further west before dissipating. Explain underwater earthquakes and the tectonic plates. Recall the experience of people in the Tamil Nadu coast of one the main characteristic of such tsunamis: how on the beaches the water receded alarmingly before a huge wave of 10 to 15 metres high came back and engulfed the coastal region.
3. Explain the origin of the word tsunami and try and give a definition, recalling how the Pacific coast is prone to tsunamis of varying intensity and is a regular occurrence.
4. Explain the measures that India decided to take to get early warning systems installed in the Indian Ocean region. As a model for India, write of the precautions that the Asia Pacific nations have taken over the years to protect themselves against this natural calamity.
5. Over ten years after the disaster, have the affected people been rehabilitated fully? Write about the assistance that poured into the area from all over the world. What were the organisations which came to assist and what they did, as in providing houses, and boats and fishing nets.

1. Analyse the response of the then district administrations when the tsunami struck. Get the views and reactions of disaster

management experts on whether the right steps were taken and what was lacking, if any.

2. Soon after the calamity, offers poured in of assistance in helping instal tsunami warning equipment. What has been the progress on this front? How much has been accomplished? Contact experts for their assessment. The Andamans were a major point of focus.
3. A few years ago there were allegations that some of the money and material which came for the tsunami victims did not reach them. A few legal cases were launched against some organisations and groups. What is their status? Have fool-proof measures been set in place to face future emergencies.

II

Let us take one more example of a news development where there were possibilities of writing news features and analyses. On 12 October 1999, the Pakistani army seized power under General Pervez Musharraf under bizarre circumstances. We have the main report detailing the drama and the attempts by the then Nawaz Shariff government to prevent the return of General Musharraf, then army chief, from his visit to Sri Lanka. To go with it, the following are possibilities for writing news features and analyses for the daily the next day or for a news weekly due out in the next few days:

1. The Pakistani army has made it a habit to seize power and derail democracy. Make a timeline, marking the duration each martial law and army rule lasted, which civilian government was toppled and how the next civilian government came into being. (For the record: Only two years ago, was there a democratic transition in Pakistan's history when one civilian, elected government handed over power to another civilian, elected government.
2. Brief profiles of the army dictators who had ruled in Pakistan, what happened during their regime, how they left the seat of power. It was Zia ul Haq who Islamised the army, bringing about a collaboration between the military and clerics which has played havoc with the country. And not all rulers handed over power voluntarily. One of them disappeared in a plane crash.

3. The impact of Zia's campaign to Islamise the military, how the country is paying an intolerably heavy price for this action, how it was during his time that religious extremism established itself firmly in the society and terrorism as an instrument of state policy began to be given shape.
4. The pro-military tilt in the policy of the US which found it easier to handle a dictator than a democrat. The impact of American military assistance, with the objective first of fighting communism and then Soviet rule in neighbouring Afghanistan. How US ignored India's protests that these arms were being used to fan separatism in this country.
5. The fate of Nawaz Sherif, now under house arrest. Will he follow Benazir Bhutto into self-imposed exile?
6. The press, which has seen much freedom in the past few years, may be muzzled but Musharraf may be wary of American and European reaction.

The following are a few ideas for news analysis:

1. Discuss the impact on India-Pakistan relations: The BJP government was warming up to Nawaz Sherif when Gen Musharraf as army chief launched the disastrous Kargil war. If Kargil set relations back by a decade, can a military government retrieve lost ground, especially taking advantage of New Delhi's eagerness to show some positives on its Pakistan card?
2. Militancy in Kashmir appears to have come down in recent months. In the backdrop of the Kargil misadventure and loss of face when forced by the US to withdraw, will the snubbed Pakistan army and the ISI try and stir up trouble in Jammu and Kashmir through their proxies?
3. Discuss the chances of a return to civilian rule: With both top leaders–Sheriff and Benazir–in the dog house, where is the political leadership in the country? What are the impediments?
4. Discuss the speculation that there can be a return to pro-Pak tilt in the US policies in the subcontinent: Washington has always found it easier to handle a military ruler than a civilian who is shackled by the real power behind the throne, the army.

Appendix 2

Basic Editing Exercises

EXERCISE ONE: ON SPELLINGS[17]

Correct words where needed. Do not rely on the computer's spell check which can check only spelling, not meaning:

1. acsent
2. anemic
3. bacalaureat
4. baggauge
5. bouleward
6. calendar
7. deceive
8. diceased
9. discreet
10. disrepency
11. eponimous
12. flouresent
13. gaol
14. hemorhage
15. misoginy
16. onomatopic
17. opthelmology
18. rapproachment

EXERCISE TWO: ON SENTENCES[18]

Correct any errors, grammatical, spelling or whatever, in the following sentences:

1. These are a few among the many that you can find on the beeches of Chennai.
2. After repeatedly giving trouble on the road, he decided to leave his car at the garage for annual service.
3. The professor that taught me has left the college.
4. Stolen jewel was found by a local wrapped in a dirty rag.
5. The intruder hit Padmavati, who was standing in the verandah, on her head.
6. CPI(M): To alienate the people from the dangerous politics pursued by the Maoists was a continuous process.
7. Twice winner of the Derby, owner C R Ramaswami decided to sell the horse to the highest bidder.
8. Raghav has been indicated for murder.
9. Each student will fill out a questionnaire outlining their lifestyle and interests and hobbies.
10. The police found the bomb under a seat in the airport waiting hall and they managed to diffuse it within minutes.

EXERCISE THREE: ON EDITING DRAFTS OF NEWS REPORTS[19]

Let us now look at two exercises for honing your editing skills.

I

Read the following report and edit it suitably.

Girl Falls Through Hole in School Bus, Crushed by Rear Wheel

CHENNAI: It was the most cruel type of accident that can happen and it happened in the city today. A six-year-old girl slipped through the floorboard of her school bus and fell on the road and was crushed to death by the rear wheel of the vehicle.

It was an accident waiting to happen and is a commentary on

the way rules and regulations are implemented. The bus belonged to the school and the authorities must have been aware of the fact that the floorboard had cracked and developed a gaping hole. The maintenance staff had covered the hole with a cardboard sheet which apparently gave way when the child stepped on it as the bus was nearing her home.

Sruti was a student of a school in Selaiyur, 22 km from Chennai, and was returning home when the accident happened around 4.30 pm at Mudichur. She died on the spot.

Unaware of the tragedy, the driver sped on despite the children inside the vehicle shouting and screaming and passersby gesturing to him. He was stopped a half km away by motorists who blocked his wat and forced him to halt. Residents dragged him and the cleaner out and beat them up. The two were rescued from the crowd by a police patrol. The driver has been taken into custody.

The bus was set on fire and gutted by the time fire service personnel came on the scene. Traffic on the highway remained affected for more than an hour as the residents resorted to a road roko.

According to the school authorities, the bus had been chartered by them from a private operator who, they said, should be accountable for its maintenance. A parent said the responsibility rested ultimately with the school management. "The school collects Rs 7,000 for every term as bus fee and the management therefore must own responsibility for the safety of the bus," he said.

The basic lesson in news writing is to tell the reader what happened in the lead para. Note that in example 1 this has been ignored. The reporter does not describe the accident that happened but how it was 'most cruel'. At the editing table, I would safely remove the first sentence and start with the second, 'A six-year-old girl ...' The reporter can talk about how cruel it was, etc. later, in the details. Again, the cliché that 'it was an accident waiting to happen' and 'is a sad commentary on the way ...' could be kept out. Do you think the phrase 'crushed to death' could be kept out? Let us not make it more gruesome than what it already is by saying she was crushed to death. We can rather say 'and was run over by the rear wheel of the vehicle'. It was indeed a bizarre accident and the report must bring these details out without resorting to hyperbole.

II

The following is an objective, matter of fact report on a debate. Try and make it more interesting, perhaps leading off with a student's comment and bring out the nature of the controversy that was generated.

Both viewpoints have value and both have a right to be expressed, ruled the chair at the end of an acrimonious inter-collegiate debate on a documentary produced by Indian-born Canadian Nisha Pahuja, titled *The World Before Her*. It was a tame end to a debate which saw strong expressions of support and opposition to the documentary, the latter a distinct but vocal minority.

The documentary, which has won a few awards, is considered a powerful film that explores the dichotomy between secularism and religious conservatism. It charts the lives and fortunes of two young women from opposing ends of the socio-cultural spectrum. One is a member of the nattionalist Durga Vahini organisation, dedicating her life to the preservation of her religion and the role assigned by it to women by any and all means. The other is a 20-year-old finalist for the Miss India contest, aiming to be crowned the most beautiful in India and enjoy all that it brings to her. Critics have said the film maker has scrupulously refrained from sitting on judgment.

The division among the debaters was stark: all black or white and no shades of grey, as clearly portrayed in the documentary which won an award for the best documentary feature at a film festival in New York in 2012. Students who supported the documentary were opposed to the so-called conservative views on the status of women in society. Many students pointed out that these "conservative" views were shared by most religions and were not confined to one. One reminded the young audience that they were the victims in a sense in both ways: the groups opposing beauty pageants belonged to diametrically opposite poles. The feminists were protesting because they feel these demeaned women while the conservatives were of the view that women belonged to the home and had no role outside.

One student recalled the attacks on pubs and clubs in some towns targeting women and said in some instances young women were pulled out of clubs and beaten in full view of the general public. There were instances of girls being attacked if they were found talking to or meeting boys.

There was clapping from sections of the audience when one girl spoke of the plans of women hostliers in a college in Kerala to defy curfew time. The women students in the hostel wanted the same timings of curfew as in the men's hostel, the speaker said, and wondered why the demand was not being supported nationwide.

Countering these views, supporters of conservative groups recalled the travails of women in liberal Western societies and warned that this "degeneration" would ultimately result in the break-up of the family. This, they said, would be disastrous especially for women who needed the protection of the family.

EXERCISE FOUR: ON INTRO WRITING[20]

Write an intro for a national paper based on the day's reports on the weather in different parts of the country:

Chennai: Blame it on climate change or on cyclone Aila which struck just when the south-west monsoon was setting in, but the fact remains that Tamil Nadu has got less rain than it would normally during the period. With the monsoon becoming active in Kerala and coastal Karnataka again, there is some 'spillover effect' in the Western Ghats of the Nilgiris and Kanyakumari, which have been receiving rain in the past few days.

Chennai: The delayed monsoon may have raised doubts about water supply in future in the minds of Chennaiites who are reeling under searing heat even in July. However, water managers are assuring uninterrupted supply to the metropolis till mid-November.

Guwahati: More than 200,000 people have been displaced and over 300 villages submerged in the past two days in Assam following flash floods, triggered by heavy monsoon rains, with Assam government sounding an alert.

New Delhi: Recent monsoon showers have brought no respite on the waterfront as the water levels in most of the major water reservoirs in the country have not gone up.

Data of water reservoirs compiled by the Central Water Commission CWE), on July 2 reveals that the water levels in several reservoirs in Punjab, Rajasthan, Jharkhand, Orissa, West Bengal, Gujarat and Maharashtra have not increased compared to last week's figures. The storage capacities of several reservoirs are still touching the dead level in these states. However, water level in the Tehri water reservoir in Uttarakhand has increased. In the southern region, except a few, the water level has not increased in most reservoirs.

Exercise Five: On Evaluation with News Lists[21]

Here is a string of important stories from the pages of the day's newspaper in a random listing. Put them in the order of importance as per your judgment. Explain why you have chosen one over another. What criteria came into play in your decision-making. Remember the interplay of criteria, when one criterion overrides another.

I

21 July 2010

1. Telugu Desam Party chief Chandrababu Naidu returns to Hyderabad after a day of high drama in Aurangabad. His protest against the Babli dam project on the Godavari raises tensions between the two neighbouring states. Maharashtra CM drops all charges against him and he is forced to fly out to Hyderabad. The water war of the future.
2. Home ministry gets an official spokesman. Aftermath of Home Secretary G. K. Pillai's remarks on the eve of the Islamabad talks. NSA Shivshankar Menon repeats remarks of G. K. Pillai on the Headley interrogation.
3. Sri Lankan Tamil MPs meet Tamil Nadu chief minister Karunanidhi, seek his help to rehabilitate displaced Tamils in their own areas.
4. Railways suffer as Mamata plays politics, says TOI. 20,000 posts linked to railway safety remain vacant. Follow-up on major railway accident at Sainthia
5. Woman held for killing lover's son. LKG boy killed by father's mistress.
6. Major international conference on Afghanistan sets 2014 as deadline for pullout of all foreign troops.

II

9 September 2009

Here is a list of eight news stories top listed by the newsroom for use the next morning. You have space for only four. How will you decide, giving reasons both for picking four and dropping the rest.

1. Gujarat govt challenges magistrate's findings in Ishrat Jahan's killing in Ahmedabad. Centre on the defensive as Gujarat cites Delhi's affidavit which described Ishrat as a terrorist suspect. (*Indian Express*, *Hindu* had it on the front page; *Times of India* in brief on front page and long story on top of inside page; *Deccan Chronicle* inside).
2. Jet pilots' strike. Goyal says he will shut down, Centre leaves it to pilots. (All four dailies have it on front page.)
3. Rahul Gandhi's visit to Tamil Nadu. (All four dailies have it on the front page. *Deccan Chronicle* has it as main lead story.)
4. YSR successor. (All except *Times of India.*)
5. Krishna, Tharoor asked to leave five star luxury. (*Times of India* top; *Indian Express* anchor; brief in *Hindu*; not covered in *Deccan Chronicle.*)
6. 'UAE apologises, India releases plane', says *Indian Express* in a must-read note on page one and story inside. *Hindu* says India is trying to settle issue amicably with UAE. *Times of India* says it has confirmation the plane was carrying arms.
7. Minister Raja in hospital gets royal treatment. (*Hindu* on brief; *Times of India* inside; others did not carry the news.)

Appendix 3

Recommended Reading

My earliest journalism hero was Frank Moraes, the first Indian editor of *Times of India* and later editor-in-chief of *Indian Express*. His column in *Sunday Standard*, the Sunday version of *Indian Express*, used to fascinate me. Titled 'Frankly Speaking'—under the pseudonym Ariel, I think—it used to carry spicy brief commentaries on men and matters, four to five topics each week. The subjects ranged from political leaders of the time (his favourite target in the late-1960s was Indira Gandhi, who he once described as the only man in her cabinet) to international affairs (the hottest issue then was the Vietnam War) and literature. In all likelihood, much of the substance of his comments must have been lost on me but his racy style and crispness of writing were a pleasure to read.

By the time I joined *Indian Express*, I had graduated to reading Frank Moraes' eagerly-awaited weekly editorial page article on Mondays. By then, I had other journalistic heroes, too, all sports writers: Vernon Ram of *Indian Express*, Delhi, a colourful personality, K. N. Prabhu of *Times of India*, known for his silken smooth cricket writing, and A. T. P. Sarathy, of *Indian Express*, Mumbai, who specialised in hockey. American news magazine *Time* was a 'must-read' every week, its play with words a rage among some of us, as was London's *Observer* published every Sunday, which used to feature brilliant cover stories and which also introduced us to the pocket cartoons of Abu Abraham—who was later to land at our desk in Chennai one afternoon and offer to draw for the *Indian Express*. Which he did with such distinction for several years.

It is indeed difficult to imagine those years–no internet, no Facebook, no Twitter, no TV, no easy-of-access online versions of newspapers and magazines, no kindle to download now and read later, no blogs. It was the time when one picked up an 800-page novel and read it through day and night for three, or preferably two days. If one had had enough of the English authors–of the Brontë sisters, Thomas Hardy, Somerset Maugham–one had others. My interest was focussed on Fyodor Dostoevsky (whose grave in St Petersburg I had the opportunity to visit), Kafka, Camus and Sartre and then Robert Conquest and Arthur Koestler and Boris Pasternak. The magazine boom in the 1980s proved a turning point. It heralded the arrival of the news magazines which proved more reader friendly, going behind the news and adding perspective to news developments.

Over the years, many editors have written their memoirs. I encountered my first editor through an article on the British journalist Leonard Woolf, husband of the more famous Virginia Woolf. He had many quotes to his name. One of his pronouncements still remains fresh in my memory: 'Nearly all good editors - like the great newspaper owners - become megalomaniacs and suffer from the hallucination that they control and exercise great power. The hallucination of power corrupts as efficiently as power.' Other journalist-authors of the past decades that I have read were Frank Moraes (whose *Jawaharlal Nehru: A Biography* was an instant success), N. J. Nanporia (of *Times of India* and *Statesman*, Calcutta), Khushwant Singh (who needs no introduction), D. R. Mankekar, Arun Shourie and B. G. Varghese (whose book *Warrior of the Fourth Estate: Ramnath Goenka of the Express*, the founder of the *Express* group of publications was a faithful recording of data).

For professional advancement there were few books to help a new entrant to journalism. More than a decade into the profession, I came across veteran T. J. S. George's useful book *Editing: A Handbook for Journalists*.[22] Much sought after also were the volumes on news writing and editing by Sir Harold Evan's *Editing and Design*,[23] a five-volume manual that included lessons on headline writing, typography and photography. But right through the years in the profession, I had but one companion: the newspaper. If a journalist ever wants to be successful in the profession, he or she should develop the reading habit early and read as much as possible. Preferably, read quality writing (in whatever language of choice). This will certainly sharpen writing skills. Today, I would recommend that a journalist in the making make it a point to read at least two newspapers, watch at least one television news channel and browse as many websites of newspapers and magazines as possible—every day. This is not a tall order. Reading and viewing must be taken as a learning experience, done with a critical eye. The aim must be to see how each outlet handles a news development and what lessons they hold for a journalism student. The possible lessons can be on the manner of presentation of a story, the choice of the lead paragraphs, the burden of the report, any unanswered questions, any biases, any comments (which are strictly forbidden), new turns of phrase, etc.

Apart from the newspapers and news magazines, there are a host of websites which one can profitably peruse whenever one has the time. These include the websites of newspapers available in the country and others such as *New York Times* and *Washington Post* and Britain's *Guardian* and *Telegraph*, magazines (if they are not firewalled), and news agencies such as Reuters, Associated Press and AFP. Websites of Nieman Lab (Harvard University's journalism laboratory)[24] and Pew Research Centre's Journalism Project (which 'assesses the state of news and information in a changing society')[25] are a few others that journalists follow.

One other reading, not recommended but mandatory, relates to the stylebooks of different publications apart from reference books such as *Fowler's Modern English Usage*. Among the more popular writing guides for journalists are those of the Associated Press and the Reuters, *Economist* and *The Canadian Press Stylebook*—which I stumbled upon recently. The guidelines in these stylebooks are both revealing and educative, revealing especially because one realises that at least 20 per cent of the words journalists use on a daily basis are redundant.

NOTES

1. Prepared by the author for this publication.
2. Prepared by faculty members at ACJ. Reproduced by permission of ACJ.
3. *Hindu*, 'Thousands throng Birla Planetarium', 23 July 2009. Reproduced by permission of the *Hindu*.
4. Prepared by the author for this publication
5. Prepared by the author for this publication

6. Prepared by faculty members at ACJ. Reproduced by permission of ACJ.
7. Prepared by faculty members at ACJ. Reproduced by permission of ACJ.
8. Prepared by faculty members at ACJ. Reproduced by permission of ACJ.
9. DHNS, 'Chennai-Bangalore oil pipeline launched', *Deccan Herald*, 2 July 2010. Reproduced by permission of *Deccan Herald*.
10. Prepared by faculty members at ACJ. Reproduced by permission of ACJ.
11. The reports appeared in the *Hindu* and *Times of India*. Staff Reporter, 'Woman Held on Murder Charge', *Hindu*, 10 March 2010; TNN, 'Elderly Woman Killed by Couple, Wife Held', 10 March 2010.
12. *Hindu*, 'Woman found dead', 5 June 2009.
13. Special Correspondent, 'Dal Khalsa will not let Sikhs forget events of 1984', *Hindu*, 25 March 2009.
14. Ajay Reddy, 'Gays take a stand with pride in Chennai', *New Indian Express*, 29 June 2009.
15. *TNN*, 'Teenagers held for elderly woman's murder', *Times of India*, 11 June 2009.
16. Dwaipayan Ghosh, 'Wife got lover to murder west Delhi businessman: Cops', *Times of India*, 11 June 2009.
17. Prepared by faculty members at ACJ. Reproduced by permission of ACJ.
18. Prepared by faculty members at ACJ. Reproduced by permission of ACJ.
19. Prepared by the author for this publication.
20. Prepared by faculty members at ACJ. Reproduced by permission of ACJ.
21. Prepared by faculty members at ACJ. Reproduced by permission of ACJ.
22. T. J. S. George, *Editing: A Handbook for Journalists*, New Delhi: Indian Institute of Mass Communication, 1989.
23. Harold Evans, *Editing and Design: A Five-Volume Manual of English, Typography and Layout*, London: Heinemann for the National Council for the Training of Journalists, 1972.
24. http://nieman.harvard.edu/ (accessed March 2015)
25. http://www.journalism.org/ (accessed March 2015)

Index